DEDICATION

I dedicate this book to my loving wife Carolyn and my son Geoffrey. Without their deep love and their continued support and patience, this long journey of mine would not have been possible...

Budd Burton Moss

Contents

11, 1976)

Acknowledgements

I am very grateful to so many friends over the past years who have worked their way into my small office in my home, who came to my rescue and to the aid of this aging Hollywood agent to finally make my second book possible.

I would like thank most importantly, my Mary Poppins, who dropped down into my chimney by way of Indianapolis of all places and spent the last year getting my travels with Rita Hayworth, M.P.A.A. president Jack Valenti, Tom Bosley, Ambassador and Mrs. John Gavin (actress Constance Towers), Sidney Poitier and Oprah, to mention just a few names, and properly placing them on these pages for you to read; THANK YOU ADDY FLEMING. I am forever indebted to you.

I never thought I would meet a brilliant author in her own right by the name of Anita Venezia on Facebook of all places. We bumped into each other talking about WW 2 and bullfighting at the same time. Why would someone want to spend hours, let alone days and weeks, reading a draft of HOLLYWOOD (hard back copy of over 300 pages) for someone you have never met before? "Send me your manuscript and I will try, without making promises, to help edit your book." Months later in the mail came my manuscript. On every page there were cut up post it's with a note to do this or to do that, or delete a few words of my masterpiece. "Delete?" I would say.

I can never forget Julie McCarron who first walked through my door with a giant 7-11 Coke and said, "Let's see this great piece of writing that your New York agent David has been raving about." I presented her with a hard copy of my first book, "And All I Got was 10%." Julie sat there for maybe twenty minutes and said, "Give me the weekend and I will call you on Monday. Looks like you have over 40 thousand words here. You sure did a lot of name dropping! Needless to say, I did not know what 40 thousand words looked like, being an unpublished author at the time.

On Monday, Julie called as promised. "I can come over at 4:00 this afternoon. Turn your computer on and we will go to work." I kept it on for over a year before she called David and said, "Budd's book is ready to send to the publishers." We waited for almost a year of submissions. I have a drawer full of some of the nicest rejection slips. Finally, between David and Julie we went to the best of all the publishers: Amazon.

Along with my loving friend Larry King, and his great family, who goes back to the early radio days in Miami, to the years that we spent with Boston sports agent Bob Woolf who was responsible for Larry's long lasting years at CNN, to today as we are planning a new TV talk show called Nostalgic created by a very talented Mark McGinley and possibly Mr. T.V. great Garry Marshall and his beautiful assistant, Heather Hall.

Over the last three years, I decided to start on my second book. Between Rita and Jack Valenti alone I had almost two books to write— my travels with Rita Hayworth from the time I put her into "L Bastiardi" with Klaus Kinsky in 1967, to first meeting Jack Valenti on his first day in Hollywood as President of the Motion Picture Association of America in 1966—and we have remained great friends over the years. In 1992, his novel "Protect and Defend" was published by Jackie Kennedy Onassis, when she was chief editor at Doubleday. My world as his agent representing his novel for a major motion picture became a non-stop journey.

When I met the "King of Broadway" agent, the most remarkable and committed agent I had ever known, Robby Lantz, I knew from the moment we shook hands that we were going to spend a long time working together with Jack and his talented director Milos Forman. Milos had already won his two Oscars, one for the Jack Nicholson classic film, "One Flew Over the Cuckoo's Nest" and Milos' remarkable masterpiece, "Amadeus."

Robby, Milos, Jack Valenti and I spent the next ten years with a few stops along the way and tried with three different production companies to put "Protect and Defend" together. After Paramount could not find the right screenplay and dropped their third option in 2006, Jack suddenly passed away from a stroke in 2007. I put the book in the closet for a long time. It took the creative talents of Connie Towers, her husband, former ambassador to Mexico, John Gavin, Mary Bonner Baker and Tom Hasting to take the book out of the closet, dust it off and bring it into this millennium and drop it right into Mexico and the tragic drug and gun wars that had killed thousands of innocent men, women and children. Connie and I took their treatment to one of the most talented Hispanic actors, writers and directors of today, Edward James Olmos, whom I have known since opening night at the Mark Taper Forum downtown where he starred in "Zoot Suit" and it made him an overnight star. Eddie, Connie and I, along with a gifted Canadian screenwriter, Nic Izzi, who has written a powerful script and still maintains the integrity of Jack's White House thriller, are now going into the film market once again in hopes that this year we will finally be able to tell Jack, Milos and Robby that their movie will be made.

Where would my life have been over the many years without knowing that Hollywood's most honored and respected public relations giant, Warren Cowan. was always there, going back to Ruth Roman's and Carolyn Jones' days, he was sitting at the next table when I went to Jack Valenti's coming-out party and whenever there was a need for some PR on "Protect and Defend," Warren was there. Finally, when I made our first development deal with French theater icon Laura Pels and her partner, Peter Bogdanovich, Warren helped set up all of our PR when Laura decided to take all of us to the Cannes Film Festival to announce her purchase of "Protect and Defend," and that production was going to start over the summer, as soon as the screenplay was completed.

As I get ready to put my book HOLLYWOOD out there for the world to read, my heart-felt thanks must go to Gayle and Bill Gladstone and their Waterside agency and Kenneth Kales, for making this book a reality. There will be many names that will come back to me once I take this opportunity to thank those who have filled these many years of my life with their love, their never ending friendship and loyalty. Once again, my two books could have never been written without my beloved wife, Carolyn and son Geoffrey sitting for hours in our living room just a few feet away from my office knowing that the years I spent with their support and blessings, writing my life adventures, is now completed.

Budd Burton Moss

Author's Note

Over the past three years, as I've attempted to write my life story, I came to the realization that going back in time some 40, 50, even 60 or more years would be a task that would be more than difficult.

I was fortunate that from the fifties onward I kept notes and held onto faxes and miscellaneous papers—business and personal. However, even with these to jog my memory, I realized that some names and places have disappeared forever into the ether. Therefore, as I finish up my adventures and get ready to send them off to my agent, it is important that you, my readers, realize that the following stories are the way I remember these persons and events affecting my life.

There are undoubtedly some errors in times, dates, places and names. While all of these people are real and the events actually happened, please remember that mistakes and discrepancies are bound to occur at this age! Such errors are mine, hopefully minor, and quite unintentional.

In Memoriam

Robby Lantz

1914-2007

His Gift to the World of Entertainment

Quotes from My Loving Friends in the Industry

"This is a wonderful and unique look at a part of the Golden Age in Hollywood TV and films that will never be repeated!"
-Larry King/*CNN Larry King Live/ Larry King Now/ Ora TV*

"Throughout my career as a film executive, as well as a producer, I loved working with Budd Moss. He always had a big smile and a kind word for everyone. He clearly loved his work. Budd's book is filled with wonderful, behind-the-scenes stories of what it's like to be a Hollywood talent agent."
-Sherry Lansing, former president of 20th CENTURY FOX STUDIOS, former chairman of PARAMOUNT PICTURES.

"Who knew in our first grade grammar school in West Los Angeles to Junior High that two school pals would go on to successful careers in Hollywood. I have always believed that you must have a deep spirit to write and to know you have friends you share that special spirit with. Budd Moss has done that—it's a must read, he had written some of the most amazing adventures in his book called HOLLYWOOD and I know it will be a best seller this year."
-Robert Wagner, Actor

"Budd Moss's new book, HOLLYWOOD brought back so many memories of all those people we both knew, it kind of took my breath away.
For those of us who lived through the 60s and into the new 21st century, Budd tells stories, I just loved to read.
He describes in detail of his personal relationship with Rita Hayworth. Both his client and a woman he loved since he was a young boy and her tragic decline into Alzheimer's.

Want to know something about the show biz titans such as Jack Valenti, former President and CEO of the Motion Picture Association of America, Aaron Spelling, TV's most successful producer, Oscar® Winners Anthony Quinn, Sidney Poitier, and director Milos Forman, agent icon Irving "Swifty" Lazar, Larry King and many more."

There are also behind the scene stories of deals that were made, were broken and heartbreaks when certain deals never became a film reality.

Budd never gave up. And then there was a moment when revenger was suddenly at his door step. Did he do it; did he not?"

-Rona Barrett, former Hollywood Gossip Columnist, Journalist, TV Host, Business Woman, Philanthropist.

"Budd Moss has written about his experience as an agent, and his career in this business, if you are looking for an enjoyable read about Hollywood down memory lane, read this book.

-Mike Medavoy, Producer, seven-time Oscar Winner.

Jack Valenti in a personal letter to former William Morris agent and president, Jim Wiatt dated Jan. 22nd 2007, speaking of Budd Moss, wrote:

"He has one trait which I find both beguiling and indispensable. He never gives up. He is always moving forward. This is, to my untutored agent's eye, the key to success."

-Jack Valenti, President and CEO, Motion Picture Association of America

Foreword

Reading my friend Budd Moss's memoirs was a wonderful trip down memory lane. Though we come from the same generation, we could not have grown up more differently. As a kid I played in the streets of Brooklyn. Budd was born at Hollywood Children's Hospital in the shadow of Hollywood Boulevard and never left. As the nephew of legendary MGM producer Sam Zimbalist and the son of film editor Lou Moss at Fox, Buddy was destined for a career in show business.

And what a career it was. As a kid, Budd swam in his uncle's pool with Katharine Hepburn and Clark Gable on Saturday afternoons. He fell in love with Rita Hayworth after seeing Blood and Sand at age 11 and vowed he would one day become a bullfighter and win her heart. I'll give the man some credit: He came pretty close on both counts!

He also married and divorced movie star Ruth Roman… along the way falling into the agenting business. It stuck. For nearly fifty years now Budd has worked with, played with and represented some of the greatest talents in show business. Broadway, motion picture and television stars… Budd has done it all. And he's still doing it! He is just as savvy today discussing my new web only show LARRY KING NOW as he was when he was negotiating deals for such stars as Sidney Poitier, Bill Shatner, Jack Valenti, Mia Farrrow, Constance Towers, Shelley Winters, Cyd Charisse, Rita Hayworth and Tom Bosley, among many names over many decades.

There are a lot of big names, big adventures and big stories in his exciting new book; "HOLLYWOOD." Over the years Budd has shared many of these great anecdotes with me over breakfast. I am delighted that they are, at last, reaching the wide audience they deserve.

Larry King ~ Beverly Hills, California

Preface

As I tried to distill my life story and almost half a century in business as an agent into a book, I eventually realized that try as I might, I was never going to get all the stories I wanted to tell into one book—at least not one of normal size! I decided that the best thing to do was split my memoirs into two volumes. As you've seen if you made it this far, Volume I ends with Carolyn and me on our honeymoon. We've now been happily married for forty-five years, and Burton Moss Management is alive, well and going strong!

HOLLYWOOD contains many of my adventures, personal and professional, since 1970. Stay tuned for stories about Rita Hayworth and her heartbreaking descent into Alzheimer's; placing clients Tom Bosley and John James in two of the most popular TV series ever: "Happy Days" and "Dynasty"; selling the rights to friend Jack Valenti's novel, "Protect and Defend" at the Cannes Film Festival; accompanying client Cyd Charisse to the White House, with President and Mrs. George Bush, for the National Endowment of the Arts Award in the Oval Office; sending Hunter Tylo to India for her first major starring role in "The Maharaja's Daughter"; a major book deal with American icon Bob Barker gone bad; Ambassador John Gavin, Constance Towers, Carolyn Jones… and much, much more.

The Burton Moss Agency was off to a great start by July of 1970, when Wayne Warga of the Los Angeles Times, calendar section, called and asked if he could write a feature story about two young Hollywood agents and the clients they represented having come full circle after leaving the big agency.

Opening Scene: A Few Words...

Nate and Al's Deli in the heart of Beverly Hills has been my home away from home for many years. At my regular booth in this unpretentious deli, watched over by motherly waitresses who bring me my order without being asked, I am surrounded by a loose group of my contemporaries, many of whom I've known for decades. Our daily breakfast meeting gives us the chance to catch up, kibitz about the latest gossip and catch up on the latest deals. As veterans of various branches of the entertainment business, every one of us has seen the great stars come and go, made and lost huge deals, triumphed and been betrayed. In short, we've weathered industry storms, and still live, breathe and eat The Business.

Our ranks thin as every year passes. Too many longtime friends and associates have gone. Old friends simply disappear from sight, casualties of fame or devastating business reversals. A few more simply fade into a quiet retirement at the Motion Picture Home out in Woodland Hills. Several have been lucky enough to go quickly and quietly in their sleep of old age, at home and at peace. But this is one tough business and the majority die long before their time is due, victims of accidents, suicide, overdoses and stress-related ailments. I know that when it's my turn to go to that big agency in the sky, Marty Baum, Lew Wasserman, Abe Lastfogel, Abby Greshler, Freddie Fields, Jay Bernstein and Robby Lantz, to name just a few, will be impatiently waiting for me to arrive and fill them in. "What have you been doing,

Budd? Who'd you sign, what's the latest?"

Meanwhile, the more things change, the more they stay the same. From the vantage point of my booth I see them every morning: ambitious young people sipping their one cup of coffee for hours, tapping away at their Blackberries and iPads, perusing scripts, all of them waiting to be noticed. Hoping and praying for some agent to come along and say… "Are you an actor by chance? There's a role in the next Focus film you'd be perfect for…" Hasn't that always been the dream?

I know, because I had the same ambitions. I was a high-school kid with an after-school job pumping gas at the 76 station directly across the street from the MGM lot. My job was to service and deliver cars for all the stars, as well as the important producers and directors. Clark Gable, Spencer Tracy, Elizabeth Taylor, June Allyson, Esther Williams, Cyd Charisse, Fred Astaire… I saw them all and knew that I, too, was destined to join their ranks. But the fates led me to the other side of the acting equation.

Marriage to a movie star changed my life from a wannabe actor/director to becoming an agent…a decision that opened the door to the greatest adventures one could ask for. Many of those stars I admired so extravagantly would become my clients, friends and lovers…and, in a couple of cases, my bitter enemies. Being an agent would become my life's blood, from that day to this, and my excitement about the business is undimmed. I'm still in the game, handling clients, dutifully trooping off to actor workshops and tiny film festivals in Ocoee, Florida…and always keeping on the lookout for the next Jerry Seinfeld or Sandra Bullock. There is nothing I'd rather be doing.

Musing over my lifetime of adventures with the famous and infamous, I had to ask myself, do I really need to write a book when there are so many other stellar accounts of the great movie stars, producers, directors and agents? Is there anybody out there who cares to read about my own personal ups and downs, tragedies and triumphs over the decades? In the end I decided to chronicle my life because I am reminded every day that the dream is still alive and well. Los Angeles is full of people chasing their dreams; though the Golden Age of Hollywood has passed, showbiz is just as exciting and vital today. May these recollections inspire all those who dream. I wish for them all to enjoy just a few of the adventures I have had, find friends like those I've been privileged to know and remain as awestruck and thrilled by this great business of show at my age as they are right now.

To put it more eloquently, these recollections are what my longtime dear friend Jack Valenti would call immortality—passing on to succeeding generations the best of what has come before. This is the tie that binds young actors, writers and dreamers together…Immortality indeed.

Budd Burton Moss

Westwood Village, California

September, 2015

Hollywood's Talent Agents Come Full Circle

By Wayne Warga
"Los Angeles Times" Calendar Section, Sunday July 12, 1970

The rumbles of pain and change in Hollywood appear to be hitting the major old-line talent agencies as well. The decline of the traditional studios and the rise of new producing outfits, the change in their nature of movies and their audiences, the potential impact of film cassettes and—perhaps most of all—the decline of the star system and of the sums and ways stars are paid is at last taking its toll on the behemoth flesh-peddling enterprises.

The earliest straw in the wind may have been the Music Corp. of America's decision—aided by the Actors Guild and the U.S. antitrust men—to make up its corporate mind: Either produce television and film or book talent, but not both. MCA chose the former, and though its studio, Universal, looks great to tourists, it's in no great shape financially.

Today the largest agencies look less than steady. Rumors persist that Creative Management Associates (CMA), one of the new and most powerful, is about to bow out of booking and move heavily into production and cartridge television. It is common knowledge the agency is trimming its staff.

William Morris, probably the most durable of the really big agencies, is reportedly having its problems. Morris people in their way are unique: In a basically gossipy business they're about as willing to admit what's going on as your friendly local Mafiosa. The agency is run under the paternal and steady arm of Abe Lastfogel.

From CMA and Morris the list—if determined by size—dwindles. There is IFA, which is in the process of merging and re-emerging and recently had two offices on each coast. Chasin-Park-Citron is a splinter group from CMA, as funny as its name sounds. But those who own Rolls-Royces make payments just like the guys with the Chevrolets.

What appears to be happening is that things are coming full circle. What began, years ago, as one or two-man operations, then grew to occupy whole buildings (or possibly whole studios), is reverting to its former state. The agent who travels lightest these days also travels the fastest. Bill Robinson and Budd Burton Moss are members of growing ranks of independent agents.

Robinson and Moss, both 39, have been independent eight and three years, respectively, and aren't hurting much.

Robinson, who got his training as head of the talent department at Ashley-Famous, keeps a roster of 12 clients. Among them: Kim Darby, Carol Burnett, Stella Stevens, Tony Bill and Van Heflin. He is also unique in that "I have no contracts with any of my clients. Very few have left and to be honest about it, those who left didn't discharge me."

Moss, who began the Matador restaurant then moved to a brief fling at bullfighting, began fighting another sort of bull at General Artists Corp., where he studied six years before heading out on his own. His clients now include Jim Backus, Ray Walston, Doris Lilly, Melvin Belli and, until August, Sally Kellerman, the girl who made a smash in "M*A*S*H." "Her personal manager has her convinced she needs the services of a big agency. It's the second time she's left," he says without rancor.

xxx

Robinson is so phlegmatic it's impossible to believe he can hustle. Moss, on the other hand, is intense and hurried. By way of history, they have been friends for years. When Robinson went into the independent business, a silent partner put up $50,000 for starters. "It was strictly without strings," Robinson says, "and I've since given him back $200,000 and will continue." Moss didn't have a silent partner, but Robinson and his business manager took him to a friendly banker and gave him an introduction worth $5,000.

"The situation right now," Robinson says, "is that there are actually very few—like maybe a total of 12—really good agents at the big agencies. Ninety-five percent of them are packagers, which means lots more money. The rest are department heads. The packagers are in trouble because, quite simply, the business is money-oriented and neither the studios nor the networks are in a mood just now to lay $10,000 per show on some packager who put the thing together. The studio and network are putting two and two together themselves. The remainder of the agents run around covering the town, peddling people they most likely haven't even met."

"And that won't work any longer," Moss interrupts. "People need attention, the biggest names aren't working. We deal in close relationships, both with our clients and with the people we sell them to."

Because of their independence and therefore their smallness, Robinson and Moss have trouble keeping the show-business world covered. To solve this problem, they meet once a week and clue one another into the action. By mutual agreement they never put one another's clients into direct competition.

"We're not in business together." Robinson says. "We don't make money from one another. But we do cover for each other. I got Hope Lange, who was at the time Budd's client, into a deal when he was out of town. When our secretaries—that's an improper term; their names are Jennifer and Joyce and they do a lot more than secretarial work— find a problem they can't solve, they call whichever of us is in town."

Moss admits they're selective in their coverage of the entertainment business. "We don't cover the junk. That eliminates fifty percent of what's going on in this town at any time."

"We don't do *The Beverly Hillbillies* and AIP pictures, for instance," Robinson adds. "There are only 12 or 13 television shows worth the attention—artistically and financially.

"We have advantages and disadvantages, just like the big ones. Natalie Wood likes 20 people working for her. Lee Marvin wants only one person, Meyer Mishkin."

A big source of income for both agents and their clients, and a bit of work they all respect, is television commercials.

"Jim Backus made $60,000 in residuals for a total of five hours' work last year," Moss admits.

"Barry Sullivan is making $100,000 per year as the voice-over for Continental Airlines," Robinson adds, "for five days' work a year and he never appears in person."

"There are no performers in the industry today, with the possible exceptions of John Wayne and Elvis Presley, who are worth the so-called big money upfront guarantee the big agencies seek. Name any other star and I'll name a recent box-office disappointment in their immediate past. This isn't by way of apology for commercials, this is just the truth."

According to Moss, the big change is now under way: "Stars as we know them opt first for film, then film with television guest spots, and finally for a TV series. Right now they're looking at TV. If you don't believe me, ask Jimmy Stewart, Henry Fonda, Shirley MacLaine, Tony Curtis and a few others what they're doing in the immediate future."

Their immediate future is already formally announced, is doing TV series.

For all their philosophical agreement and cooperation as agents, Robinson and Moss have remarkably divergent ambitions. Casually holding a recent weekly meeting in Moss' office, which is located two Beverly Hills blocks from Robinson's, they teased one another about their respective ambitions:

"Look, no one ever believes me, but I only want to be an agent," Robinson says, "I don't want to become a producer. I'm not good at it and I'm not interested. I'm not what you'd call wealthy and I never will be. But in three years, I'll be semi-retired."

Moss, if he has his way in the next three years, not only will not be retired; he'll be producing pictures.

"My whole family is in the business. I want to produce, I've studied the business all my life because it was there at the dinner table every night. Quite simply, I want to put things together."

"The basic difference between Budd and me," Robinson quips, "is that Budd will gamble, gamble big. I won't. But for Budd, just as it is for everyone else, most of the gambles don't pay off. That's the name of the game. But I figure one of these days he'll hit and I'll just trot my client list for him."

Moss, recently tried—at his own expense, because the bet was worth one good Mexican dinner—to assemble *Or I'll Dress You in Mourning*, the book on Spanish Matador, 'El Cordobes,' for TV producer Chuck Barris (who owned the rights) and his former boss and present head of ABC Pictures, Marty Baum, into a picture. The arrangement, courtesy of the Spanish government and a few greedy other people involved, sank like a taco in a deep fry pit. He remains undaunted:

"My goal right now is to get Melvin Belli cast as *The Godfather*. Attorneys must be actors to convince a jury and Belli is a long shot but a perfect candidate as the Italian Mafia patriarch. He has the warmth, the guts and talent. It's a terribly logical idea, but then logic has nothing to do with it."

Logic does, however, have a lot do with Robinson and Moss. Robinson's annual income is well into the six-figure category and Moss hopes to break the barrier within the next two years. Both men are unanimous in their approval—self-respect wise—of their respective work.

There is an apocryphal story going around town about a big talent represented by an independent agency being wooed by a large, important agency.

"You'll be represented in every city in the world," the big agency tells him.

"Yeah," replies the superstar, "and when I'm unemployed, I'll be unemployed in every city in the world. Can you get me a commercial?"

Chapter One

Rita Hayworth Goes to Spain 1967

It was late Friday afternoon and I was heading over to the Polo Lounge to meet some friends for a drink before I headed home. The phone started to ring and I asked my secretary, Carrie, to grab it as I stood in the doorway of my office.

"It's Ed Feldman for Warner Brothers calling."

What does the president of Warner Brothers want from me at this time of the day? I have known Eddie on and off over the years going back to his days with Ray Stark at Seven Arts. I had also met him at various events with Jack Valenti.

"Hello Eddie, how are you?"

"Budd, I have a rather sensitive matter to speak to you about.

You represent Rita Hayworth?" "Yes?" I replied.

"Tell me a little bit about her today. I hear she is difficult to work with, I hear she is a big drinker?"

"Ed, there are so many rumors out there when you are as big a star as Rita has been over the years…why do you ask?"

"This is not for publication, but I think we are going to have some serious problems with Joan Crawford and a film we are planning on making in Spain in September or October, and we might have to replace her and we are putting a very short list together. Is she available?"

1

"Ed, do me a favor please? Send me the script tonight to my home and let me read it and then I will call her attorney, Leonard Monroe, who along with Judy Ault, his assistant, makes all the decisions for Rita." "Here is my home phone number, call me after you read the script." Ed said.

I thought how strange it is today that a giant actress like Joan Crawford would have "script problems" and she was going to be replaced by another "giant" actress who could not work out the creative problems at this point in her illustrious career.

"L Bastiardi" was waiting for me when I arrived home a few hours later. I called Judy Ault and gave her a heads up on what happened earlier that day.

"How exciting, Budd!"

"I am not too sure how exciting this is, as I need you to tell me how Rita is doing these days?"

"Ed, I have to be honest with you. She has had some great days and then there is a day or two that she slips and becomes very difficult, but this new medicine seems to be of help."

Remember this was 1967 and not too many people knew the word Alzheimer's.

"Let me read the script after dinner and if it is not too late, I will call you; if not in the morning."

"No, please call me at any time, I want to know how good the script is!" Judy eagerly said.

"L Bastiardi," "The Bastard," aka "Sons of Satan, " directed by Duccio Tessari, revolved around two brothers brilliantly played by Klaus Kinski and Giuliano Gemma. Martha was to be played by Joan Crawford. The brothers, Adam and Jason, specialized in jewel heists, overseen by their alcoholic mother. Jason is betrayed by Adam, who steals his girlfriend and has him beaten and left for dead. A female doctor, Margaret Lee, nurses him back to health, and sets about planning his revenge.

After reading the script, I could see where Joan Crawford was unhappy with the role of Martha. She was not a nice character, which I shared with Judy that night when I called her at midnight. "Do you think Rita would want to play that role?" she asked.

"When did she last work?" I replied.

It was around 9:30 the next morning when I called Eddie back and told him my thoughts about the script and what it would take to get Rita to do the film.

"Budd, I will know Monday morning if we are going to make an offer to you. I must tell you that there is an offer out to another actress who has to give us an answer by 10 Monday morning. If she passes, I will call you with the offer."

"That sounds great. I know we can work out a deal that everyone would be happy with. My recommendation is that Warner Brothers make the same deal, point by point, that Joan Crawford was going to get!"

There was a long thirty-second pause and then Eddie said, "Let me see what I can do."

Monday morning the phone rang at my office around 9:30. Carrie had yet to arrive. "Mr. Moss, this is Edna, Mr. Feldman's assistant. He asked me to call you and tell you that he has arranged for business affairs to call you at noon, if that is convenient for you?"

My heart skipped a beat, since this was going to be a great credit for the new Burton Moss Agency.

"If you would hold on Edna, I am going to give you the phone number of Ms. Hayworth's attorney Leonard Monroe. He will be the one to work out Ms. Hayworth's contract for the film."

I quickly gave her the phone number and while I had it in front of me, called Judy.

3

"Hold on to your hat, Judy. Put Leonard on so I can give him some information prior to speaking with Warner Brothers business affairs."

Leonard was just as excited since this was going to be Rita's first important job since she worked with Tony Quinn earlier that year in "L'avventuriero," or "The Rover." Before that, she had only worked in 1965 with Glenn Ford in "The Money Trap." I told Leonard to insist that Rita receive the same, favored nation's deal that had been offered to Joan Crawford point by point. That should make it easy for everyone.

Eddie had sent over that afternoon a beautiful arrangement of flowers to Rita, along with the script and a very warm letter welcoming her to Warner Brothers. Rita looked so lovely when I went over to meet with her, Leonard and Judy later that day. I had insisted with business affairs that Warner Brothers provide three first class tickets so Judy could come with us, but Judy had not been well and her doctor suggested she not travel at that time. I was so disappointed, knowing how Rita depended on her, but I made sure we had a standby in Madrid who would be with Rita when needed.

It was now late September and we had to be in Madrid by October 10th for two weeks of filming and one week in Rome for post-production..

Chapter Two

Rita and Budd Go to Madrid

Having lived in Madrid for almost two years when I was married to Ruth Roman, I had a lot of favorite spots to take Rita while we were there. I made arrangements for us to stay at the Palace Hotel across the street from one of the most beautiful fountains in all of Madrid: Neptune sitting on his royal throne surrounded by mermaids and dolphins. We could almost see the Prado just down the street from our large balcony. The manager who was there when we arrived took us to the royal suite reserved for visiting royalty and presidents from around the world. It was indeed breathtaking as royal suites reside on the top floor of the hotel.

I had arranged with Luis Sanz, Ruth's agent, to help look after Rita while we were there from our arrival at Barajas Airport, with a large group of press waiting to see one of the truly great legends of the silver screen come back to Madrid. Rita's director, Duccio Tessari, was there also to greet this great star. He rode back to the hotel with us. He spoke excellent English, which made everything so easy for Rita.

My loving friend, Vicente Ibanez, was also there to take photos of Rita for our personal collection while the press spent almost twenty minutes asking her a million and one questions.

By the time we got to the Palace Hotel, Rita was beginning to slowly fade and wanted a drink, which turned on my light bulb. Duccio excused himself and said he would see us later along with several members of the cast. "Let's get upstairs and rest, since production has arranged a small cocktail press party in the Hemingway suite of the hotel. We can have our welcome drink upstairs, Rita," I said.

The next two days were filled with wardrobe, makeup and press. Both her "sons," Giuliano Gemma and Klaus Kinski, had sent two giant arrangements of flowers and various fruits and were around her all the time, helping, needless to say, to make her comfortable and to make her feel welcomed and wanted.

Before you knew it, Rita and I walked on to the sound stage, and were welcomed by the crew as well as her fellow actors, including actress Margaret Lee and Claudine Auger, and producer Turi Vasile. I made sure that her dressing room on the stage was well appointed and with a large sofa so at any time, in between shots, she could relax. Rita had very few script problems since Duccio was always one step ahead of her when she needed help. He solved the problem before it happened.

Her director's chair was waiting for her. What a smile Rita had on her beautiful face. As she sat down, Klaus and Giuliano lead the group of well-wishers by her and thanked her for coming all the way to Spain to make this film together. I stood off to the side, knowing how important this moment was for Rita.

Rita was in and out of make-up, wardrobe and hair and in front of the camera, and said to Duccio with that great magical look that made Rita Hayworth one of the greatest movie stars in the world, "READY WHEN YOU ARE, DUCCIO!" I could feel my heart skip a beat. I was here. My dream was coming true. I could say to myself, "Look what you have done, Buddy Moss!" For the next week, I never left the set. As Rita got into the script with her two sons, there were many moments where Duccio would say, "CUT," and walk over to Rita, sit her down and speak to her ever so softly so she felt secure with what he was telling her. Before you knew it, she was back in front of the camera with a quick smile at Duccio and saying, "Let's do it!"

As the days went by, I started thinking about Rita's birthday that was on

Tuesday, October 17th, 1967, and what to do on that special day. She had worked late the day before and the director told me that they were going to give her the day off for her birthday and had arranged a special birthday cake on set that night.

She was touched and very pleased that the company had thought about her. Everyone sang Happy Birthday to her. I had told Rita over the weekend about my years in Spain with my first wife Ruth Roman and her five-year-old son Richard, and how much we loved driving to Toledo for the day. It was about fifty miles from Madrid and if we left early enough that day, we could drive there in an hour or so depending on the traffic, have lunch, do a quick tour of the Great Cathedral, see some of the famous Velazquez paintings, visit El Greco's home and see his famous painting *"El entierro del señor de Orgaz,"* and maybe the synagogue of Sta. Maria la Blanca built in the 12th century. Then a quiet lunch at Los Cuatro Tiempos (The Four Seasons), which was next to the imposing cathedral founded in the 16th century. The National Heritage building still had some old wine cellars and caves.

We ended up having lunch in one of the oldest rooms. We had their paella and some of the best tapas in Spain, along with their special partridge roasted in their antique ovens.

I was so pleased with my plans that day and thought all was going well until after lunch, we were sitting near El Greco's home and from out of nowhere, a Spanish paparazzo popped out from behind the corner and took a photo of us relaxing in Toledo. As it turned out, it made the Madrid papers the next day and was not a bad photo of Rita or me! It said she was with her agent "Mudd Morton Boss," my new name in España.

I told her how nice it would be to have a low key day in Toledo for her birthday and then if she would like, we would go with some friends of mine, including Vicente Ibanez, the famous photographer, to *El Corral de la Moreria,* the best flamenco club in Madrid. Ruth and I spent many a happy night there over the years. It was the best of all the flamenco clubs in Madrid.

We had a great afternoon in Toledo and on our way back, since Rita was not tired at all, I suggested we make a quick trip to the Valley of the Fallen (Valle de los Caidos), about eight miles north of El Escorial, the home of the great kings of Spain.

I explained to Rita that General Franco started to build this monument to be a tribute to commemorate all those soldiers that died during the Spanish Civil War (1936-1939). About 40,000 Nationalist and Republican soldiers are buried there. However, when he started to build this complex from 1940-1958, it was going to have a basilica, like that of St. Peter's in Rome. When General Franco died in 1975, he was buried there. Rita was deeply moved when we went into the basilica. She said it reminded her of St. Peter's in Rome. She must have crossed herself a dozen times when we were there. I had never seen so much gold around the basilica; it was really a shrine to Franco.

I told her that the cross, which was built on top of a rocky cliff known as Risco de la Nava, is 1400 meters above sea level. The Holy Cross of the Valley of the Fallen is the largest in the world. You can see it from twenty miles away as you are driving there.

It was time to head back to Madrid. Rita had dozed off on the way back to the hotel, where she was greeted with at least a dozen floral arrangements from so many of her friends, including Cayetana, the Duchess of Alba.

We decided to take a nap and then get dressed at 10 p.m. to go for a little birthday supper and some flamenco dancing at *El Corral de la Moreria*. Before we left Rita's wardrobe lady, Mercedes, came over and helped her get dressed for the party. Yes, Rita did get on the tables with two of the male dancers and did a terrific flamenco dance for the guests in the restaurant.

This was one of my most memorable days with Rita—sharing her 50th birthday after all the years I had known her and traveled around the world with her. I am sure if we go to the Spanish newspaper archives, we will find some great photos of her dancing with several of the flamenco dancers at *El Corral*.

Before we knew it, it was almost 2 a.m. and Rita was slowly fading. She was still gracious and beautiful and had very little to drink that night. Our friends, the Ibanez's, drove us back to the Palace Hotel.

As we went up in the elevator, Rita put her head on my shoulder and said, "Thank you Roomy," which was my nickname, "for the best birthday anyone could ask for."

We went into our royal suite and I walked her to the door of her bedroom.

"Can I get you anything?"

"No," she said, "just unhook me so I can get to bed."

I leaned over and gave her a kiss on her cheek as she smiled at me and said, "Thanks for my best birthday party, ever" and she kissed me softly on my lips, much to my great surprise.

I crossed the large living room with a smile on my face and stopped and looked out at the magnificent Neptune Fountain below our suite.

I walked over to the fridge and grabbed a couple of bottles of soda water and the bottle of Fundador, a Spanish brandy, which was on the bar. Within minutes, I found myself in bed slowly thinking of what Rita and I did in one very long and special day, to say the least.

I must have been asleep for several hours when I saw the light go on in the living room from a crack under my door. Slowly my door opened and I could see Rita's silhouette coming toward my bed, she paused for a moment, which gave me enough time to smell the Arpege perfume she loved to wear at night. She sat at the end of the bed for a moment and then slowly slid under the covers next to me. I did not move or say anything. As she came close to me I could hear her whimpering.

"I need you to hold me please, Roomy," she said as I laid there.

My head started to spin. I could see myself at the screening with my mom and dad. I was eleven years old and I saw this beautiful woman with flaming red hair, just like my mom's. I was in love as only an eleven-year-old boy could be. I saw her in the commissary at Fox Studios with the great Darryl F. Zanuck. I was a busboy wanting to be the man she was with.

I could feel her warm, sweet breath on my neck. Here I was with one of the most beautiful women in the world—a woman who has been made love to by some of the most famous and wealthiest men in the world. She was truly the greatest sex goddess ever and I was holding her. Was it time finally to fulfill my lifetime dream and make love to her? I could feel myself getting harder and harder. I had her left breast in my hand. I could feel her hard nipple between my fingers as she laid there quietly. What would have happened had I reached over and kissed her like I wanted to? Could she feel my hard, hot penis next to her soft body? Did I dare tell her I have loved her all these years and wanted her more than any woman I had ever gone to bed with? Seconds, and then minutes passed. She turned over with her back to me as we started to cuddle. I said to myself, what if she starts to scream or haul offs and hits me? It would be the end of our relationship, which I did not want to happen. I pressed my body next to her and held her tight as we started to doze off. I could hear her softly starting to whimper for a few seconds and then she started to cry, almost like a lost child being held by her mother.

As the morning light tried to break through the nightshades, I rolled over and looked over on my side. Rita was gone. The smell of her body still lingered on my pillow. A new day in Madrid was just beginning.

The days went by rather quickly. Rita knew deep down inside how important it was to finish the film without any problems. She always managed to be on time and seemed to be eager to help out with the other actors when there were script problems or when one of her "sons" was concerned about how that one scene went, and could it be better if they did another take.

We were almost through filming with just a few scenes left. The PR people that were handling the press had one more interview to do with Rita about her going to Rome the next week. They wanted to do a big splash for her arrival at Leonardo da Vinci Fiumicino International Airport first, and then check into the famed international Cavalieri Hilton

Hotel on top of one of the seven hills, one of Rome's few hotels that had one of the most beautiful swimming pools in all of Rome.

As our limo pulled up in front of the Castellana Hilton Hotel in Madrid on the beautiful Paseo de la Castellana for our press conference, I was taken by surprise to see one of my beloved friends from California, Sidney Poitier, and his four beautiful daughters, Beverly, Pamela, Sherrie and little Gina, and of course Mrs. Hester James, their longtime friend from the Bahamas, housekeeper and governess.

I am sure that Sidney was taken by surprise too when he saw me get out of the limo with Rita Hayworth, who was dressed to kill on a bright and sunny afternoon.

I called to him and said, "I think, Mr. Poitier, that the Beverly Hills Hotel is back that way?"

He was caught off guard and then he let out with one of his great laughs and said, "Buddy Moss, what are you doing in that limo with this gorgeous lady?"

Rita had known Sidney over the years and there we were, all eight of us, kissing and hugging right there on the Grand Paseo.

You would have thought that we had just landed on the moon. "What are you doing in Madrid?" I asked. "And what are you doing here Budd?" As if he didn't know.

"Off to a press conference!"

"We are staying here!" said Sidney.

"I will call you later! Let's do drinks!" and off we went into the hotel.

The press party went very well. Rita was a bit nervous but handled most of the questions well when all she had to do was answer with a yes or no, or *si* or *muy bien*.

For some of the questions that she could not answer quickly, either Luis Sanz, her agent, Turi Vasile, the producer, or Duccio Tessari, Rita's director, would respond.

Once the event was over, Rita wanted a drink which I had no problem with after her having done an excellent job with the press, and all we had to do was go back to the Plaza Hotel which was just minutes away.

Turi told Rita and Luis how well the dailies looked and was anxious to get to Rome for the week of editing with her and her "sons." He told Rita that she was going to like staying at the Cavalieri Hilton Hotel, which was perched atop one of Rome's Seven Hills, overlooking the Eternal City. Having stayed there with my wife Ruth and her son Richard a few years ago, I told Rita that the hotel was like a mini museum with some of the greatest artwork, including the Tiepolo triptych that was on the soaring lobby ceiling and the exquisitely hand crafted antique tapestries.

Rita seemed interested but said, "I usually stay at the Hassler on top of the Spanish Steps!" But I was quick to add that usually this time of the year, September and October, was still very hot and this hotel had one of the few great swimming pools, knowing how Rita enjoyed swimming.

Chapter Three

Guess who Came to Dinner At Casa Botin with Rita

Once Rita and I were back at the hotel, she wanted to rest for a while. I suggested that I call Sidney around five or so to see if he would not only have drinks with us, knowing he did not drink if I remembered correctly, but might like having dinner with us around 9:00 or so since Rita had an early day the next morning at the studio and then we were off to Rome the following day. I suggested we go to Casa Botin where we had been twice since we were in Madrid. She loved the restaurant, especially having dinner in their famous cave.

I spoke with Sidney around 6:00, catching him resting. He had spent the afternoon at the Prado with the girls and a guide, which was just on the other side of where our hotel was. "I am tired. I cannot keep up with these young ladies but we all loved the Prado and we had a great guide who took us everywhere."

I told him that we would love seeing them for an early dinner since no one eats in Spain before 9:00 or 10:00, which he thought would be a great idea. I told him all about Casa Botin and he said, "Let's pass on the drinks and we will meet you there at 9:00 or so." I told him I would make the reservations and call him back and that I was sure his limo driver knew exactly where to go.

I quickly called downstairs to the concierge and asked if he would please make a reservation for a party of eight at Casa Botin for Ms. Hayworth, and in the cave, at 9:00. "Right away Señor Moss, but that is rather early? You might have the whole cave to yourself," he said jokingly.

Rita slept for an hour or so and then she was dressed and ready to go. "I am hungry, Roomy, let's go!"

It was only 8:30 and I told her I was going to make a few calls and the limo was going to be downstairs in a half an hour. Rita was fine with this and she took her book and went into the living room to read for a while, which she did quite often.

Years ago I had heard something about carrying a book with you at all times as it would make you look like you were very intelligent! If I remembered correctly, it was told by her husband, Prince Aly Khan.

It was a little after 9:00 by the time the limo got us to Casa Botin. The manager had been waiting for us at the front door. He was very excited as Rita and I came through the door. "Ah, Señora Hahhworth," he pronounced her name. "Señor Poitier and his family are downstairs waiting for you! Please come this way."

He led us down the stairs to this three-hundred-year old cave and there was Sidney and his ladies, waiting patiently for our arrival.

The waiters had already put a lot of tapas on the table, several bottles of water and a couple of bottles of mineral water. The girls were already on their second cokes—picking up and tasting or smelling these strange tapas but enjoying them, not quite sure what they were eating.

Sidney had gotten up and took Rita by her arm and said, "Sit here my dear lady!"

He had Mrs. James on his left and Rita on his right. The maître d' had moved a couple of tables around so we had a large round table towards the end of the cave, which worked out perfectly. I found myself

14

surrounded by his four beautiful daughters, Pamela and Gina on my right and Beverly and Sherri on my left with Mrs. James. The girls were lost for words, sitting in this very old cave underneath the streets of a very old Madrid, wondering about the history of Casa Botin and how many famous people had been in this historic cave before them.

"What brings you here, Buddy B?" (that was the name Sidney would always call me).

We all got a kick out of being on Angelo Drive one day and then half way around the world the next day at Casa Botin. Ah, the wonders of show business, I said to myself. I briefly told Sidney and the girls what history I knew of Casa Botin. It was considered to be the oldest restaurant in the world, going back to when the owners from France served their first meal here in 1725. "I am sure you will find it interesting to know that the first meal consisted of *cochinillo asado*. Roast suckling pigs."

"Euuwwww!" the girls said.

Legend had it that even Francisco Goya was said to have worked there as a waiter while waiting to be accepted into the Royal Academy of Fine Arts, and even Ernest Hemingway made mention of the roasted suckling pigs in his novel, "The Sun Also Rises."

The waiter brought menus when Sidney suggested that I order, knowing that he likes lots of veggies and rice, pasta and fish. Rita wanted a nice turbo and a mixed salad, as did everyone else. I had the waiter bring a carafe of sangria—that was fine with Rita. That was followed by a couple of thick filets, a few roasted chickens and several orders of their fresh giant shrimp a la parrilla, almost like small lobsters. A great dinner was had by all. Needless to say, the girls were curious to see the baby pigs that the waiters brought to them. They looked like they were wrapped in their blanket, sound asleep.

As we were finishing dinner, a group of Tunas college students strolled in, wearing traditional costumes and knickers, singing and playing traditional songs of early España and some flamenco music and songs from La Mancha, the south of Spain, like the Gypsies.

Sidney and the girls were so excited to have their own private musical review. This was topped off with the best flan (caramel pudding) and a chocolate and vanilla cheesecake—the best in all of Spain. No one could move for almost half an hour as we said our farewells and promised to meet for dinner again as Sidney and the ladies were going to be in Rome, the same time as we were. I told them if it was warm there, and it should be, to get a bathing suit and come swimming at the Hilton.

Sidney and I embraced and looked at each other as our limos pulled up, both of us sharing a private second of our years going back to when we first met on the set of "Blackboard Jungle." Eight years later, I opened The Burton Moss Agency, and here we were together with Rita Hayworth and his children on the streets of Madrid.

Our last days in Madrid were very hectic as Rita wanted to go by the set and say goodbye to the cast and crew and then head for Rome. We also said our farewells to her agent Luis Sanz and my loving friend Vicente at the airport, with our thanks and appreciation for all their help and for giving La Rita the special love and attention she deserved.

Chapter Four

Adios Madrid, Ciao Roma

The flight to Rome was very relaxed and Rita only asked for one drink, which I felt she deserved. She worked very hard on the film and wanted her work to be recognized and for it to be known that Rita Hayworth was still a dependable actress. Before we knew it, we were circling Leonardo da Vinci Fumicino International Airport. As expected, once we were at the gate, two agents from Alitalia came aboard and introduced themselves to us and explained that they were going to escort us to their VIP lounge once we were taken through Immigration and Customs. They asked us for our passports and luggage tags and told us that Duccio and their press people from Madrid were waiting for us in the VIP lounge along with some twenty in press from Rome.

With the help of the two agents, we were the first off the plane and were whisked through Immigration and Customs. As we headed for the VIP lounge, I could see Duccio walking towards us to put his arms around Rita to reassure her that he was going to help her through the interview and answer as many questions as possible about the filming of "L Bastiardi" in Madrid. From the moment that Duccio opened the door to the private room that had been set up for Rita, there was a barrage of photos and press asking questions. Duccio was a master at calming things down and quickly explained that there was a limited amount of time available since she had to go to Cinecitta Studios straight from the nference. I looked at Rita to make sure she was OK. I could see was somewhat nervous, so I quickly asked Duccio to get started. The press in Rome are always very explosive to say the least. Most of the questions were about the film. When was she last in Spain and Roma? Did she like working with Klaus Kinski and especially Giuliano Gemma, who was Italy's own up and coming superstar that Duccio was responsible for discovering and putting him into his first major role in "Arrivano i titani"? Visconti then wanted him for "Il gattopardo" and years later became almost as big in Italy as Clint Eastwood in their "spaghetti westerns," having changed his name to Montgomery Ward. Duccio was able to answer most of the questions the press asked and many of the questions about Hollywood, Tony Quinn, whom she had last worked with, were all answered with a series of yes or no's or "I can't remember."

I knew that it was time for Duccio to thank the press for coming and with a wave to the two agents who escorted us to the lounge, Rita waved, smiled and said ciao to the press and we were on our way out the back door with Duccio and a quick walk to our waiting limo.

Rita was now anxious to get to the hotel and, I am sure, wanting her vodka on the rocks, which we both could use at that time. Duccio had the hotel manager waiting for us in the lobby, and had us pre- registered and were taken to our two-bedroom suite looking over the historic city of Rome and the Vatican. It was truly one of the most majestic sights in the world. It was now over two hours after we had arrived in Rome and we had the production people come to our suite to discuss our three days, which consisted of looping, some additional wardrobe stills and a few interviews. I made sure that Rita had time to do a little shopping if she wished and to see Sidney Poitier and his daughters. I could see that Rita was ready to come to a stop. Duccio could not have been nicer and thanked Rita a million times for being so helpful and generous with her time and made her feel like she truly was "A Great Star!"

Once everyone left, I suggested that Rita relax and told her that I had made arrangements with the manager to have the maid come and take care of the unpacking that was needed for her stay in Rome. I made sure that the other two cases were locked up until she got back to Beverly

Hills.

It was late afternoon on a very warm day when I got a call from Sidney. They had just got back to the Grand Hotel, and were exhausted from their shopping on Via Condotti at the bottom of Spanish Steps. They had their bathing suits in hand, and asked if this was a good time to come over.

An hour later Sidney called from downstairs and I told him I would be right down and take them to the pool. I quickly called the front desk and asked the assistant manager to arrange a cabana for them to change in. Within minutes the girls changed and in they went, screaming as they jumped off the diving board. Sidney and I sat by the pool with Mrs. James for a little while and much to my surprise, Rita came down in her lovely Pucci wrap-around, all in browns, beige and rust, her favorite colors that matched her glowing red hair.

She seemed pre-occupied and managed to say hello to the girls as they splashed around and then quietly walked down to the deep end of the pool, slowly slipped into the water and started to do a few slow laps like a pro. There were very few people around the pool and I am not even sure if anyone knew that it was Rita.

When she finished, she came over to dry herself off and told Sidney how nice it was to see him and his lovely girls again, what a fun night we had in Madrid and that she hoped to see him back in Beverly Hills. Sidney suggested we all have dinner that night, but Rita said some old friends were coming to the hotel for an early dinner, much to my surprise, and had two busy days ahead of her with looping, additional stills and a stack of interviews, which of course Sidney was the first to understand.

I suggested to Sidney, as he was ready to take the girls back to the hotel, that maybe we could have dinner together, since I now had the evening free? "Let me call you later," he said. It was almost 7:00 when Sidney called back. "Budd, the girls are beat and want to order in and maybe walk up and down the street for a while so come and pick me up at eight and we will have an early dinner too!" "See you out in front at eight," I said.

I walked across our suite, stopping to look at Rome with a million lights flickering over this beautiful city at night. I knocked softly on the door until Rita opened it. "I am going to meet Sidney at eight for an early dinner. Are you sure you are alright?" Rita smiled and said her friends were coming at nine and "we are going to eat in the main dining room, so have a great time with Sidney." For some strange reason, I was not too sure what Rita was going to do but I knew she would be ok if she stayed in the hotel.

I quickly changed and called downstairs to make sure our limo was there. On my way out I stopped by the manager's desk and made sure that one of his assistant managers would stop by a couple of times to check on Rita. In minutes I was on my way to pick up Sidney "P" for our dinner in Rome. It turned out to be one of my greatest joys having an evening just with Sidney—a little dinner at my favorite Sabatini's in the old Piazza del Santa Maria in Trastevere. I ordered linguini and clams for both of us with a side order of grilled langostinos and a bottle of Pinot Grigio, even knowing that Sidney would not take a sip of the wine. Sidney was amazed at where we were when I told him that this was part of the oldest section of Rome and about the history of this famous church, Del Santa Maria, completed in 1143, in front of us. It was almost 10:00 when I told him that I had made arrangements with one of my Italian actor friends, Umberto Orsini, to take us to the most famous disco in Rome called the Hippopotamus. From the moment Sidney walked into the disco and was spotted by all the gorgeous young Italian women, he found himself being invited to dance with at least a dozen of them during our brief two hours there.

Finally Sidney looked at me and said, "Let's get out of here or we'll be here all evening." I managed to say goodbye to my two Italian friends and found our limo and took Sidney to the Grand Hotel. As Sidney got out of the limo we said our farewells and promised we'd go to Spago's when we got back to Beverly Hills to re-wind the film of our bumping into each other in Madrid of all places.

When I got back to the hotel and found my way to our suite, I was surprised to find a waiter's cart in front of our door with a stack of plates with food on them—a salad that was half eaten, a dried-up piece of cold salmon that looked like it was not touched with a few veggies scattered around, a full cold pot of coffee and two lowball glasses that smelled of vodka. I could only assume that Rita did not have guests for dinner and just wanted to be alone.

Rita and I were happy to be leaving Rome, her three days of film editing went well and she was looking forward to spending time with her daughter Yasmin for a couple of days. It was quite the whirlwind trip and we both needed a little rest.

Looking back at my first adventure with the legendary Rita Hayworth, thinking of all the years that I had wanted to know her, to spend time with her, to share my thoughts about her as I was growing up, I will always remember those three weeks with her and our adventures in Spain together with great fondness. A young man's dream came true.

Yes, I could see that there were some problems that could be looming in the distance. I was not aware at this early date that one day, this legendary goddess of the screen was going to be stricken with a tragic illness that would linger inside of her for years to come, and I would be witness to it as I continued to be her friend and agent, and there was nothing on God's Earth I could do to save her from death's door at a very early age.

What I was pleased about was that the filming was a success. I was able to prove, as her agent, that Rita was still able to be a creative and productive actress. There were very few problems that had to be handled and the end result was that my friend and head of Warner Brothers, Edward Feldman, had a very successful film that showed to the world that Rita Hayworth was still out there, thrilling her audience and fans with an outstanding performance. And I was able to fulfill all of my dreams of being a part of this great star's life for three weeks together.

Chapter Five

This Is What Happens When You Go on a Blind Date

Sidney Beckerman was a fast-talking Sammy Glick-type agent from Brooklyn who was trying to turn himself into a cool Hollywood producer. He did so well as the years went by that two restaurants, Dan Tana's and Matteo's, named one of their famous dishes after him: Chicken Beckerman. Sidney and his wife Marion and friends were always at the Factory Disco on Sunday nights, which was the night to be seen there.

One night I bumped into Sidney and noticed his wife seated at their table. Marion was speaking to a very tall, attractive blonde lady. I asked Sidney who she was. Sidney laughed and said, "They are longtime personal friends and if you think she is hot, wait until you meet her sister."

"Really?"

"She's in the middle of a divorce and would probably like to go out with a famous Hollywood agent. If you like I will call her and set it up."

A week later, Carolyn Gerry was on the phone. "I am sure you have been to the Factory." "Oh yes, too many times," She answered.

"Well, I am not sure if you know that on Sunday nights they have a celebrity night. Next Sunday, Vikki Carr is singing there. She happens to be married to my brother Danny and we are having a few friends to see the show. I plan on inviting Sidney and his wife. Want to join us?"

I could not remember, as I drove down Sunset Boulevard to Palm Drive, when I was last on a blind date, but here we go. I turned right on Palm Drive and pulled up at a Beverly Hills classic red brick home. It was large, as large as 907 Beverly, but all in brick with an interesting slanted roof. I parked in the sloping driveway and walked up to the front door and hit the chimes.

"Hi, are you Mr. Morris?" asked the kid who opened the door.

He looked to be about six years old.

"Moss, kid, not Morris."

"OK, I'm Bobby. Come on in."

As he led me into the den, another kid came from out of nowhere.

"Hi, I'm Jimmy. Wanna Coke or a beer, Mr. Morris?"

"A Coke would be fine. Moss, not Morris."

He disappeared as quickly as he arrived. All of a sudden, he walked in with my Coke on a tray.

"Hi, I am Susan, Mr. Morris." I started to correct her and say Moss, but didn't feel like going through it again. As I sat there admiring the warmth of the house, I could feel someone staring at the back of my neck. I quickly turned around and there was yet another kid, this one a teenage boy with long hair and the "gang look" of the day. He smelled like cigarettes.

"Hey," he said in a low whisper. "I'm Steven. What time are you bringing my mom home, Mr. Morris?"

"Hi," I said, and reached out to shake his hand. He was not expecting that.

"Can you keep her out late?" Steven asked. "We got some girls coming over at eight."

"I'm Budd," I told the kid. "Wish I could help but this is only my first date with your mother. But I'll try."

Just as I was asking Steven, "Is your mom here?" I heard someone running down the staircase. Into the room came a young girl dressed in all brown leather and covered with a Gucci scarf, Gucci chains and Gucci boots. "I'm Carolyn, the mom," she said as we shook hands. She had the greatest smile I'd seen in years.

In a flurry of goodbyes, she yelled at Steven to get home early, kissed Susan and looked at her as if to say, "What do you think of this guy?" and reminded Jimmy to do his homework. As we walked to the front door, little Bobby came running to say, "You didn't finish your Coke, Mr. Morris".

"Never mind that," Carolyn said. "Go upstairs and tell Olla May to get you into the bath…Love you," she called out to everyone, and we headed for the Factory and a night with Vikki Carr. "Great," I said to myself somewhat grumpily as I helped her into the car. My first blind date and probably my last. As lovely as she was, I sensed that this might be an early evening. There were just too many kids!

The dating started and it was joyous to say the least, kids and all. It was just what I needed after the adventures with Ruth and the Hollywood scene with Ms. Jones as I was on my way to becoming a famous Hollywood agent. Little did I know what a wonderful woman Carolyn Gerry was and what pleasures awaited us as I fell deeply in love with the mother of four and most importantly for me, "a non-pro," which is what I needed at that point in my life. All she wanted to do was to make me happy and share the special gift we had: our new love together.

A year later, when Carolyn and I decided to get married, Melvin Belli offered to host the wedding at his apartment. "Come on up and we'll do the ceremony on my terrace overlooking San Francisco. Invite whomever you wish."

Sam Rolfe, producer of "The Man from U.N.C.L.E." and his wife, Hilda, Arthur O'Connell, a character actor I'd known for many years, Joan Sheldon, from Mills College days, and six or seven other close friends attended the small ceremony.

Carolyn and I were married on Melvin Belli's terrace overlooking the magnificent city of San Francisco on September 27th 1970. Stanley Mosk, a judge who eventually became Supreme Court Justice of California, performed the ceremony. Sidney Poitier and his then-fiancée, Joanna Shimkus, stood up for us. After the ceremony, we all headed to a Mexican restaurant for a celebration dinner in the Cannery that lasted late into the night. When I finally reached for the head waiter and asked for the check, he said, "No check, Señor Moss. Compliments of Señor Belli!"

The next day, Mel came by our hotel and said, "Here are the keys to my Rolls. It's stocked full of food and champagne. Have a wonderful honeymoon." We had made a reservation at a hotel in Carmel, the Tickle Pink, hidden behind the famous Highland Inn near Big Sur. Carolyn and I did not know how to thank him for everything he had done for us. The next morning, Carolyn and I took off for Carmel, and on the outskirts of town, I noticed a Warner Bros. studio truck parked off the highway. I couldn't imagine what it was doing there, so I slowed down to investigate.

"What are you doing? Don't stop, Budd!" Carolyn said.

"It might be somebody famous; I want to see what's going on," I told her. "This will only take a second."

"Budd, this is our honeymoon," she sighed.

"Two seconds, I promise," I told her, and pulled in behind the truck. I jumped out to investigate and heard a familiar voice say,

"Budd Moss, what the fuck are you doing in that Rolls Royce?"

It was my old friend Clint Eastwood giving us his famous squint. It turned out he and Jessica Walter, a client of our agency, were shooting the famous death scene in "Play Misty for Me" that day. "Stick around," Clint invited. "Watch us do the scene."

Carolyn looked at me. "You're not going to stay? Today of all days?" she asked.

Needless to say, it was several hours before we were back on the road and headed to our honeymoon. That was my first day as a married man. What can I say? I was a famous Hollywood agent!

Chapter Six

Jack Valenti/U.S. Congressman Wayne Hays, Elizabeth Ray Scandal 1976

It was a late Friday afternoon and I was returning my daily calls when my private line started to ring.

"Budd, Jack Valenti." It was never just Jack.

"Can you talk for a moment?"

"Sure," I said. I buzzed my secretary.

"Please hold my calls for a while."

"How are you, Jack?"

"Great. I'll be coming out to LA next Wednesday for two days, let's do lunch on Friday." "Great," I said.

"Budd, do you know the photographer, Tom Kelley?"

"Sure, we all know his famous Marilyn Monroe nude on the red satin sheets with the one rose."

"A friend of mine has an actress friend that has always wanted to have her photo taken by Kelley, just like the Monroe photo." "Oh," I said.

"I don't know the girl, never met her, but I understand she is quite attractive and has a great body. Can you call Kelley and see if he can set up a photo session for her at the end of the month? Her name is Elizabeth Ray and she will call you next Monday, OK?"

"No problem," I told Valenti.

I found Kelley's phone number and put a call into his office.

"Tom Kelley! Hi, this is Budd Moss calling. I was wondering if you could help me? An actress friend of mine from New York is coming out here at the end of the month and wants to have her photos taken by you. I guess you get a lot of calls since you did the Monroe photos."

Tom said, "I charge $1,000 for the session. It will take about a half hour, including make-up and its cash."

"I will call you back on Monday once I have her schedule, and thanks, Tom. Her name is Elizabeth Ray! Here is my phone number for now."

After I hung up from Tom Kelley, I thought for a moment; in all the years I had known Valenti, this was the first time I'd got a call from him about an actress wanting to have some nude photos.

"Oh well," I said to myself.

Monday morning, the phone rang bright and early.

"Hi Budd. This is Elizabeth. Did Jack call you?"

"Yes, he did and I called Tom Kelley for you."

"Oh, God. Did you really?"

"When are you going to be here?"

"I come in on Monday and will be there for two weeks. I need a couple of days to work out before I take my photos. How much does he charge?"

"$1,000 for the session."

"Cool," she said. "I thought it was going to be like $5,000. I brought a lot of cash. Will the photos be on the same red satin sheets?"

"I don't really know. Those photos of Marilyn were taken a few years ago. I think in May of 1949. He might have bought some new red satin sheets for you." "Really?" she said.

"I gotta grab a casting call," I said, trying to get rid of her. "Where will you be staying?"

"I think my boyfriend, Wayne, had Jack's office put me in the Beverly Hills Hotel. Is it nice?" she asked.

"Yes, you will like it!"

"Has it got a spa? I will call you when I get in. Maybe you could set up a few casting meetings for me also?"

Once again, I sat there trying to sort this one out. I decided to call Tom Kelley, and since she was coming in on Monday, I would see what dates Tom had available.

"How is Thursday morning at 11 a.m. or Friday at 3 p.m.?" Kelley's assistant asked.

I opted for Friday afternoon.

"Thank you," I said. "Elizabeth Ray will be there."

The next day, Jack called, having just gotten into town. "I have her set up with Tom Kelley on Friday afternoon at 3 p.m."

"Thanks Budd, I know her friend is very appreciative." "I hope he is. I bet he can't wait to see the photos." "Me too," Jack said, kiddingly.

"They won't be as good as Marilyn's, I can assure you," I said.

Jack and I had lunch on Friday as scheduled. We spoke briefly about

Elizabeth.

"I think I told you, Budd, that I have not met her. Just spoke to her a couple of times, but her boyfriend wants her to try and get a shot in Hollywood."

"I told her I would try and get her a couple of casting meetings if at all possible." "Thanks," Valenti said, as he signed the check and said he had to get to Universal to see Lew Wasserman at 3:30 and then catch the "red eye" back to D.C. Sometimes he would arrive in LA at 10:00 a.m., have a car take him to the hotel, have three meetings there, go out to see Wasserman at Universal and catch the last TWA flight back to D.C.

When Elizabeth called me from the airport on Monday, she said she was grabbing a cab and wanted me to come by the hotel for a drink before I went home.

"I will try," I said.

"I am so excited, Budd, I can't wait to meet you."

It was almost 6:30 p.m. when I called my wife Carolyn and told her I was going over to meet Elizabeth for a quick drink and then I asked her to meet me at La Scala at 8:00 for dinner. Carolyn was terrific about last minute changes.

I would always park on the Crescent Drive side of the Beverly Hills Hotel, especially when I had to get out of there in a hurry. I called up to Elizabeth's room but there was no answer. As I walked into the Polo Lounge, there she was, sitting at the bar with two guys climbing all over her. She wore a white summer dress that dropped to the floor in front. To say she was big breasted was an understatement. Attractive, hmmm, no. Sexy? No. A quick turn on? Most definitely.

"So you are Budd Burton Moss!" she said as she threw her arms around me. She was on her second scotch and soda.

I spotted Mario, the maître d', the "seeing eye" host at the door and asked if he could find me a table in the back. Mario knew who Ms. Ray was already. She must have dropped Valenti's name a dozen times or more. I told her I could not stay long; besides, it looked like the two bodybuilders at the bar had dinner (and possibly breakfast) plans for her.

"I have studied for so long. I know I am a great actress. I just need someone to believe in me besides Wayne and Jack." (Jack had said he'd never met her.) "When I go to New York, Jack is always so nice to let me use his apartment at the Lombardy Hotel."

"Well, let's see how these Tom Kelley pictures turn out first," I said to her and I guzzled down my Corona beer. I told her about some casting people that I had called.

"Did you bring some headshots?"

"Yes, they are up in my room. Want to come up and see them?"

"Not now," I said. "Gotta go, Elizabeth. Got a dinner meeting." She walked me to the door.

"I got the check, Budd. Don't worry."

I slipped some money into Mario's hand as I headed out the side door to my car. "Take good care of Ms. Ray."

Mario winked. "I don't think I need to."

Elizabeth called after lunch on Tuesday, sounding a little hung over. I didn't want to know what she did the night before.

"Can I come over at five to show you some of my headshots?"

Five was okay. Her headshots were not. They looked like they were taken in Omaha, Nebraska by her drama teacher getting ready to do a production of "Our Town." They were black and white and as flat as the Salton Sea.

"You could use some new photos besides Tom Kelley's. I will try and set up a photo session next week."

"Oh please do," she said as I walked her to the door. My secretary Nicole kept looking at me.

As the door closed, she said in her best French, "Boy, someone really must be taking good care of her."

Little did I know at that time what was soon to happen in the months ahead.

I had Elizabeth see a few casting guys I knew that would get a hard-on when she walked into the room. When they gave her a script to do a cold reading, they were very kind to her but when I called them later, they said, "We only did this for you, Budd."

The day had arrived for Elizabeth to go to Tom Kelley's. She was so excited that she was up most of the night doing exercises and then into the spa early in the morning. This was her greatest moment to lay on the red satin sheets, spreading out and thinking that this was where Marilyn Monroe had been. For a brief moment in her life, she was "Marilyn." I called her to wish her good luck and reminded her to tell the cab driver that the address was 736 Seward Street in Hollywood between Santa Monica and Beverly Blvd., in the back. As I hung up I found myself thinking of Marilyn. She was so broke in those days that rumors were such that when she needed money for her rent she would go up to Sunset Blvd. near Highland and turn a trick for fifty bucks. She turned Kelley down twice to do some nude photos until finally he offered her $50.00 and she took it. The vast fortune Kelley made over the years from his famous nude photos put him into an early retirement for sure, just from selling the calendar rights alone around the world. I am sure that Hefner probably paid a lot for those photos of Marilyn. Hef was so in love with Marilyn that he bought the vault next to her at the Westwood Memorial Cemetery in Los Angeles so when he dies, he said, "I would be able to sleep next to Marilyn Monroe for eternity."

I arranged another couple of meetings and one dinner with a part-time producer who wanted to meet her. He took her to La Scala. It seemed that he hit on her, according to Elizabeth, and said he wanted her to go down on him at their table in the back of the room, just like Warren Beatty in the feature "Shampoo."

"I am not happy with Hollywood. All the guys just want to jump on me."

"Oh, come on Liz. I think you are creating some things that just look that way. You are a great looking girl and your Tom Kelley photos are the best I have seen." (In real life, they turned out OK, but they were not Marilyn.) "You can't make it in Hollywood in ten days, but you did great and should come back after the summer and get an apartment, and stay for a couple of months and study with some of the best coaches we can find for you," I said.

"I'll think about it. I have to see what Wayne wants me to do."

This was March 1976. Valenti called and thanked me. He said he had yet to see the Tom Kelley photos.

As April clicked by I felt like there was a bomb ticking and was ready to go off any minute inside the capitol building.

In May, 1976, The Washington Post broke the story quoting Elizabeth Ray, Wayne Hays' former secretary, saying that Hays hired her on his staff and later gave her a raise as part of his staff for almost two years, in order to serve as his mistress. Hays had divorced his wife of 38 years just months prior, and married his veteran Ohio office secretary, Pat Peak, in early 1976 shortly before the scandal broke. Liz let a reporter listen in as the Ohio congressman told her on the phone that his recent marriage to another former secretary would not affect their arrangement. Time Magazine reported that Liz chose to tell her story after Hays decided to marry Pat Peak and did not invite her to the wedding. It was just five weeks after the marriage that the scandal broke.

Elizabeth had previously had a chance encounter with Marion Clark, a

35

Washington Post reporter, on a train that had gotten delayed by a paint factory explosion. As the passengers swapped stories, Liz said that she had quite a few sexual escapades in the nation's capitol, including with several congressmen. Clark tried to keep in touch with her but lost track when Liz briefly went west to try and make it as an actress. Liz remembered Clark, however, and was eager to spill the beans on Hays, which eventually removed him from his office.

Liz said that she had been working on Capitol Hill since 1972, starting as a hostess and then working for a few congressmen. She began working for Hays in April of 1974 as a clerk for the House Administration Committee. As Ray told it, though, "work" was too strong a term for what she really did. Basically, she told reporters, that she was a hired mistress, coming in only a few hours per week to have sex with Hays and receiving $14,000 a year for the administrative duties she never performed. "I can't type. I can't file. I can't even answer the phone," she said.

Chapter Seven

Who Do I Have to Screw, Congressman Hays?

Liz said she knew other girls working for congressmen who also had to submit to sex to keep their jobs and made references to "orgies" at the Capitol attended by congressmen. She said that on one occasion, Hays referred to the Fanne Foxe incident by saying that any woman that embarrassed him in such a way would be "six feet under."

Clark and Post reporter Rudy Maxa took Liz up on the story and personally witnessed her dinner dates with Hays on a couple of occasions. Liz also allowed them to eavesdrop on a phone call from Hays. When Liz asked what the state of their relationship would be after Hays' wedding, Hays replied, "if you behave yourself, we'll see." He also advised her to start coming into work more often, since he was afraid that Bob Woodward, one of the two Post reporters who managed to crack open the Watergate scandal, was after him (Woodward was looking into Hays on restaurant expenses, but not the affair with Liz). Liz asked, "Do I still have to screw you?" Hays answered, "Well, that never mattered."

The Post ran the story on May 23, 1976. It included Hays' response to the question of whether he had been having an affair: "Hell's fire! I'm a very happily married man." However, the personal witness accounts of the reporters, including a transcript of the phone call, made the denial ring hollow. The story also accused another committee staffer, Paul Panzarella, of living with Hays' niece and receiving a paycheck for doing virtually no work. In later investigations, Hays was accused of giving two other men annual salaries of $25,000 and $10,000 for minimal contributions to the committee.

Two days after his denial, Hays admitted to having a "personal relationship" with Liz, but maintained that she had done work for the committee and had not been hired solely for sex. Time opened that Liz was not the most sympathetic character, described by past boyfriends as "nutty, spacey, neurotic, or dim," but that Hays' overall crustiness made him a particularly worthy subject to be knocked down a peg or two. In July of 1976, the Ohio Black Political Assembly called for Hays' expulsion, saying the House had set a precedent for expulsion for misconduct with the Powell decision and needed to be consistent, noting that Powell, dead since 1972, had said "he could come back to haunt those who had removed him because they were guilty of the same sins." A lawyer later referred to Liz as "the ghost of Adam Clayton Powell."

In June, Hays was hospitalized after taking an overdose of sleeping pills, an action he insisted was accidental. The same month, he resigned from the Democratic Congressional Campaign Committee and Committee on House Administration, an action that automatically removed him as chair of the Joint Committee on Printing. He said he was resigning due to the accusations and the state of his health, but that he was convinced he would be exonerated and possibly restored. In fact, Hays was easily able to win the Democratic nomination for the 1976 election that month.

Instead of proceeding, Hays announced in August that he would not seek re-election.

"The polls show I'd win, but I don't want to give that woman another chance to make an appearance," he said. By this point, a book on the affair entitled "The Washington Fringe Benefit" had been published under Liz's name. Liz herself said she regretted her actions and that she had not intended to bring about Hays' downfall. She even declared, "He's suffered enough. He's gone through enough torture."

On September 1, Hays resigned. The House Committee on Standards of Official Conduct immediately dropped its investigation since they no longer had jurisdiction in the matter. Hays had reportedly asked for the ethics committee to look into the matter in order to show that Liz had actually worked for her salary, though other sources say the resignation was explicitly to escape the committee's investigation.

This was not a simple matter of infidelity, however. There was still the question of whether Hays had thrown away government money on useless employees. For a time, the Justice Department looked into whether Hays could be charged with conspiracy to defraud the government or conversion of public funds to private use. In October, three lawsuits seeking to recover Liz's salary were dismissed, and in December the Justice Department closed their investigation without pressing charges. An anonymous source said there was a lack of evidence against Hays, and that Liz's credibility was also an issue.

Liz said to her friends, "I was good enough to be his fucking mistress for two years, but not good enough to be invited to his fucking wedding." She pouted for days.

One night, around 11:30, Carolyn and I were watching Johnny Carson and the phone rang. It was Valenti. All he said was that if I got a call from the press, "You don't know Elizabeth Ray or anything about Wayne Hays." Click!

I am not too sure how much longer it was before a tell-all paperback came out called "The Washington Fringe Bandit." Liz had called me to ask me what I thought about the book.

"On page 28 and on page 122 and on page 187, you mentioned meeting your agent Buddy Morris, a friend of Jack Valenti, and that he did this and this for you. My agent, Buddy Morris, arranged my Tom Kelley photos, etc. Wait a minute, Liz. My name is Budd Moss, not Buddy Morris. Why did you spell my name wrong?"

"Don't you know Budd, I did that for you and some of my close friends that I wanted to protect?"

"Better you spelled my name right and not worry about protecting me."

The book was trash and Liz turned out to be trash. After making unsuccessful attempts at being an actress and stand-up comedienne, Elizabeth Ray faded back into obscurity.

Chapter Eight

Rita Hayworth Goes to London 1976

It was Super Bowl weekend, January 1976. It was the Cowboys and the Steelers, as I sat with Rita Hayworth and her secretary/traveling companion, Judy Ault, in the TWA red carpet lounge at LAX. We were watching the pre-game show from the Orange Bowl in Florida. As great as the game was going to be, we were about to board for our flight to London. We were able to get the scores on the plane as we were flying across the Atlantic.

I had booked Rita on the Russell Harty Show, one of England's top TV interview programs, and Rita was very excited about going to London where she had so many friends to visit. We were staying at the world famous Savoy Hotel overlooking the Thames River and the National Theatre.

What I had done as her agent was to put together a twenty-minute film clip of her major movies, so that during a half hour TV interview show, they could start and stop and ask Rita various questions about each film. The concept worked very well since Rita did not have to give long answers to each question. We did the same show in Buenos Aires in October of that year with not many problems, even though there were a few emotional breakdowns.

Those who knew Rita were concerned about her serious drinking problem and were concerned when she traveled. I was aware of all of these problems but I would tell Yasmin, Rita's daughter with Aly Khan, that there was more to her "just one drink." We all found out years later that it was the combination of "that one vodka on the rocks" and the various medications that she took when she was traveling caused her to "explode." It was years later before everyone knew that what was happening to Rita was the very early stages of Alzheimer's slowly crawling into this magnificent lady's brain and body.

Judy Ault had promised Yasmin that she would keep an extra eye on her even when Rita went up front to the bathroom on the plane to change into her nightgown and sleeping jacket, which she would always do prior to taking off. Did Rita have a small silver flask stuck away in her flight bag filled with vodka? I did not think so. In the old days of flying first class on the new 747's, the airlines had built a piano bar room upstairs, or an intimate dining room with five or six small tables for an elegant five-course dinner on fine bone china plates, a bottle of a fine Bordeaux or a classic Chardonnay if you preferred white wine, and all the Krug Grande Cuvée you could drink in flight.

Before we left, I had reserved a table for the three of us, but by the time we took off, it was getting late and Judy decided to go right to sleep, so it was just me and Rita for dinner.

I helped Rita up the spiral staircase and into this small dining area. There were only two other couples and they seemed to be halfway through their dinners. I knew Rita was ready for her second vodka and I was the one who said to the stewardess, "Please bring Ms. Hayworth a vodka on the rocks."

In the late afternoon sun, Rita looked lovely. She seemed very relaxed and spoke about Yasmin and hoped on our way back from London to stop off at the Carlyle Hotel in NYC to visit with her for a few days.

As Rita pushed the rocks around in her vodka with her forefinger, you could hear the clinking of the ice in the fine crystal low-ball glass. The stewardess then brought over a small dinner menu with just three choices, Dover sole, a fillet mignon, or Duck a l'Orange.

Rita looked at me and said, "You order for me, Budd."

"I think we both will have the Dover sole as long, as it is really from Dover," I said to Cathy our stewardess. She gave me a semi-dirty look, as if it was a personal affront.

"They are from Dover, Mr. Moss."

"Oh, and a glass of Chardonnay with just a little ice!"

"Sir," she said, "the wine is cold."

"I know, but I am famous for ruining some of the great wines of the world by putting ice in them."

Rita and I had just finished the prawn salad and were quietly waiting for the Dover sole to arrive, when from out of nowhere Rita stood up, accidentally pulling the tablecloth with her, causing what looked like Wedgewood china plates and crystal glasses to go in five different directions.

"God damn you, Gary!" She was on the verge of screaming. "This is the last fucking time I am going to wait for you." She was pointing her finger at me. Her face was turning red and her eyes seemed to be on fire.

"You will never treat me again like you do all your other slutty girlfriends. For three hours I waited. What was I supposed to do?"

I said to the stewardess, "Quick, get Judy Ault up here right away."

I tried to put my arms around Rita and slowly sat her down. She was shaking like a child that had just gotten out of a cold shower as she started to cry, "Gary, don't leave me again...please...I love you...you promised...you promised."

By that time Judy was upstairs with her flight bag. She was trying to get some pills out of the bag. She held Rita's mouth open the best she could and put the pills into her mouth, with a glass of water the stewardess was holding— and then we waited.

The three of us sat there for what seemed ten or fifteen minutes. Not a word was said. Once or twice, Rita took a few deep breaths and sighed and then started to whimper like a little girl having just lost her favorite doll.

By this time, the other two couples had quietly gone back downstairs. The first officer had come to speak to Rita, but she just wanted to go downstairs and sleep. He slowly, with the aid of Cathy, the stewardess, helped her down the spiral staircase and into her oversized first class seat next to mine. Judy was just across from us. We had agreed to switch seats during the flight depending on how Rita was doing.

Rita slipped into a deep, deep sleep. She started to whimper again as I put my arm around her and tried to hold her tight for a few hours.

Somewhere during the flight, I heard the captain say, "For you Steeler fans, Pittsburgh 21…for you Dallas fans… (a long pause) 17," and then I dozed off again.

Around six or so, Judy nudged me and pointed upstairs. Rita was still asleep so I joined Judy for a large glass of orange juice and some scrambled eggs.

"What do you think?" Judy said. "Shall we call Yasmin when we get in?"

"I think Rita is going to be okay. Let's wait until we get to the hotel." Little did I know at this time what was ahead of us.

Chapter Nine

Just When You Thought It Was Safe to Go Back in the Water

The pilot said, "Good morning. In about an hour we should start our descent into Heathrow Airport in London. Our estimated time of arrival is 7:35 a.m. Greenwich Mean Time. The weather in London is slightly overcast and a light rain is expected." Judy and I started our way down the spiral staircase that was between business and first class. As we got to the bottom of the stairs, I could hear Rita's high-pitched laughter. I thought she was asleep. What was she doing up?

It seems that the couple sitting in front of us was on their honeymoon and the captain had sent them a bottle of Krug with his compliments. The couple and Rita were toasting to their new marriage. I had to guess that Rita was on her second or third glass of champagne by the time Judy and I got to her.

"Hey Rita," Judy said. "Here, let me take your glass because it is time for some tea and breakfast." Rita pulled her glass away from Judy, spilling some champagne on Judy's slacks. "Now look at what you have done, Rita!" You could see that Rita was getting upset as the champagne was beginning to mix with her medication.

We sat Rita down again for a few minutes. I had the stewardess bring some hot tea and some bread for her. Once we felt Rita had calmed down, with an hour ahead of us before we landed, I suggested to Judy that this would be a good time to take her into the bathroom and get her changed into her street clothes, which had been hanging in the front closet near the side door of the aircraft.

Even though Rita seemed a little wobbly, Judy managed to make sure she looked ready for the landing. She helped Rita comb her hair and brush her teeth. She had very little makeup on because we had hoped to get through customs fast with the help of the TWA rep and into our limo without any problems.

Little did we know what was going to happen next.

The stewardess was starting to bring to the first class passengers their coats and jackets that had been hanging carefully in the front closet along with Rita's ten-thousand-dollar full-length mink coat.

As we started to feel the slow decent into Heathrow, the flight attendant had Rita's coat outstretched for her to stand up and slip in to it.

"What the fuck are you doing with my coat, you cunt! I caught you trying to steal it!"

The flight attendant stood frozen in her tracks, and before you knew it, Rita had hauled off and slapped her on the side of the face. The flight attendant started to fall as I quickly grabbed her and the mink coat. Judy had hold of Rita who was shaking again and trying to grab the flight attendant, yelling, "You stole my coat, bitch! I am calling the police!"

Finally, we calmed Rita down. Judy had another pill in her mouth with a quick sip of tea. "Easy, Rita. All is well. Nobody has taken your coat." Rita started whimpering again.

The flight attendant had disappeared. She had slipped upstairs to the cockpit and, I am sure, gave the pilot a full report of what just happened. I knew the pilot was calling ahead to London to give them a 911 warning that there was a problem aboard the flight as we got closer to landing.

I looked out the window below and there was the plush English countryside, sailing by our plane. Little red houses started to get bigger as we made our approach. You could see there was a slight drizzle coming down as the streets below looked wet and shining. There were a few bumps here and there as we started our final approach to runway #37 at Heathrow. I could now see small black cars making their way through the wet countryside of England.

We had landed our giant aircraft on English soil. The engines started their back-spin, the flaps were down and the brakes were grinding away, bringing our flight to a slow stop at the end of the runway.

I thought we were sitting there a little longer then you usually do after you land, as if the pilot was waiting for some special instructions from the tower. A moment later as we still sat there, the captain and another flight attendant came over to us.

"Mr. Moss, I am Captain Edwards and this is our first cabin officer, Nancy Hillboro. I trust Ms. Hayworth is feeling better?" Rita was sitting silent, with her head on her chest as if she was meditating.

"Yes," I replied, "She is resting."

"I wanted you to know that at the gate, there are about twenty in press, waiting to see Ms. Hayworth when she disembarks. They know that something has happened on the flight."

"How did they know unless someone on this aircraft called The London Times?" I asked.

"I don't know, Mr. Moss. I am only telling you this as an advance warning and wanted to find out what you wanted to do before we help you off the plane?"

I quickly told Judy that there was no way I wanted the press to see Rita as she was. "How long can we keep her on the plane?" I asked the captain.

"After everyone gets off, maybe a total of a half an hour."

I told Judy that I was going to try and go out and speak to the reporters, tell them that Rita was under the weather and was not able to do a press conference when she got off the plane.

Judy did not think it was going to work but we had very few options. Shortly we were at the gate. The captain came back and said he would walk me out to where the press was waiting at the gate. The rest of the passengers were put on hold, having been told that there was a security problem that would take just a few minutes. I took a deep breath and headed out the door down the tunnel to the gate.

Chapter Ten

"Ladies and Gentlemen, May I Have Your Attention"

The captain said in a soft voice to a few of the reporters that were close by, "This is Budd Moss, Rita Hayworth's agent, who wanted to say a few words to you."

There were more than twenty people of the press waiting for Rita; I counted close to thirty or forty. I asked if they would be of help to us as Ms. Hayworth was not feeling well and asked them if they would come to the Savoy Hotel that afternoon around 4:00 for cocktails and a brief press party with Ms. Hayworth. You could tell that they knew something was really wrong.

"What happened on the plane, Mr. Moss?" A few flash bulbs went off.

"I am not too sure what you are talking about but please, please respect Ms. Hayworth's wishes, and mine, and come to the hotel this afternoon."

"We want to see Rita as she is! Right now!" They were not going to give ground, I could tell. I thanked them for coming and walked back into the aircraft as the passengers that were in first class started to come off the plane, grumbling under their breath. I knew for sure that at any moment, one of the passengers was going to give a full report as to what happened.

Once back in the first class cabin, the first officer approached me and told me that he was going to try and be of help to us by getting Rita off quietly. What the captain was going to do, once the aircraft was empty, was bring a moveable stairway to the back of the plane. He asked that he take Rita's passport, and with Judy now in Rita's fur coat and hat, try and let her be the decoy if only for a brief amount of time, to get the photographers and press out of the gate area.

Was it going to work? I hoped and prayed it would. Fifteen minutes later the cleaning crew started spraying the aircraft with disinfectants, getting the plane ready for its return to LAX.

The first officer said, "Customs will clear Ms. Hayworth and Ms. Ault. Let me have their passports and we will make arrangements to put your entire luggage in your limo."

All of a sudden, there we were at the backdoor of the aircraft. Rita only had her traveling suit on and Judy's rabbit fur coat. It was windy and the rain was now coming down. There was no time for umbrellas. There was sheer panic on her damp face.

The captain said, "I'll take one side and you take the other side. Be careful, the steps are slippery."

As we made our way down the stairs, step by step, I could see in the distance what looked like a golf cart coming our way. I thought for a moment it was part of the service crew but much to my surprise, as we got to the last ten stairs, off jumped a small man in a grey trench coat, with a Canon camera flashing away at poor Rita, who did not know where she was or what she was doing there! I tried to shield her but it was too late.

Her legs were like rubber. The flashes continued for what seemed forever until the limo driver pushed him away and opened the door so we could slowly get her into the back of the car.

I tried to thank the captain but all he could say was to take care of this beautiful woman, whom he had admired over the years as one of our greatest movie stars. He knew she would be fine once she got to the hotel, and then he was back up the stairs and into the plane. As we drove away, you could see the crew moving the stairs away from the aircraft.

I held Rita in my arms the best I could. She knew, like a wounded animal, that something was wrong. She trembled and whimpered again as we drove off the tarmac, through security and into a slow and cold London rain, making our way to the Savoy Hotel. I thought about Judy and wondered how she was doing?

In the morning traffic, going into London, it was a slow drive. Mini cars were speeding by us, people on motorcycles were passing us and cars were leaving a high trail of water behind them that would spray the limo's windows.

"How long do you think it will take to get into town?" I asked the driver.

"Not too sure, sir" he said, "maybe a half an hour if the traffic stays this way."

Needless to say, I could not wait to get to the hotel, get Rita into her room with Judy and take a hot shower and wash this long, frustrating trip off me.

I was concerned about the press waiting for us at the hotel. The driver said that it was all arranged for us to go into the garage parking lot under the hotel, and security would then take us up the back way as the hotel has done over the years for royalty and VIP people from around the world that wanted to come and go unnoticed.

The driver found the side entrance of the Savoy Hotel and an iron gate appeared with two in security. As it slid open, the security checked the driver and in we went, with a small mini cart falling in behind our grey Rolls limo.

"You're here, Mr. Moss. The lady in the cart will take you and Ms.

Hayworth up to your suite. I have been advised that Ms. Ault will be here in about twenty minutes or so."

"I have no pounds on me." So I handed him a twenty-dollar bill. "Sorry sir," he said, "I have no change." "Not to worry," I said.

"Thank you, sir. I was glad I could be of some service to you both. Good luck to you, sir." And he tipped his hat, and smiled and said to me, "She is one of a kind, sir. Don't let anything happen to her. England loves her, sir! Here is my card in case I can be of additional service to you."

Chapter Eleven

"Welcome Ms. Hayworth to the Savoy Hotel"

"Hi, I'm Terri York and I will be with you this afternoon if you need anything!" A cheery strawberry blonde woman said. "The manager told me that there were a lot of press people waiting for Ms. Hayworth, but security was able to get most of them out of the lobby and into the street for now. The lift is just down the hallway, sir. It will take us to a private entrance to your suite on the 6th floor. We have arranged for security to be there also for the time being."

I thanked her and started to hand her another twenty-dollar bill.

"There is no need for that, sir!" she said in a very stiff and proper manner.

Rita looked like she was getting a little stronger. I had her arm locked in mine and Ms. York was on the other side with the driver of the cart following us just in case.

Within minutes we were in our lovely suite on the 6th floor. Rita wanted to know where Judy was. "I just sent her downstairs to bring up your luggage, Rita." I took her into the master bedroom and sat her down in a Queen Anne chair next to the bed. "Here Rita, let me take your coat and your shoes. I will get you a blanket until your luggage comes upstairs."

Before I knew it, there was Terri with a soft cashmere blanket with what looked like the royal seal of England and not the logo of the Savoy Hotel. I walked into the living room and opened the double doors to the terrace. It had stopped raining and our suite needed some fresh air. There was a lingering stale odor of smoke.

As I passed the front door, there on the floor were two or three envelopes all marked "Rita" or "Rita Hayworth" or "Mr. Moss." I walked over and picked them up and opened them as quickly as I could:

"Mr. Moss, call the front desk. Urgent!" "Mr. Moss call The London Times, Editorial Desk. Ask for Ernest!" The other envelope was a large 8 x 10 with a note attached inside, "For your eyes only."

I slowly pulled what seemed to be a black and white photo out. "Good God," I said to myself. "They got Rita. What a ghastly, horrible photo of her." It was taken just before we took the last step off the aircraft. Rita's hair was in shreds. Her quivering hand was to her face. She looked like death warmed over.

"Mr. Moss," the note said. "Unless I can see you and Ms. Hayworth this afternoon, no later than 6 p.m., this photo will be sent to the A.P. and U.P. and it will go around the world in less than sixty seconds."

The phone rang. It was the front desk. "Mr. Moss, Ms. Ault is on her way upstairs with Ms. Hayworth's luggage. What do you want me to do with all these messages?"

"Please turn off the phones. No incoming calls until notified."

Judy and three porters brought in our luggage. She looked like she had not slept either. Her lipstick was smeared. Her mascara was running down her face. I can imagine how tired I must have looked. Ms. York asked if she could do anything else as she handed me her card, before she quietly slipped out the door.

Chapter Twelve

"The Photo That Went Around the World in 60 Seconds"

Here we were arriving first class in London, in one of the most expensive hotels in Europe, with one of the world's most famous actresses and sex goddesses and we looked like we had just come from the front lines with battle fatigue. Judy rushed into Rita's room, only to find her sitting on the bed in her terrycloth bathrobe, watching an old English film with Vivien Leigh and Laurence Olivier on the television.

"I am going to get Rita ready for a nap. Off we go to the bathtub!" she shouted with a laugh. Rita half smiled and off she went. I told her that I was going to order some lunch for all of us; three big bowls of hot tomato soup, some eggs and bacon and lots of tea and coffee.

It was almost noon, London time. The events of the morning still were framed in my mind: the long trip, our aborted dinner in the VIP dining room, the champagne party in first class, Rita slapping the stewardess. God, did this really happen? I stared at this tragic face before me. How could I, as her agent, protect her any more than I had? How could I prevent the photo from going around the world? No matter what I agreed to, I was sure it would eventually leak out through some cheap National Inquirer type of magazine.

By the time room service got into our suite, Rita was back in bed, having spent a relaxing time in the bath. Judy had made sure that she was well scrubbed. Her hair was wrapped in a towel and she was in her oversized bathrobe. I brought her lunch into the bedroom so Judy could eat with her.

What to do? Once Judy had finished her brunch, she turned off the TV and told Rita to rest for a while. Rita was asleep in five minutes. Judy had also changed into her nightgown and bathrobe. I was in my jeans and my UCLA sweatshirt that I traveled with. "Do you think they will send this photo out?"

"No question about it," I said.

I told Judy that I thought it was important that we call Yasmin in NYC right away before she got the news first. There was a five-hour time difference between NYC and London. It was early morning in NYC, just going on 7:30 a.m. "Let's wait until 9:00 NYC time before we call," I said.

I had dozed off for a while, and when I woke up, I looked at my Porsche watch and saw that it was almost 9:00. I thought something was wrong for a split second, and then I realized with all the confusion coming into London, I had forgotten to reset my watch. I went into Rita's room as Judy was going through all the phone messages that had piled under the front door. "Press, press, press," Judy kept saying. Jack Hawkins had called. He was one of England's truly great actors and a longtime friend of Rita's.

"Give me that one, please," I said to Judy.

Russell Harty, the English TV show host that Rita was supposed to do his show with, was on Wednesday. Here it was Monday afternoon, almost 3:00.

I asked Judy to call the operator and put a call in to Yasmin before she saw the New York Post or Times or got a call.

Five minutes later, the phone rang and I answered it. "Your call to the States, Mr. Moss," said the very proper British operator.

The first thing Yasmin said was, "What's wrong? Is mom okay?"

"She is fine, but we had a few problems coming into London." I tried to keep it low key. I only told her about the stewardess bringing Rita her fur coat and Rita slapping her, thinking she was someone else. After a long pause, Yasmin said, "Budd, I think you should bring her to New York right away and I will take her to my doctor. How is she now?"

"She is sleeping quietly."

I told her about the photo and that the press wanted to see her at the end of the day or they would print the photo.

"What do you think they will do?" said a very nervous and upset Yasmin.

"Give me a few hours and I will call you back." "What about the photo?" she asked again.

"Yazzy" (that was what Rita always called her), "My personal guess is win, lose or draw, they will print it. I promise I will call you back by noon your time. I had a call from the TV show and also from Jack Hawkins, a close friend of Rita's."

I sat there for what seemed like an hour thinking this out. Let's call Jack Hawkins first," I thought.

"Mr. Hawkins, Budd Moss. I am Rita's agent."

He spoke in a very soft whisper. "What happened, old boy?" he said in his most proper English voice. "I heard on the radio this morning that there was a problem coming into London? What can I do?"

"Please, let me call you back once I speak to Russell Harty's office."

"Thanks, old man. Please tell my lovely Rita that I called and that we should go to the golf course and hit some balls!" I promised him that I would, but not right away.

"Operator, may I have an outside line, please?"

"Yes, Mr. Moss, right away."

The phone at the other end rang two or three times and then,

"The Russell Harty Show, may I help you?"

"Mr. Barrett, please."

"May I ask who is calling Mr. Barrett?"

"Budd Moss, Rita Hayworth's agent." Within seconds Mr. Barrett picked up.

"Mr. Moss, Nicholas Barrett here. How is Ms. Hayworth?"

"She is fine," I said. "She is on the phone with her daughter in New York," I quickly said.

"We hope she is alright and that what we have heard is just rumors."

"Not too sure what you heard Mr. Barrett, but she is fine and looking forward to meeting you and Russell Harty tomorrow. What time is rehearsal?"

"Whatever time is convenient for Ms. Hayworth. We only need about an hour for a walk-through and to set the film and, of course, Mr. Harty would like to take you all to lunch at the White Elephant tomorrow."

"Let me get back to you in a couple of hours." I hung up the phone.

"Judy, let's go over a few things." Rita was watching another old movie. "Keep her away from watching the news. I am sure it is all over the place."

"What do you think we should do?" Judy asked.

"Yasmin thinks we should pull the plug and take her to New York tomorrow on the first plane out."

"She seems so quiet right now. I know this will pass over by tomorrow."

I agreed with her and told her that I had an idea, knowing that Jack

Hawkins said he wanted to hit some golf balls with her.

"What would happen if we could get Russell Harty to host a press conference with Jack Hawkins at his golf course? That way, the press could see her and that she looked great," I said.

"Do you think Hawkins would do that?" asked Judy.

"Let me find out."

I called Jack back and told him the whole story, starting with the dinner upstairs in the small dining room, and then the champagne party and her hitting the flight attendant, and how the pilot managed to try and get us out of there without the press chewing her up. "Sorry to hear that, Budd. What can I do to help my lovely lady?"

"The press has been after us to give an interview. How far is your golf course from the hotel?"

"By car, less than an hour, on the way to Eaton."

"Let me call Russell Harty's office back."

"Do you want me to call Russell? We are old friends."

"Let me make the first call to Nicholas, and then we can go from there."

Nicholas said he would contact the press and would suggest Russell Harty get a double decker bus to take everyone out to Jack Hawkins' golf course to meet Ms. Hayworth and watch them hit some golf balls and do an interview there with Russell and the press. "A great idea," said Hawkins. The next day, there was Rita dressed in a green wool jacket and sweater with golf club in hand, with Russell on one side and Jack on the other, waiting for the press.

The press seemed to be kind, but every once in a while someone would keeping asking, "What happened at Heathrow? What happened on the plane?"

"Don't know what you are talking about," Rita would say and would move on to another question. When the press started to push Rita, Jack Hawkins stepped in and said, "Gentlemen, Rita and I are going to play a few holes. Time to get back on the bus! Thank you for coming out here."

No more photos, no more questions as we whisked her away and out towards the first green.

Judy and I gave a big sigh of relief.

Rita looked very beautiful as we drove to the Russell Hardy show. However, I noticed that she was becoming very nervous. Then I held my breath for the next half an hour. Judy couldn't bear to watch Rita, and had to turn away. Rita bounced gracefully on to the stage; however, when Russell introduced her she seemed bewildered.

Russell said after the interview, "She seemed lost, drained and very tired."

During the interview, Russell attempted to avert disaster by naming the great movies Rita had starred in. Throughout the interview he would play clips from her movies including clips from "Blood and Sand," "Sadie Thompson," and "The Loves of Carmen." Eventually, he announced that they would play a clip from Rita's movie, "Gilda," a film known for the fact that Glenn Ford "drool[ed] in the background." While the clip played, the camera cut to commercial, giving Russell the opportunity to slowly walk Rita off-stage into my arms. By this point, he was speechless.

Judy and I led her to her dressing room and gave her a glass of water and two pills. We then sat with her for a while until Russell's assistant came in and asked if she could do anything for us. I told her that Ms. Hayworth was fine and to make sure the limo was ready for us to leave.

She replied, "Ms. Hayworth's car is at the door already, sir."

"Thank you, and please thank Mr. Harty for everything."

Within minutes we had Rita back in the limo and were on our way to the Savoy Hotel for a quiet dinner in our suite so Judy could get Rita to bed early. Rita was quiet throughout dinner, as she knew there had been problems during the show. Judy reassured her that the show was excellent and she had done a terrific job. As Judy and I finished up our packing, we spoke about what happened not only on the show, but what had taken place over the last forty-eight hours. We knew that Yasmin was going to have to take Rita to a lot of doctors to try and find out what was wrong with her. Needless to say, we had no idea about what was ahead for our beloved Rita.

Soon we were off to New York on a noon TWA flight. Yasmin was waiting for us at the door to the Carlyle Hotel when we returned, and welcomed her mother with open arms.

Chapter Thirteen

Evita Meets Hollywood and Aaron Spelling 1978

When "Evita" opened on June 21st 1978 at the Prince Edward Theatre, it was an overnight smash. Tim Rice and Andrew Lloyd Webber had their biggest hit to date. The play starred Elaine Paige as Evita Peron, Josh Ackland as Juan Peron and David Essex as Che, and Hal Prince directed this masterpiece.

I was in London on business later that year and was having dinner with my two special friends, Janet Suzman, star of the Royal Shakespeare Company (and recipient of an Oscar nomination for "Nicholas and Alexander") and her husband, Trevor Nunn (director of "Cats" and "Les Miserables") at the Ivy restaurant, in the heart of the West End, London's famous theatre row. Both had been knighted separately by H.R.H.

Listening to them speak about "who's who" and what was the latest "smash" on the West End, and what and why this play and that play "crashed" was like listening to a BBC news report.

It was my last night in London. I had a late flight back to LAX the next night. Sadly, I did not get to see any theatre that past week due to a very tight business schedule with dinner meetings almost every night. What time I had free, I managed to see a longtime friend from college and former client, Robert Vaughn from "The Man from U.N.C.L.E"

TV series at MGM when I was his agent at General Artist Corp.

I ran into Bobby my first night in London at a party that I had gone to; we chatted and he asked where I was staying. When I told him I was at the Brown's Hotel, he suggested I check out in the morning and take a cab to the address he was writing down; he said he had four extra bedrooms and would love the company. He had rented a 19th century houseboat on the Thames. Typical Robert Vaughn.

When in London, why not stay on a houseboat? What a delight it was for the week that I was there. A little difficult to find from downtown in a cab, but they knew where the Hogarth roundabout was in Chiswick and I would have loved to see the taxi driver's face when we pulled up in front of this beautiful houseboat.

Robert had several cocktail parties in the evening at twilight time, and always managed to have several of London's most beautiful women there, along with a host of upper class English actors and writers. Just to sit on this historic site, right on the Thames where history was written over the past 400 years or more, was fantastic. My favorite moment, and it came as a big surprise, was my first morning there. At around 6:00, there was a distant tap…and then another tap…a little closer and then a tap…tap…tap. I sat up, trying to figure out where the taping was coming from. Bobby did not want to tell me that every morning, around this time, the local ducks and swans came banging on the side of the boat waiting for you to go up on the deck and throw them their morning bread, which I ended up doing for the remainder of the week, with great pleasure.

"Budd," Janet said, as she was finishing her cognac and coffee, "you must go and see Evita before you leave, it's a must!"

"But Shakespeare," (my nickname for her), "I am on the TWA redeye back to Beverly Hills tomorrow night."

"Well, go to the box office tomorrow before noon and get yourself a seat, even in the balcony or SRO, but go!"

Trevor nodded and said that David Essex stole the show playing "Che," and to hear Elaine Paige sing "Don't Cry for Me Argentina" would bring tears to your eyes. I thanked my loving friends for a great dinner. I took their advice and found myself getting out of a cab in front of the Prince Edward Theatre around noon the next day. As I approached the box office, there hung a sign over the head of a very old ticket seller, "TODAY'S PERFORMANCE SOLD OUT."

"Sold out?" I said to him. He pointed with a wiggling finger above him, without saying a word, hard at work with what looked like a week-old London Times crossword puzzle and a pen in his shaking hand, not even looking up at me.

"Sir," (that got his attention), "You don't understand. I know Trevor Nunn and Janet Suzman from the Royal Shakespeare Company and they said that I must see this play. I am leaving tonight for the States and I can't go without seeing "Evita.""

He looked up for a brief second and said softly, "Sorry," and pointed up to the sign one more time.

"Shit," I said, hoping he heard me as I walked away from his box office.

I found myself pacing back and forth at the front of the Prince Edward Theatre, like someone who was protesting the fact that the play was sold out and I could not get a ticket. Me, a famous agent from Hollywood.

I started to walk down the street and noticed around the corner from the theater was a pub on Greek Street, The Coach and Horses, and decided to run across and do some serious planning. I was thinking about the logo of "Evita" above the entrance to the theater. I decided to order a shandy (draft beer and lemonade) and think this one out.

The lady bartender was serving the couple next to me a Shepherd's Pie which looked really good, and all I'd had when I left the houseboat that morning was a large piece of French bread and some Spanish

67

manchego cheese that was left out from the cocktail party Robert had the night before. "I'll have one of those," I said as I pointed to his plate.

"Coming up, duckie," she said through her smoked-stained teeth.

The pub was filling up as it got closer to lunch with those who were heading to see "Evita" without me, I thought to myself. I had just finished my second shandy and the Shepherd's Pie that looked better than it tasted.

It was now 1:30 p.m. as I walked back to Old Compton Road and crossed the street again to the theater. I almost bought it as I was not thinking when I was looking the wrong way when the cabbie hit his brakes. I went back up to the box office window and slowly pulled out my wallet. I took out my Burton Moss Agency card and a U.S. five-dollar bill and handed both to the ticket taker at the same time.

"Sir," I said again as he was taken aback by the bribe. "Please give this card to Ms. Paige and tell her I have to see the play today, as I am on a flight back to America tonight." I could see him picking up what looked like a house phone and spoke for the first time, "Archie, can you come to the box office?"

Within a few minutes, an aging stage door man, in an aging blue jacket with several gold buttons missing, appeared from out of nowhere. The ticket taker handed him my business card and pointed to me, standing quietly near the billboard of the play. He nodded and headed back to nowhere with my card in his right hand, limping along.

It was now 1:40 and then 1:50, as I was giving up hope and wished I had not given the old man at the box office the five dollars.

All of a sudden, as I looked at my Cartier watch that read 1:59, Archie appeared from out of nowhere with a ticket in his shaking hand and said, "Compliments from Ms. Paige, who is expecting you backstage after today's performance."

I thanked him and told him to tell Ms. Paige that I would be there. I did not have another five-dollar bill to give him and did not want to hand him a twenty that I had tucked in my wallet and ask for change.

What a shock as I was led to my seat by a heavyset, rather small lady. I was seated in the fifth row center. I said to myself, "Job well done, Budd." What then took place for the next hour and a half was one of my greatest experiences in the theater. From the first sound of the inspiring music to Che coming out on the stage and unraveling the story of "Evita," I was mesmerized. I was transported to a Buenos Aires-like experience almost instantly.

By the time the curtain came down, I found myself mentally and physically exhausted. I could honestly place "Evita" in the top 10 of all the musicals I had seen over a 50-year period, and I did see some of the great ones.

I saw an usher standing close by as I was heading for the front door. I told her that I was a guest of Ms. Paige and wanted to go backstage. She took a quick glance at me to make sure I was for real and said, "Come this way, it is a shortcut and you don't have to go outside." She walked toward the stage and on the right behind some aging maroon velvet curtains, a small doorway opened that took you right into the backstage area, and for a fleeting moment I found myself standing right where Evita sang, "Don't Cry for Me Argentina."

We were now at the stage door, and she announced me to the old backstage man whose gold buttons were still missing from what looked like his World War One uniform.

"I am Budd Moss, and Ms. Paige is expecting me."

He then realized that I was the Hollywood agent that he had given the ticket to. He buzzed down on his interphone, "Mr. Moss is here," as if I was Laurence Olivier. "Prudence is on her way to collect you!"

Prudence looked like she was in her sixties and looked almost like Edna May Oliver, a film star going back to the 30's and 40's. She was out of breath taking the stairs two at a time, so I wouldn't be kept

69

waiting.

"This way, please. Ms. Paige is looking forward to meeting you, sir!"

Prudence led me into a small sitting room, if you could call it that, and then disappeared. Out came Elaine Paige; as attractive as she was, there was no resemblance to that giant star on stage singing, "Don't Cry For Me Argentina."

"What a powerful performance, Ms. Paige, and thank you for the ticket. Please let me pay you for it."

"Don't be silly, especially if you are really a Hollywood agent. Tell me how you got here this afternoon."

I told her of my long relationship with Janet Suzman and Trevor Nunn. She knew them both and had admired their great work at The Royal Shakespeare Company over the years. Little did we both know that one day Elaine was going to star in one of England's other great musicals, "CATS" directed by Sir Trevor Nunn.

We chatted for a few moments about Hollywood and about The Burton Moss Agency. She had a dream to go to Hollywood and be in the movies and I told her it would be an honor to represent her. We exchanged phone numbers and fax info and I promised I would stay in touch with her, and she promised she would send me headshots and resumes. I told her of my friendship with Hal Prince over the years, and was going to call him the first thing Monday to tell him about her and one of the truly great performances.

"Promise now, you'll find a movie for me, love!"

"I will do my best, Ms. Paige."

"Call me Elaine, please!"

A small handshake that led to a kiss on the cheek and I was back in a cab to my houseboat on the Thames to get my luggage and head to Heathrow.

The flight back to Los Angeles was a long one but filled with fond memories of my London trip, Robert Vaughn's charming houseboat on the Thames, the swans and ducks knocking at the side of the boat requesting their breakfast in the early mornings and a most fortuitous dinner with Janet and Trevor taking their advice to run, not walk to see "Evita" before I left London.

Back in LA, I could not wait to tell Carolyn about the play and how I wished that I could have at least one client in this brilliant musical. My first day back in the office, I called Hal Prince's office and left word that I was calling regarding "Evita." His secretary said Hal was traveling but would get back to me when he returned to New York. It was just a few days later that he called. I went on and on with Hal and told him how I came about going to see his musical at the suggestion of Janet and Trevor. He was pleased that I called and even remembered to ask how Ruth Roman was. I promised him that on my next trip to New York I would come and see him and looked forward to seeing "Evita" again.

If I thought the London production was a masterpiece, I was overwhelmed by Patti LuPone as "Eva Peron." She was truly one of the most exciting actresses in the American Musical Theater and an unknown actor to me. Mandy Patinkin as "Che" almost walked away with the show along with Bob Gunton as "Juan Peron." Hal Prince directed both the London production and the New York production that officially opened in 1979 and played 1,579 performances before closing in 1983.

It was during late 1978-1979 that plans were being put together for the first of many national tours. As casting lists were being put together both in New York and Hollywood, I had done some research about some of my clients who could sing, and I remembered that Jon Cypher had an excellent voice. Jon had some excellent Broadway credits, having appeared in several successful musicals. I remember him starring in a TV special of "Cinderella" with Lesley Ann Warren, playing the handsome "Prince Charming."

71

As casting was ready to see actors for the national tour, I suggested to Jon that after having seen the play at least three times, I thought he would be perfect to play "Peron." Jon had mixed emotions about doing a national tour. He would have rather auditioned for the replacements coming up for the New York company.

Jon finally agreed to audition for Hal Prince, after he saw the play; and after the fourth time, Hal told him that he would love for him join the company when it started up in Los Angeles.

As an agent over the years, and as I learned this from my boss, Marty Baum, whenever there was an important meeting where the agents' presence was needed, especially for support, I would be there. When there was a special event, in this case the signing of Jon's contracts with Hal Prince for "Evita," I felt it of major importance to be there to witness the historic moment.

I flew in from the coast and checked into Jack Valenti's suite at the Lombardy Hotel on East 56th Street just off Park Avenue. Over the years, Jack was very generous, sharing this lovely apartment with his special friends when he was not in New York. Looking back at the years that I went to the city, which at one time was every four to six weeks, especially when I had clients in plays or daytime series, it was a direct savings of thousands of dollars.

Chapter Fourteen

Hal Prince, Jon Cypher, John James, and Tommy Cruise

I will never forget the day I walked into Hal Prince's office that was located just behind Rockefeller Center, the home of NBC. From Hal's office you could look right down on the beautiful gold trimmed ice rink where skaters and lovers, both young and old, would come to hold hands and skate to some of the most beautiful music that glided with the skaters through the air.

As I introduced myself to Hal's secretary, I turned around and saw this young, attractive man with a two-week growth of hair on his face.

"You must be playing "Che,"" I said with great confidence.

"How did you know?" he said with a surprised look on his face.

"Oh, I have seen the play now four times. I know you will be great in that role. Do you have an agent?" I asked.

"Only in New York," he said.

"Well, knowing what a big star you could be from this part, I would like to meet with your agent while I am in New York." I introduced myself to him and gave him my business card. "What is your agent's name?"

"Her name is Dolores Sancetta and her agency is called D.M.I."

"I am staying at the Lombardy Hotel and here is the phone number. Maybe I could meet her at the end of the day tomorrow?" Just then, Jon walked into Hal's office and we greeted each other warmly, knowing that "Evita" was going to be an exciting and rewarding experience for him and all the actors. Within a few minutes, Loni Ackerman, who had been one of the understudies for Patti LuPone, came in and we gathered in Hal's office for this festive occasion. Hal could not have been more gracious and took the opportunity to tell everyone of our early friendship and how my going to see "Evita" in London brought us all together that day.

The next day, after receiving a very warm phone call from Dolores Sancetta, I went over to her office on West 57th Street. She took me by surprise when I first met her. She was nothing like I expected a New York woman agent to be. She really looked like a beautiful, warm, lovely and sensitive Italian mother that had only one concern in life, and that was to make sure her children were taken care of and nobody was going to harm them.

We spoke for an hour or so about Hollywood—my agency, my career, my clients and how I worked with producers, directors and, most importantly, casting directors. Dolores was the first to admit that she did not have a lot of contacts in Hollywood and would like to find a way for us to work together, especially since she knew that Jon Cypher was a client and I would look over Scott while he was in the play, and send him out to meet as many of the casting people in town while he had this great entrée to Hollywood as one of the stars of "Evita."

Dolores and I spoke about some of her clients, including John James, a tall, very attractive and talented actor that had been doing very well in the world of soaps in daytime TV. She recently had John meet and audition for Joyce Selznick, one of the major casting giants at ABC.

It was Joyce's job to play talent scout and find the best actors and actresses in New York; she would put them under an exclusive contract for one year at the sum of $40,000, which would put a hold on the actor while ABC went searching for a TV pilot for them. The actor was free to do movies or TV at any of the networks, but they were exclusive to the network as far as TV series.

Dolores and I met the next day with John James, whom I liked almost instantly. She also introduced me to a scrubby, kind of uptight young actor, who I expected to say to me, "Well, what can you do for me in Hollywood?" Here was this very young Tommy Cruise, along with John. Dolores brought in an actor and friend of Tommy's, Patrick St. Esprit, who Dolores saw as a young Clint Eastwood.

My primary concern was with John James and Dolores. We had worked out a very simple business arrangement. Dolores and I became partners and we would share a 50-50 split on all commissions that came in on monies earned, not only by John but other clients of hers that I would represent on the West Coast. John had been starring on "Search For Tomorrow" and now it was time to bring him to Hollywood to make the rounds.

The list of casting directors from Lynn Stalmaster to Fred Roose and Mike Fenton met John. I took John to Fox, Metro, Columbia and Universal Studios and he was endorsed by the studio executives as a very promising young actor that should end up in a major TV series that season.

As Hollywood folklore tells you, after my six-year relationship and engagement with Carolyn Jones that sadly broke up towards the end of 1967, I had spent a lot of time repairing my friendship with Aaron Spelling, who had been married to Carolyn for almost 13 years before they divorced.

From the time I moved into 907 North Beverly Drive in 1963, Aaron and I did not get along very well. He would constantly get upset with Carolyn when he would call the house and I would answer the phone. He would say, "Who is this?" "It's Budd!" I would say.

"Put Carolyn on the phone. Carolyn, Godammit. It doesn't look good when Budd answers our phone!"

This went on for a long time and finally Carolyn had to say to Aaron, "Get a grip, Aaron. Budd is living here and is sleeping on your fucking side of the bed and from time to time we fuck in your bed, so unless you can call and be nice, don't call!" and hung up on him.

When I brought John to see Aaron for a new series he was going to make called "Oil," dealing with a rich oil family and their early days in Texas looking for that first big strike, Aaron liked John and called Joyce Selznick to tell her he wanted to test John for the lead role of "Jeff Colby," along with John Forsythe, Joan Collins and Linda Evans. Soon the pilot was sold and before you knew it, the series became known as *Dynasty*. John, Dolores and I had a great eight-year ride, filled with a lot of bumps as far as John's character and his relationship with his fellow actors that, towards the end, caused a lot of friction within the camp.

Chapter Fifteen

Just When You Thought It Was Safe to Go Back in the Water (Not Again?)

Somewhere along the latter part of the series, Aaron called me and asked, without saying anything to John, to come over to his office and meet with him, Doug Cramer and the Shapiro's, who created the series. Needless to say, I saw red lights going off as I drove down Santa Monica Blvd. to the famous Goldwyn Studios on Formosa Avenue in the heart of old Hollywood.

By this time, our relationship had mended and we found ourselves embracing as I came through the door, and there were the Shapiro's and Doug waiting for me.

"Please sit over here, Budd, as I want to show you a few quick clips of a couple of the most recent shows and then tell you why we asked you here," Aaron said. The lights went out and there before me was John, in several brief scenes, with various leading ladies, holding them and kissing them. He looked bored as he went into an embrace. His dialogue sounded flat and showed little or no emotion at all. This went on for four or five minutes.

"Well, Budd, what do you see?" Aaron said to me.

I was not shocked at what I saw, but I knew there was great concern from the Shapiro's that their leading man on the silver screen was not a lover. He came across cold and flat. He looked like he did not have a hard-on when he took these young maidens in his arms. His lips were sealed. There was not even a sign of our leading lady's tongue trying to get into John's mouth.

"Budd, you know the brass at ABC. Tony Thomopoulos, president of ABC TV, has expressed some concern. They aren't too sure what to do with John. Do you have any idea when he was last laid?" asked Aaron. "We asked you to come in because we have known you for a long time as a friend, and as a respected talent agent you can understand our dilemma."

"Maybe you could find an expensive hooker. We would pay for it," said Doug Cramer, the executive producer, "and take him to Palm Springs for a weekend and fuck his brains out. Not to be crude, but the ratings are down and we have thought about replacing him or having his car go over a cliff."

"Aaron, give me a couple of days. Let me call Dolores when I get back to the office and bring her up to date. I know she will want to get on a plane and come out here ASAP." Esther Shapiro looked at me and said, "We love John but he has got to put some life into his acting."

And I said as I walked out, "And put something hard into his pants."

Doug Cramer was going to put a call in to Dolores also, but I asked him to wait until I spoke with her first. He nodded to confirm that he would. I knew the minute that I called her, she would get on a plane. She agreed with everything I told her about John and my meeting with Aaron, Doug and the executive producers and writers. John was becoming a problem and was developing a star attitude.

Dolores was in LA two days later. She first went to meet Esther Shapiro at her home. Esther suggested that John also get a good acting coach. Dolores told John that the Shapiro's were really planning on developing his character and focusing on his being an "intense lover," but with the new problems, they could just as easily write him out.

Dolores took John out to dinner the next night and, like his mother and agent, told him the facts of life and did not pull any punches. She was determined to convince John that he had to change his attitude and go back to being that lovable guy that they first met and fell in love with.

John was furious, Dolores told me the next morning when we met for coffee at her hotel. It took some time to calm him down, especially since he told his girlfriend what was happening and she said, "You are a great fuck, darling," and to tell that to Aaron and ABC.

Looking back on this, Dolores told me that she strongly felt this was the beginning of the end in their long relationship. He felt that what Dolores was telling him was coming from "his mother" and not Aaron, Doug or the network.

Dolores and I put a lot of time into making sure his contract was locked in for a few more years, even with the network's options. We had taken John's salary and doubled it from $9,000 to $20,000 a show. At the same time of those negotiations, we went on record that if there were a "spin-off" that John would be a part of the new show (soon to be titled "The Colby's" with Chuck Heston and John James.) We made sure that if the spin-off did not sell, John had to go back to "Dynasty" at the salary he was getting at the time of the spin-off.

All this time, behind our backs, John had been having meetings at the William Morris Agency. John had become a TV star overnight, and the Morris office kept promising him that if he came to them, they would make him a movie star. Those were the words that got to John. Now, the test was coming. Would this caring, young, talented actor think about what Dolores had done for him the past nine years? Would his loyalty and integrity, which we all thought he had, overrule the smooth, cunning pitch of the Morris office? Or would the pitch block out what had been done for him and make him change from Dr. Jekyll to Mr. Hyde? Would he become a weak, spineless actor without any balls and tell Dolores that he had to give them a chance? If that happened, we would still be "protected" on our commissions for what was done for him contractually. "Shit, I hate this fucking business when that happens," I thought to myself.

I had lost all my respect for John and could not believe he would treat this loving and talented woman this way. I remember telling him either by phone or fax that he had destroyed her confidence in him, and that she felt she was left on the side of the road for all the passing world to step on and shit on. How embarrassing this was for both of us.

Dolores felt that her career as an agent had become too emotional for her to handle any longer, that John had taken all the joy and excitement out of her. He had put an end to her life as an agent and her talent agency. She remained in pain for months. Much to my regret, I had placed John with my business manager, who also had been Tom Bosley's manager. I called him when this tragedy started to take place. He, too, had become spineless and said, "Budd, you put John with me and I have to do what he tells me to do, or he will get another manager."

"Bullshit," I said as I slammed the fucking phone down. I was pissed.

I had tried to explain to him what a terrible thing John was doing to Dolores and to try and use some common sense to get him to realize that the Morris office was doing their job in trying to steal a hot young actor from his small, powerless agents and come with "the big show."

By the time that John went to the Morris office and Dolores and I went to the Screen Actors Guild to file for arbitration, months had passed. The Morris agent who stole John from Dolores had lied in court that he had not used the expiration of Dolores' contract with John or the spin-off of "The Colby's" as a means to move in and try to get a new deal for the Morris office. The arbitration became nasty and then nastier, and John had avoided testifying. Each day, he would walk by Dolores and not even look at her. Finally, when it ended, I managed to make sure that since John was at his third year of "Dynasty" that his salary should not start at his first year salary, but at his third year of $42,000.

The agent at the Morris office took the credit for boosting John's salary and was commissioned for the difference. However, they never got John that movie to make him the star that they had promised him.

I have to do some research as I write the tale of an agent innocently going to see a production of "Evita" in London in 1978, the road I took to New York and how my eagerness as an agent to use this event as a stepping stone led me to Jon Cypher going into the National Company of this great musical, meeting Scott Holmes and his opening the door to meeting Dolores Sancetta—a lovely and brilliant talent agent who brought John James and Tommy Cruise into my life. And look what took place from 1978 to 1985. In six or seven short years, look at the lives that were touched and moved around and around; some with overwhelming success with millions of dollars in the bank, and the emotional experiences that took place by my meeting John, Patrick and Tommy, and this most gifted, special and blessed lady, Dolores Sancetta.

I always wonder, looking back on my life and history, what would have happened if I could not have gotten that ticket to see "Evita" that one day in London. Looking back at the early days with John James and Dolores Sancetta and "Dynasty," I found myself concerned about her other two clients that I was looking after—Patrick St. Esprit and Tommy Cruise. I never felt comfortable with them, especially Tommy. There was this constant pressure that I felt coming from him.

I also said to Dolores on several occasions that the overnight success of John probably did not sit well with Tommy and Patrick. I know that Dolores kept telling them both that it was just a matter of time before they "hit it big."

Chapter Sixteen

What Are You Doing At My Office, Tommy Cruise, At 8:30 in the Morning?

I remember telling Dolores that one morning, knowing I was always there before nine, I found Tommy sitting on the back staircase to my office on Beverly Drive, above the Hamburger Hamlet restaurant. Tommy was in his usual uniform, a smelly sweatshirt, torn Levis and dirty Adidas jogging shoes.

"Tommy, what are you doing here so early in the morning?" I said with great surprise. "Gotta talk with you," he said almost as part of a speech he was going to make.

"Come on in and let me put up the coffee!"

Carrie Landfield, my secretary from General Artists Corp., was now working for me and usually came in around ten. It took me only a matter of five minutes to get the Braun coffee pot dripping into our coffee mugs.

"Tommy, you're upset?" I said as we walked down the short hallway, past my conference room into my office that overlooked the Hamlet parking lot.

Tommy dropped down on the grey couch and managed to put his dirty Adidas shoe on the pillow. I grabbed my original Tone French rocker that Carolyn Jones had given me as a birthday present when I was at

General Artists Corp. Kind of looked like the one that Jack Kennedy used to sit in when he was in the Oval Office, pondering the problems of the world.

"Budd, I am not happy with what is happening in my relationship with Dolores. I am indebted to her for taking me out of the modeling world and turning me into an actor.

I owe her everything but I feel like she is my mother and not my agent. She is always telling me what to do and how to dress and..."

"Stop, Tommy. I have been an agent for a long time and I am stunned at what you are telling me. Her world as an agent in New York is not like mine in Hollywood. She discovered you, told you what knife and fork to use and gave you the basic groundwork on what acting is about. And for this you want to leave her?"

"I like you, Budd and would like to stay with you, but I have to leave DMI and Dolores!"

"You could not stay with me without Dolores. Do you understand the word integrity? She brought you, John and Patrick to me and I could not work any other way. Please give this some serious thought. You know it would kill her if you left her after she put so much of her life's blood into you and your career. Please, let me speak with her about this. Give us another 90 days, as I know she is hard at work trying to put a deal together for you."

"Budd, I am getting calls from Stan Kamin at the Morris office, Mike Ovitz and Ron Meyer at CAA. I am going to meet with them tomorrow."

"Take your meetings with them if you have to, but slow down and give us some time to put a couple of deals together for you, please?" He was walking down the hallway before I even finished what I was saying.

What took place in the summer of 1984 with Aaron Spelling, Doug Kramer, the Shapiro's and John James was probably the turning point in John thinking about leaving Dolores and me in the months to come.

After my meeting with Aaron, I started to rewind the film as to what took place from the time I saw "Evita" in London, New York and through Jon Cypher going into the National Company—I met Scott Holmes, Dolores Sancetta, John James, Patrick St. Esprit and Tommy Cruise.

Dolores made a test deal for Tommy for a film called "Taps" that starred George C. Scott, Timmy Hutton and Sean Penn. It was a film that followed a group of military school students who decide to take over their school in order to save it from closing. Tommy played the powerful and cruel "Cadet Captain Alex Dwyer," a role that launched him to stardom the following year when the film opened in 1981.

I thought about how quickly things happened with John and Dolores. She had negotiated the ABC holding contract with Joyce Selznick and then with Maurice Morton, head of ABC affairs. Dolores had gotten John an unprecedented $40,000 for the one year holding period to find a TV series for him.

It was shortly after John's test to play the role of "Jeff Colby" that the offer came in to star in the new series called "Oil," at the time starring Dale Robertson. Soon it was changed to "Dynasty" with new additions and changes to the cast. Dolores and I encouraged John to take this series since it was sold where several other pilots were still hoping to be picked up.

Dolores had traveled back and forth at least six times that year, meeting with Esther Shapiro to see what could be done about expanding his role. "Jeff" was not a very important character at that time. We encouraged him to give it his all and set a meeting with John and Esther to promote the expansion of the Jeff Colby character.

John had a good deal from ABC and Spelling for the present, but Dolores and I spoke about re-negotiating in the following year if the show was successful and John's role increased as it did—1980 first year and then the 1981 second pay period on original deal. In 1982 we started discussing our re-negotiating the entire contract, which took over three months and brought Dolores out to California on at least four more trips.

In May of 1983, a new deal was in place from Marvin Katz, attorney for

Aaron Spelling Productions. The deal basically was doubled from John's original salary and extended the contract with a seven-year deal with increases and the standard renewal options.

As the years passed after the ugly arbitration was over, and John was sitting at home waiting for the Morris office to call with that "Star Breaking Role" that was going to launch him into major stardom, he was soon forgotten, at least as far as I was concerned. I can't speak for Dolores, as I know how painful it had to be for this very lovely, very sensitive and caring woman.

Someone asked me a few years later who was fully aware of this typical Hollywood story, "Looking back on the whole drama, were you glad you finally got your ticket to see "Evita" in London that Saturday afternoon?"

Chapter Seventeen

Rita Hayworth Goes to Argentina and Rio de Janeiro (October 4 - 11, 1976)

I had received a call from Celebrity Services in New York one morning shortly after I got to my office in Beverly Hills."Mr. Moss, this is Frank with Celebrity Services. How are you today?" "Fine," I said, having dealt with them in the past.

His company specialized in keeping the film industry up to date as to the whereabouts of movie stars, producers and directors in Hollywood, New York and even Paris, Rome and London.

"You are listed as Rita Hayworth's agent?"

"Yes," I said, knowing that something very interesting was about to happen.

"A Mr. Juan Abraham called from Buenos Aires this morning wanting to find the agent of Rita Hayworth. I know you have worked with her in the past. He gave us his number in Buenos Aires for you to call."

"Many thanks, Frank. Please tell the boys in your office I send my thanks and appreciation for finding me."

I checked the time difference between L.A. and Buenos Aires, and California was three hours behind.

It was just after 12:00 p.m. when I returned Mr. Abraham's call. He worked with Editorial Abril, at the time the most important publisher of magazines in South America, and with Channel 13. Channel 13 in Buenos Aires had a morning TV special called "Lunch with Mirtha Legrand," which starred Argentina's biggest TV and movie star. Many called her the "Rita Hayworth of Argentina."

"Mr. Abraham, this is Budd Moss calling you regarding Rita Hayworth. How can I help you?"

"Gracias," he said in a very thick Spanish accent.

"We would be honored if we could invite Ms. Hayworth to come to Buenos Aires as our guest to appear on our biggest TV show, "Lunch with Mirtha Legrand." She is the most famous star in Argentina and many refer to her as the "Rita Hayworth of Argentina." What a thrill that would be for us!"

"Would you explain to me what the offer is and the dates that you would like her there for this show? Also, send me a fax explaining the type of show that it is so I can show it to Ms. Hayworth, if you would please?"

He explained that the offer would be ten thousand U.S dollars to be given to her after the show. I told him that the only way Ms. Hayworth accepted these types of interviews was if the monies were transferred to her lawyer's account fifteen days prior to the event, or she would not travel. He was taken aback but said he would speak with the head of the TV network, Channel 13, regarding our request.

"We require three first class tickets from Los Angeles to New York, a hotel in NYC for one night and then a three-bedroom suite at one of the top five-star hotels. We also need 24-hour limo service, and not a town car but a limo. All meals, beverages, tips, phone calls to the States when needed and most importantly, twenty-four-hour security service since I have heard that your government is having some serious problems with the military, is that correct?"

There was a brief, thirty second pause and then he said, "We are having a few minor problems but I can assure you, Ms. Hayworth will not notice any changes since she was last here many, many years ago, I promise you!"

I first put a call into Leonard Monroe's office to tell him and Judy Ault, his assistant, about the call from Buenos Aires.

Within a few days, Leonard and I were able to structure our plan, with the help of Juan Abraham. He had spoken to his producers and they agreed to have a cashier's check for the sum of $10,000 in Leonard's trust account.

Rita had promised to see her daughter, Yasmin, in New York prior to our leaving for B.A., so I arranged with Juan to put us up at the Carlyle Hotel for one night and do a limited photo shoot of Rita getting ready for this exciting trip. I suggested we do a "Gilda Returns to Buenos Aires" theme, since her film Gilda was one of her greatest successes and it was to have taken place there, even though she never left stage seven at Colombia Studios in Hollywood.

A gala lunch was hosted by Rita's longtime friend and one-time lover Jorge Guinle, at La Grenouille. He was the owner of the famous Copacabana Palace Hotel in Rio De Janerio. He invited us to come to Rio after our four days in Buenos Aires.

Jorge Guinle made his mark over the years as one of the era's great lotharios, having had the following lovers: Marilyn Monroe, Jayne Mansfield, Lana Turner, Hedy Lamarr, Ava Gardner, Anita Ekberg, Veronica Lake and, yes, Rita, to mention just a few.

The lunch at La Grenouille was a beautiful affair. Yasmin brought four of her closest friends, including the First Lady of Canada, Margaret Trudeau, as did Jorge. I believe there were twelve very chic and elegant guests there. Plates of the Masson family's most famous dish, their escargot, wrapped in a fine thin paper were placed at both ends of the table, and in the middle were plates of every kind of hors d'oeuvres your mind could conceive of. There were bottles of Chateau Margaux and Montrachet on ice at each end of the table, and even several buckets of Dom sitting there quietly waiting for the waiters to reach over to serve you at the snap of your fingers.

The luncheon lasted almost three hours. Mr. Guinle had asked the chef to fix six of his most favorite dishes to be served to his guests as we luxuriated in this magnificent cuisine and setting. The restaurant was famous for surrounding their guests with some of the most beautiful floral arrangements of the day and romantic lighting that made every woman in the restaurant look beautiful and at least ten years younger.

Judy and I had to laugh quietly because just the other day she had come over to my offices on Beverly Drive to go over our pending trip, and decided to go downstairs to the Hamburger Hamlet for lunch and have their famous Lobster Bisque soup and two hickory cheeseburgers with bacon, and now here we were dipping our French bread in the garlic sauce with their French snails, at one of the truly great French restaurants in New York, if not in the world.

Juan arrived while we were having our espressos and hot tea from Ceylon with just one of his photographers to take a very limited number of photos at our table with everyone's permission.

Fortunately we all held up very well as far as our drinking was concerned, especially Rita, whom I was worried about as she bounced around the table taking photos with each of the guests, especially Jorge. Juan was now off to B.A. that night to prepare for our arrival in two days. Now off to Buenos Aires, Argentina.

The next day we all met one of Juan's partners at JFK for a few additional photos for his magazine, and then we were on our way to Buenos Aires on Aeronavis Argentina Airlines, but we were delayed several hours due to bad weather in South America—especially in Brazil and Argentina.

The flight was bumpy most of the way and you could hear several people throwing up in first class. Most of us thought we were going to crash in the Andes Mountains. I am Jewish, and even I was saying my prayers, hoping God would come to our rescue.

We finally arrived safely at Ezeiza Airport in a torrential downpour at 6:00 a.m. As we taxied to the gate we could see a few dozen people standing near the arrival area holding up handmade signs with the paint running down them: "Gilda has returned." "Welcome Rita." "Te amo Rita." They were soaked, but had to see this great legend get off the plane. In those days, the door opened and you would walk down the stairs and through the gate to the terminal.

From the moment the door opened, it was a shock. There stood three armed guards with what looked like submachine guns, and a very wet Argentine Airlines rep came into the cabin and asked for me. I was already at the door waiting for him.

"Mr. Moss, welcome to Argentina. Sorry about the rain. We have some security waiting to get you and Ms. Hayworth into the terminal and to meet Mr. Abraham who has been waiting a long time for you."

Rita and Judy had been up for hours. Judy had fixed Rita's make-up and hair and had her ready to depart. She seemed, after this long flight, to be in rather good shape. She quietly noted the crowd outside but did not comment on the welcome signs. It seemed that there had been hundreds of fans earlier that night but were driven away one by one by the storm.

The airline reps had umbrellas waiting for us and down we went on the slippery steps into the terminal.

As soon as we got into the smoke filled terminal, a group of ten people along with several photographers were there to take photos and greet Rita.

I asked Juan if we could limit the photos for the time being since Ms. Hayworth was tired after a long trip.

"No problem," he said, and he asked the photographers to stop.

"Mr. Moss, I want to explain, since you had some concerns about coming to Argentina at this time, that we have our private security to stay with you, Ms. Ault and Ms. Hayworth at all times. They will take you to the hotel as soon as we can collect your luggage; if you will give your tags to the young lady she will get your luggage to your limo as soon as possible. Here is your security. Diana will be with Ms. Hayworth and Judy. She speaks perfect English. If you remember Diana Rigg as "Mrs.

Emma Peel" in the TV series, "The Avengers."

She was all in black leather and under her leather jacket, next to her rather large left breast, was a German Luger, just in case. "I am here to be of help to all of you...meet Juan Justo, Otero Ricardo, Gorini Aquiles Antonio, Don Bosco and Enrique Angel." She introduced us to the security team; they were different ages and sizes, and none of them looked like they belonged there.

They all carried various kinds of weapons ready to fight an army to protect us.

The terminal, even at 6:00 a.m., had armed soldiers up and down the walkways. Every 25 yards or so a wave of fear came over Judy and I. Rita did not comment or even notice them as we worked our way to the front of the terminal. By the time we got there, we could see three limos in front of a deserted terminal.

Mr. Abraham and his assistants said that our luggage was in the back of the two limos and the security would go with us to the Sheraton Hotel, and to our suite that was waiting for us.

It was now close to 7:00 a.m. and there was still a slow downpour as we headed for the limos. Judy and Rita climbed in back with Diana and I got in front with Raul who was driving with Alberto. The other three security got into their limo behind us as we waved goodbye to Mr. Abraham, who looked relieved that we were now on our way to the hotel.

The moment the doors closed and we started to move, Otero reached into his overcoat and pulled out his gun. He said to Diana in Spanish, "Better that I have them ready." I broke into a cold sweat, as did Judy.

We drove out of the airport; Gorini was on his walkie-talkie in Spanish, I could understand a lot of what he was saying...code green was the keyword.

"Verde, verde," he kept saying, and there was a lot of crackling in the walkie-talkie.

"Are you having a nice day?" the new voice said. Gorini answered, "Verde, we are going to see the school teacher or professor. We are going to be late because of the rain and will not be going the usual way to school because of the weather. Say hello to the professor for us." I understood some of this.

I asked Diana what was happening. She asked Otero something and then she said, "We are taking the long way into town as there have been some reports of some snipers shooting some of the military trucks along the main roads. Not that they are looking for limos, but Raul wants to be safe. As you know, Sr. Moss, we now have a military government since Isabel Peron was removed from her office recently."

I had heard all about this and had read as much as I could because many of our friends at home suggested we not make this trip to Argentina. It was not revealed until much later, while we were in Argentina and years beyond, that we had arrived at a very serious time in Argentinian history—there was a secret war going on, to be known as THE DIRTY WAR.

From the time that Isabel Peron left power, the country was taken over by the military and the new man in power was President General Videla.

The ride into Buenos Aires on a clear day was maybe half an hour or so; it was now almost an hour and we still had a long way to go. In those days, everyone smoked and I asked them to hold off until we got to the hotel in the nicest words possible for Ms. Hayworth's comfort.

Soon, we started to see the change as we got closer and closer to the city. Small buildings started to get bigger and some of the wagons being pulled by horses started to change to buses and trucks. People were now walking on the streets and there were army trucks passing us in both directions every few minutes.

Soon we were in the city and at 8:30 a.m., people looked like they were making their way to work. Stores, office buildings and markets seemed to be all around us.

"Up front on the right Sr. Moss is the Sheraton Hotel," said Enrique, taking his gun off the dashboard and handing one of the guns to Diana, who placed it in her leather jacket, again, next to her left breast.

We slowly passed the front of the hotel on our right. In front of us and off to the left looked like a park or large plaza with a clock tower at the end of the park. Later I found out what it was; "La Torre de los Ingleses," a gift from the British people living in Buenos Aires for building a new train station nearby. Some called it "Argentina's Big Ben." As we continued to pass the hotel, we then drove around the back, and passing some watchful eyes as the gate lifted up and into what seemed a garage entrance. We started to go down to the second level, and then the third and then the fourth level. It was dark and all we could see were several hotel people standing there with luggage carts and two military men with their machine guns.

More sweat covered my body. I now could see Judy's face and she too seemed concerned. Rita had been very quiet the whole trip into town. Judy said she had dozed off for about a half hour when all of a sudden, Rita said, "Here we are, Roomy," which was my nickname from Rita when we travelled.

The two hotel employees took one luggage cart to the back of our limo, and there was our second limo waiting for their luggage. How did they get there before us? The three security men from the other car were standing around our car, in front and on the side where Rita, Judy and Diana were getting out. Don Bosco and I got out as Otero moved around the car in a hurry to help me out. I took a deep breath and said, "Thanks, and nice to be here!" or something dumb and stupid.

The two military soldiers and our security walked down a dimly lit hallway with Diana staying close to Judy and Rita—there at the end of this hallway was the elevator. In I went with Rita, Judy, Diana and Otero. He said in Spanish and broken English, "We will be in the other elevator and see you on the top floor."

When the elevator opened its doors on the top floor of the hotel, there were two more guards at the elevator and one standing by the door to our apartment. It was good to walk after so many hours in the plane and then in the limo. One of the hotel managers was standing there too to greet us: "Welcome, Ms. Hayworth. We are honored that you and your guests are here with us!"

"Gracias!" said Rita with a very lovely but tired smile.

As we walked into the large suite, we were surrounded by over a dozen or so arrangements of flowers of all varieties. Roses, mixed flowers, orchids, more roses and more arrangements, as we walked into a sitting room. There, off to the right, was a dining room with more flowers. Rita kept saying, "How beautiful...how lovely!" The drapes to the suite had been closed and Rita found herself walking over to the window to pull open the curtains, and started to say, "Oh...how beautiful it is!" when all of a sudden, at the given moment that her hand touched the drapes, the hotel started to shake and tremble as if there was a 7.6 earthquake below us!

A bomb had just exploded in front of our hotel. Diana sailed across the room like Wonder Woman, pulling Rita to the floor of the suite and covering her with her body. Alberto had also pulled Judy down and by that time, I was on the floor also, surrounded by the security guards.

We waited and waited and waited and finally, Raul said, "Let's be quiet and relax. The other security has all gone downstairs to see what happened."

Diana said to Judy and Rita, "Let's go into our bedrooms," which was also surrounded with more flowers and bowls of exotic fruits. Not having smoked in almost five years, I wanted to start all over again.

"It's also time for a drink," I said, as the two luggage carts came into the apartment.

The first thing I did was to get a call out to my wife, Carolyn, before she heard it on CNN BREAKING NEWS that Rita Hayworth was in a bombing on her arrival to Buenos Aires. It seems that security came back and told us that there were other military, security officers and bomb experts that had been looking for a bomb and found it and had tried to defuse it when it accidentally went off, seriously injuring three soldiers, but there was no damage to the hotel as it had gone off across the street in front of the tower.

We walked down the hall followed by the two luggage carts. As we walked into Rita's room, we noticed it was surrounded with at least another dozen flower arrangements. Diana asked Mario to have the boys take them out into the hallway. She left a dozen red roses next to the bed, and several large arrangements of mixed flowers.

I said to Judy, "Let's order some breakfast for us and three large pots of coffee with a lot of coffee cups."

I called room service and ordered some scrambled eggs and some bacon for Rita and Judy. Also, several orders of toast along with my three five-minute, soft boiled eggs and juice, lots of soft drinks and a dozen large bottles of water to go around for everyone.

Judy's room was adjoining Rita's, and mine was on the other side of Judy's. There was even a spare bedroom next to mine. Rita's was the largest of the four bedrooms with a nice sitting room next to a large bathroom with an extra-large tub and a big walk-in shower. The luggage was taken off in the hallway and brought into Rita's room. Judy told the porters where the bags went. Most of them were left in Rita's room. Two bags went to Judy's and the Valpack with my three suits went down the hall to my room. Diana quickly escorted the porters out of the suite.

Judy had helped Rita change into the hotel's large terrycloth bathrobe and helped in getting her washed. Security came into the bedroom and told Diana that room service had arrived and she was setting all the food on the dining room table along with the three large pots of coffee. Judy quickly fixed a plate for Rita and herself and took them into Rita's bedroom and promptly closed the door.

The security quickly took one of the large pots and coffee cups and went into the large living room where there were several tables and chairs for everyone. The phone started to ring. It was the hotel manager who politely said that he was sorry to bother me, but Mirtha Legrand had called several times since word of the bomb blast had gone all over Buenos Aires and the TV world knew of it, too.

I took her phone number and told the manager to continue to hold the calls until notified.

"Mr. Burton," said Mirtha, "we were so afraid for Rita. Are you sure she is all right?"

"She is fine and resting for a while."

"I would like very much to come and see you later this afternoon? We have arranged a small cocktail at 6:00 p.m., if that is okay to meet the press and our producers from 13 and maybe an early dinner?"

"I think for Rita's first night here, she would like to order in the room and get to bed early, even though I think there is only a three-hour time difference from Los Angeles. She is very tired after a long and very bumpy plane ride."

"I completely understand, Mr. Burton. See you at 6:00!"

"Please come at 5:00 so we can meet privately before the cocktail party for Rita. I know she is looking forward to meeting you.

She has read so much about you and your show "Lunch with Mirtha.""

"Hopefully, tomorrow night, subject to your approval, the president of the TV network would like to have a small dinner party for Ms. Hayworth at the finest steak house in Buenos Aires, "La Cabana." He has arranged for the dinner to be in one of the elegant private rooms."

It was the favorite room of Isabel Peron when they had small groups of friends for dinner.

"I will speak to Rita about the dinner and I am sure it will be fine. Looking forward to seeing you at 5:00 p.m."

We had our breakfast at the large table in the dining room. It turns out that this was the presidential suite and there were three staff in the kitchen to help serve our breakfast. The hotel was doing their best after the bomb went off to make things comfortable for Rita.

Judy made sure Rita had eaten and then to the bath. Diana asked if she could be of help, but Judy told her that she was fine. It was time for all of us to get some rest. Diana said that she and the boys had rooms down the hall and she, Juan and Don Bosco were going to take the first break for a few hours, until Rita was up and dressed for the 5:00 p.m. appointment with Mirtha. I could not wait to take a hot shower and get some sleep in the big king size bed.

It was almost 4:00 p.m. when Judy knocked on my door. "Are you asleep?"

"No, I am now awake. I was not too sure where I was for a few seconds."

"Rita is up and watching TV; she saw the photos of her arriving at the airport and at the hotel, and heard about the bombing on the 4:00 p.m. local news. The military was everywhere in the park and in front of the hotel on the news. She watched with some interest."

Judy had Rita's make-up on already and had laid out a casual but chic outfit for Mirtha and the cocktail party. We told her that it would be a quick half hour or so, and then back upstairs for the evening. Rita smiled and nodded.

There was a quiet tap at the door and Diana and the security came back into the suite. I explained that at 5:00 p.m., Mirtha Legrand and the general director of Channel 13, Mr. Montero, were coming to the room to go over Rita's schedule since I was not able to get them to tell us what they wanted us to do before we left New York. All I knew was that tomorrow we were going to go to the studio of Channel 13 and do a walk-through with Judy and Rita. We were also going to see the set, meet the crew and get an overview of the TV show, "Lunch with Mirtha."

At 5:00, the phone rang and it was the front desk announcing that Mirtha had arrived. Security was going to bring her and her producer up to our suite.

Mirtha Legrand was a stunning blonde version of Rita Hayworth, Betty Grable and Lana Turner all rolled into a 50-year-old TV star. She entered the room as you would walk on stage at the Palace Theatre in New York.

Arms outstretched, she said, "Hola, Rita. We are honored that you have come to our country. We have been waiting for you since you made the great film, "Gilda" (pronounced "jill-dah!")." All of this was in Spanish, which Rita understood pretty well. However, it always comes as a great surprise that Rita did not speak Spanish. A *si* and *gracias* and *como*, but no Spanish as she had done over the years in all of her films that were translated into Spanish. It came as a shock to many, even Mirtha, who had been warned prior to our coming to Buenos Aires.

Mirtha had made such a grand invitation to have dinner the next night with the general director of Channel 13 that we found it difficult not to accept it. Rita had been a little down, or better yet, uptight, after the run through of the show at the TV studio. Maybe she thought that Mirtha was too pushy, trying to get everything done her way. One important issue I had when I noticed that "Lunch with Mirtha" really was lunch with four other guests and she really had food serviced where you and your guests were supposed to eat your lunch and try to speak about your career at the same time. I knew that Rita was not going to be able to do both.

I first went to Juan, who almost knew what I was going to say as I walked over to him. Without any hesitation, knowing I was right, he went right over to the producer, who was taken aback for a moment at this last minute request, knowing that Mirtha was going to flip out when she was asked not to serve Rita during the taping. But, because she knew by now that her idol was human and she sensed that Rita was a little off balance that day, she quickly agreed and they worked it out to just serve her some hot tea during the hour they were at the table taping.

Mirtha was in charge of opening the introduction by telling her audience about "Hollywood's greatest actress and sex goddess on the silver screen," and that she had been waiting all her life for this historic meeting between the two of them, not realizing it was going to be on her television show.

When Mirtha told the audience that they were in for a grand surprise, they started to applaud when they were told that they were going to see some of Rita's greatest roles on the screen, from her first moment when "Dona Sol des Muire" from "Blood and Sand" was holding Tyron Power in her arms, to her sexy matador dance with Anthony Quinn, with her flaming red hair in his face, and the hot Sadie Thompson dance, too. Her greatest moment on the screen was doing her glove striptease for "Gilda" with a handsome Glenn Ford drooling all over the camera. The audience was standing up and cheering for "LA RITA!" What more could Mirtha and Buenos Aires want?

Rita was also very excited and pleased and found herself signing some one hundred or so pictures that were provided by Mirtha. She, too, made sure she had her photo before we insisted that we take her back to the hotel to rest if she was going to go to La Cabana for her "greatest steak dinner" that was promised her.

Judy made sure from the time we got back to the hotel that Rita remained quiet. We both kept telling her how great she was and that her appearance on the show was going to be a well-remembered performance for a long, long time. You could see that she was still excited about doing the show and kept asking how did she look and how was her hair?

"What time is it, Judy?" she asked. "I think I would like to have a little drink and then lay down for a while."

It was only three in the afternoon and dinner was going to be at nine. Juan suggested 10:00 p.m. but I told him that was too late since Rita's day started at 7:30 getting ready for the TV show. Nine it was, knowing that nobody was going to order dinner until after 10:00.

I had heard and read a lot about La Cabana. It was the Gallaghers of New York, The London Steak and Chop House of Detroit, The Cattleman's Steak House in Las Vegas and Wolfgang Puck's CUTS at the Beverly Wilshire Hotel in Beverly Hills.

There was not another restaurant in Buenos Aires that had the celebrities get right off the plane, drop their luggage at the hotel and race to La Cabana for one of the most famous steak houses in all of South America, if not in the western hemisphere, according to their publicity. Years ago, on any given night, you might have seen Eva and Juan Peron, Fidel

Castro, Sofia Loren, Pele, Luis Miguel Dominguin, Vivian Leigh and years later, Richard Nixon and Bill Clinton, to mention a few names.

As you came into the entrance of La Cabana, there were two stuffed Hereford cows waiting to greet you and have your photo taken. "Be sure you touch their tails for good luck," said the captain. "It will be your lucky charm," he promised.

As you started to work your way into the restaurant, there on your right was a large six-meter window staring you in the face. It takes another ten seconds to realize that you are looking at three rows of half-carcasses hanging from giant hooks, with Aberdeen Angus on top, then Hereford in the middle and Shorthorn at the bottom.

"What is your pleasure tonight, sir?" the captain would say, waiting for you to pick out your "cut" for dinner.

As Judy was getting Rita dressed to leave for La Cabana, she came into my bedroom twice letting me know that Rita seemed very edgy. When she started to get that way we knew she could have an attack at any time. Needless to say, we were both concerned as it got to be close to 9:00 and we had to make an appearance. That was a must.

Juan called from downstairs that the limos were ready. As we got to the front door, there was Diana in her ever present "Miss Peal" leather outfit. She would get your attention a hundred yards away. "Good evening, La Señora," she said to Rita.

The other two guards, Otero and Gorini, were at the end of the hallway holding the elevator for us. As we went down, you could smell the pungent odor of four people having just put out their strong Argentina cigarettes.

We were just a few minutes without any traffic to La Cabana. As we pulled up in our two limos, Diana was first out to open the door for Rita, who was taken by surprise as she was greeted by the two stuffed Hereford cows. Before she knew it, the restaurant's staff photographer was waiting for her along with two of the photographers from Channel 13 waiting to get a photo of Rita smiling with the cows. She enjoyed that as she pulled on the cow's tail for good luck. Judy and Juan looked at me and we thought we had a little bit of a rest period as we made our way to the Patagonia private dining room that was just ahead of us. I let Judy walk ahead of us and quietly said to Diana, "Stay close to us in the event we have to leave early."

La Cabana had several large private dining rooms that gave you the feeling of being in the Pampas with the Gauchos. The Molinas Campos room held their famous painting of the Gauchos horses. The Pampas room and the Patagonia room were done in beautiful red and rust colors, and everywhere you looked there were leather carved saddles and antique chests and objets d'art that were there to remind us we were in the land of the Gauchos.

As we entered the private dining room, we were once again greeted by Mirtha Legrand and Mr. Montero, the general director of Channel 13. The dining room must've been filled with some thirty of Buenos Aires' most social elite, who one by one came by and quickly introduced themselves to Rita. Juan was standing to help with some of the introductions.

I could see from the moment we sat down Rita was very, very agitated and looking around to make sure that Judy was nearby. The director was on Rita's left and Mirtha was on her right. I wanted to make sure that Judy and I were directly across from her in the event we noticed something going wrong.

Since the dinner menu had already been planned, the waiters started to serve a combination of tapas, wines and salads that were quickly and quietly placed in front of everyone. Judy had made sure that from the moment Rita sat down, she had her drink, but as the minutes ticked by, Rita was not comfortable speaking to the director and Mirtha.

She had hardly touched her salad and I knew from looking at her that she was not happy. From the moment that Rita asked the waiter, "Bring me another drink right away," and picked up her glass of wine I said to Judy, "Go over and stand by Rita." We held our breath for what seemed almost an hour of dull, boring conversation between Rita, Mirtha and her boss. I could see Judy really did not know what was happening to Rita, she kept looking to me for some answers.

I had already in my mind made the decision that we were going to gracefully attempt to get Rita out of there in the next ten minutes since I could feel that the time bomb was close to going off.

As Judy made her way around the long table, I excused myself from this Spanish gentleman on my left and said, "I will be right back." I then walked to the door where the maître d' was standing, and asked him to quickly get Ms. Hayworth's security to the door and wait for me.

By the time I walked back to where Judy and Juan were standing behind Rita, some five minutes had already passed and Rita was close to standing up when I said to Mirtha, "You're going to have to forgive me, but Judy has to take Rita to the restroom."

As Judy reached over and took Rita by the arm and said, "Come with me," Rita was somewhat surprised, as was the director and Mirtha, but she got up and quietly worked her way to the back of the room where there was another exit. Without saying anything to anyone else I walked back to the maître d' and there was Diana with Gorini. Judy and Rita were back in the hallway with Juan and Diana. I walked over and took Rita by the arm and I said, "Let's get her into the limo as soon as possible." I then said to Judy and Juan, "Please come back in five minutes and quietly make Rita's apologies that she had suddenly taken ill and needed to go back to the hotel." Juan knew what he had to do in speaking to Mirtha. I told Judy I would be back in an hour.

The ride back to the hotel was a matter of minutes before Diana and I had Rita upstairs and into the room before she realized what happened, and finally said, "I need a drink, quick!" I explained to Rita, who looked like she was in a daze, that we were back in the hotel and it was time for her to rest as Diana walked her into the bedroom. I managed to get Rita to take the two pills that were in the ashtray that Judy kept close by.

For the next ten or fifteen minutes I left Rita with Diana and asked her to do the best she could in getting her undressed and into her bedclothes, which I knew was not going to be an easy chore. Rita kept saying,

"Where's my drink?"

Finally, after almost a half an hour, Diana convinced Rita to lie down and rest.

Once I could see that Rita was tranquil and the pills were working, I said to Diana, "Stay here in the room until she's asleep and I will come back as soon as I can. And then standby in the living room until I come back. Check on her every ten minutes or so."

As I walked into the hallway, there was Otero waiting for me and we took the limo back to La Cabana and back to the private dining room looking for Judy. As many of the guests were departing, they asked me what happened and how Rita was. All I could say was she took ill and was now resting.

I could see Juan and Judy talking with Mirtha, who was very concerned and upset that this evening did not turn out to be a special night for her, her director, and most importantly for Rita Hayworth. I made whatever apologies were needed and thanked her for this memorable trip to Buenos Aires and hoped that one day we could return.

Judy, Juan and I grabbed the limo back to the hotel and then I said goodnight to him, who completely understood everything that was happening. All he could say was, "I am sad for you and Rita" as he left with the limo. I told Juan "All that really mattered was that Rita was a success on the TV show. Nothing else was really important. That was why we were here."

Judy and I were upstairs in a matter of minutes and walked into Rita's bedroom and found her sitting watching TV, and noticed that the walk-in closet where her clothes were was wide open and there were flowers on the floor leading into the closet. She had taken three or four of the large arrangements of flowers and had smashed them and threw them into the closet in a quiet rage that Diana must not have heard. When I confronted Rita asking her what had happened, she looked like a little girl and said to me, "I guess little Rita was a bad girl, wasn't she?"

The next morning around 8:00, I worked my way into the living room where Judy was already talking with Don Bosco, Diana and Gorini. They were making plans to try and take Rita shopping to some special stores that Mirtha's office had arranged with special prices on some leather coats and purses. I decided not to go shopping and to keep Rita busy watching an old Lana Turner movie in English with Spanish sub-titles.

As we prepared for the special cocktail party that Ambassador Robert C. Hill was hosting for Rita at the Bosch Palace, the home of the American ambassador and embassy, Juan took time to tell Judy and I about this French neoclassic mansion that was commissioned by Elisa and Ernesto Bosch in 1910. Bosch had just returned to Argentina following a tenure of six years as Argentina's ambassador to France.

The palace was completed in 1917 and became of interest to U.S. Ambassador Robert Woods Bliss during a reception there in his honor, and in 1929 was sold by the Bosches to the U.S. State Department for use as the embassy and residence of the U.S. ambassador to Argentina for around US $3 million. The Bosch Palace was, indeed, everything that you could imagine either in Paris, London or Rome.

Juan had said he would call when he was downstairs at 6:40 p.m. We had to be in the car at 6:45 p.m. in preparation to be at the iron gates of Bosch Palace promptly at 7:00 p.m., where we would be greeted by four U.S. Marines in full dress.

There, in front of us as we got out of our limo, was the American flag waving ever so proudly. Once we were inside the gate, we were again on U.S. soil.

I saw out of the corner of my eye a big smile on Rita's face knowing how proud she was to be an American. How proud we all were at that moment to be Americans, not being aware of the turmoil that surrounded Ambassador Hill at a time when that country's internal affairs were being torn apart by terrorism and political unrest.

It wasn't until years later that correspondence and official documents from the embassy provided an excellent view of this unfortunate period of Argentina's history. Once, for example, the embassy residence was machine-gunned while the ambassador watched from behind bulletproof windows months later after we left. The tension of living under such unstable conditions undermined Hill's health, and he resigned from his post in 1977, returning to his home in Littleton, New Hampshire where he died in 1978.

I quickly introduced myself to the Marine major who quickly requested our group follow him to the entrance of the palace. Juan said that this was as far as he could go and would remain there until it was time to pick us up.

As the three of us walked a brief ten yards or so, there was Ambassador and Mrs. Hill waiting for us along with two of his aides with outstretched hands to welcome us to their home. "How delighted we are, Ms. Hayworth, to have you here at Bosch Palace," said Ambassador Hill. "May I introduce you to my wife, Cecelia, Ms. Hayworth." And "Yes," Mrs. Hill said without a blink, "You must be Judy and Mr. Moss. Please come in and make yourselves at home!" I had to say to myself, it was like walking into the White House with President Bush saying the same thing. "Take your jacket off and relax," a little difficult to do at the time.

We were overcome by the grandeur of the main living room. One of Ambassador Hill's aides joined us as Hill took Rita by the arm and slowly introduced her along with Judy and I to the various heads of different sections of the working embassy, along with their respective wives or husbands.

One of the women, who was originally from California, said to Rita, "Ms. Hayworth, I hope you were able to recover from your welcoming party the other day at your hotel."

"Hotel?"

Rita was not too sure what she meant and Judy jumped right in and said, "Yes, it was a giant welcome. We did not expect to be greeted that way!"

Once the door was opened, a young man from Cleveland said, "We at the embassy could not believe that you would come here knowing what was happening with the new military takeover!" I tried to look like I knew what was going on and quickly said, "I checked with the State

Department in D.C. and they basically said there was an advisory to be cautious but at that time, it was safe to travel to B.A."

Needless to say, they all looked at each other as if they were saying, "How stupid these Hollywood people must be?" My mind must have been a blank not knowing that these embassy staffers were trying to tell us something about what was happening all around us.

Once again, and it was not until years later when I was doing some research for my files regarding my trips with Rita, that I was made aware that between 1976 and 1979 alone, 8,353 Argentinians were killed or had "disappeared." We were in the midst of what was soon to be called "The Dirty War" and hardly anyone knew about it.

From 1976 to 1983, documents showed that the Argentine military believed it had U.S. approval for its all-out assault on the left in the name of fighting terrorism. The U.S. Embassy in Buenos Aires complained to Washington that the Argentine officers were "euphoric" over the signals from high-ranking U.S. officials, including then-Secretary of State Henry Kissinger.

In September of 1976, one month before we got there, Ambassador Hill reported that Argentine Foreign Minister Admiral Guzzetti said, when he had seen the Secretary of State Kissinger in Santiago, the latter had said he "hoped the Argentine government could get the terrorist problem under control as quickly as possible."

Just after we left B.A. on October 11th for Rio de Janerio, I read from documents released in August of 2002 from our State Department that after a second meeting between Kissinger and Guzzetti in Washington on October 19th, Ambassador Hill wrote a "sour note" from Buenos Aires complaining that he could hardly carry human rights demands if the Argentine foreign minister did not hear the same message from Kissinger. Guzzetti went to Washington fully expecting to hear some strong, firm, direct warnings on his government's human rights practices. Instead, he returned in a state of jubilation, convinced that there was no real problem with the U.S. over that issue, wrote Hill.

Another embassy staffer came over and said to Rita, "I just happened to see you on TV yesterday with Mirtha having lunch with her. You were excellent and those film clips were so great. I knew you were a marvelous actress, Ms. Hayworth, but what a great dancer you are, especially with Fred Astaire." Rita had her beautiful smile on and thanked the young lady, as we moved on.

Here we were, just a little band of strolling actors and helpers roaming the streets of Buenos Aires during one of Argentina's darkest hours, not knowing about this historic time that was taking place. How lucky we were to be leaving the next day for Brazil, Copacabana Beach and the legendary lover of the 40's, billionaire Jorge Guinle.

Our visit with Ambassador and Mrs. Hill lasted a little over an hour, and on several occasions, looking back at our reception party, I remember moments where I could see other staffers coming in and coming out of our cocktail area. Before we knew it, Ambassador Hill and two of his aides started to thank us for allowing the embassy to host us if only for a brief time, back on U.S. soil. Soon, Mrs. Hill and one of her aides also came over and thanked us for coming into their home and being so generous with our time to say hello to all the Americans that worked at the embassy. In my mind, I sensed something was happening. Something was URGENT and we should be leaving... or were we being escorted out due to an extreme emergency?

Hill was truly a great American and a great ambassador, having served our country in Spain, Mexico, Costa Rica, El Salvador and finally Argentina.

From the time we said goodbye to our hosts, Ambassador Robert C. Hill, his lovely wife, Cecelia Bowdoin Hill, and his staff, there was a changing of the guards with the U.S. Marines walking us back to the front of the embassy where Juan and our security had been waiting for us. As we said farewell, we started thinking about our trip the next day to Brazil, our host, Jorge Guinle and the legendary Copacabana Palace Hotel where Fred Astaire and Ginger Rogers had danced their way through the grand ballroom in "Flying Down to Rio."

As Rita, Judy and I got into the first limo with Juan, I looked at Rita. Did

I do the right thing in bringing her down to Buenos Aires for Lunch with Mirtha? I thought I heard Rita let out a sigh of frustration. I looked back at her and Judy. Alberto sat up front with Gorini and me as he drove away from the high iron gates of the embassy and a piece of the U.S. American flag waving fading in the distance. Juan asked how everything went and Judy was the first to say how charming the Hills were and how much she and Rita enjoyed meeting all the staffers that made up the American embassy in Buenos Aires.

The ride down Avenida Alvear with some of the other old mansions turned into embassies from around the world seemed so quiet at 8:30 in the evening. We turned on to Avenida 9 de Julio, one of the widest streets in the world, named in honor of Argentina's Independence Day from Spain.

There seemed to be a brief stillness as we headed for our hotel. It was 8:35 p.m. when behind our car, there was a bright flash like 1000 bolts of lightning had struck all around us. Abel's car seemed to speed up as did our car. Diana started to grab Rita and we could feel the ground tremble ten times greater than when the bomb went off at the hotel on our arrival. I could see behind me a large cloud of white dust in the air and pieces of concrete flying everywhere. Small pieces were bouncing off the top and the front of our car as we sped down the avenue. Strange, there were cars coming the other way and most of them were screeching to a stop, but there was no traffic in front of us until we got to the Sheraton.

What a shock. I looked at Juan and Diana who were speaking in Spanish to Raul.

"What could it have been?" I asked, my voice shaking.

Juan said, "There are a lot of big business offices from around the world here on this avenue. Oil and major gas companies, Fortune 500 companies, diamond dealers, gold dealers, car companies like Mercedes, Rolls, Saab, Fiat and even many U.S. companies like GM, Ford and other big businesses. The rebels find ways to get into their worlds and put them out of business for a few days to make a statement. We will find out in a little while what has happened when we get back to the hotel."

I wanted to tell them to forget about going to the hotel, to keep driving to the airport, even without our luggage. Rio de Janeiro was waiting for us to arrive.

Chapter Eighteen

Adios Buenos Aires, Hello Rio de Janeiro

Our 2:00 p.m. departure to Rio from Buenos Aires was mixed with emotions, especially as we said our goodbyes to Diana and our security guys. Judy had been on the phone earlier with Jorge Guinle's office at the Copacabana Palace Hotel confirming our departure from Ezeiza Airport and flying to Galeao International Airport. The flying time was almost three hours and we were looking forward to enjoying the next three days on the famous beaches of Rio and Copacabana, right in front of our hotel. I was going to look for that "Girl from Ipanema" that Jorge had arranged for one of his most famous all-time lovers. Even Rita said on our way to the airport, Jorge was one of the most generous and loving men. "All he wanted to do was to make me happy in our time together."

We promised our team that we would stay in touch and thanked them again and again for protecting us those past four days. I suggested that since Juan was coming to the airport that we take only one limo and Diana said she wanted to go with us just in case, since the hotel was having our luggage go in their van to the airport.

The ride back to Ezeiza started off like any normal day in Buenos Aires. The traffic seemed light since most citizens were at their lunch tables. The road we took back was not the one we came in on just four days before. Today, Diana was not on her walkie-talkie. There were no suggestions that there might be snipers in the area.

We were only twenty minutes out from town when all of a sudden, the traffic started to get heavy, Juan noted. Soon we were slowing down as we started to see military motorcycles and trucks on both sides of the roadway. Then there were the soldiers in groups of five, and then ten with their rifles and machine guns handy.

I looked at my watch that said 12:30. We were due at the Vargis counter in thirty minutes for a 2:00 p.m. flight to Rio for three glorious days on the beach. Sirens were now screaming as our limo came to a stop. Rita had been dozing, and Judy had her hand out the window having just lit a cigarette: "What happened Diana?" as if to say, "Are we going to make the plane?"

"I'm sure everything is ok, but I am calling security to find out." It was 12:40, and then 12:50. Diana was getting a lot of static and sounds of "rouge, rouge, red, red" as our limo was crawling along at a snail's pace and now there were soldiers on both sides of our limo. More sirens, and then they stopped.

We could now see a large crowd of soldiers, jeeps, trucks and ambulances along the side of the road. We could now smell what seemed to be burning gas or oil. There was smoke all around us as well, so we rolled up our windows and the driver turned his air conditioning up high.

As the jeep in front of us pulled ahead and then on the soft shoulder to move ahead, there in front of us laying on its side was what looked like a farmer's truck covered in bullet holes and smoking badly, with the front right wheel still spinning slowly. There seemed to be two dead cows or bulls on the soft shoulder also covered in bullet holes and a rusty looking pool of blood coming from their mouths. As we were instructed by three or four serious-looking soldiers waving us to stop, we could see the remains of an elderly man, maybe in his fifties, and what was once his very white hair, leaning half-way out the window of the truck, was now a mixture of blood and white. The side of the truck's door was covered in blood and mud.

Judy asked very quietly to Diana, "I guess he is dead?"

We both looked at Rita, who was so quiet and seemed to be just observing the whole situation and probably thinking to herself, just another day in Buenos Aires.

Two of the soldiers opened the driver's door and the door where Juan was sitting and in Spanish asked very quickly who we were and where we were going.

Diana had her walkie-talkie in one hand, as she handed several cards to the soldiers.

They said a few brief words in Spanish again and waved us through, telling the driver to stay on the soft shoulder as long as we could. Diana also said she had been in touch with airport security and since we were now late, the Vargis rep would be waiting for us to pull up in a matter of minutes.

Once we arrived at the Ezeiza terminal, everything moved at lighting speed. There were six soldiers with their machine guns ready and waiting. Diana ran around to the other side to open our door. Juan was there too, eager to get us right out to the gate. The airline representative, who was there to greet us on our rainy arrival, asked very politely for our passports. Three baggage helpers were there to get our luggage out of the hotel's van and onto their carts and through two unmarked doors.

In minutes, we cleared customs with only a "thumbs up" from the rep. There were police and military all around us, as if they were waiting for an attack and possible kidnapping for ransom for us. I found it amazing what goes through one's mind after our four wild and unexpected days in B.A.

Juan had been walking ahead of us with the rep. They were taking us directly to the Vargis gate so we could have an early pre-board on our waiting Boeing 737 to Rio. Due to our delay on getting to the airport from the terrible traffic jam, Juan had arranged this for us.

"This, my dear friends, is as far as Diana and I can go due to Brazilian security. You will be taken very good care of by these people."

Juan and I embraced and promised we would stay in touch. Diana gave Rita and Judy a warm embrace, as did Juan with an extra kiss on the cheek for Judy, which she loved.

Rita said to Diana, "We sure kept you busy, didn't we?" as the rep took her by the arm to the portable ramp and up the stairs to the front of the cabin.

Diana called out, "Muchas gracias, La Rita, for coming to our country. We will always remember you."

I had been holding my breath for what seemed like the last twenty minutes and then I let it out with a large noise.

"Good God," I said to myself. Little did I know when I was just eleven years old and seeing Rita for the first time in "Blood and Sand," which sent me on this long journey, that it would come to this.

Chapter Nineteen

Finally We Were on Our Way to Rio

For the next fifteen minutes, the three of us just sat in the first class cabin by ourselves. The two stewardesses were all over us with warm towels, hot and cold tapas from Rio. Rita was enjoying what looked like a double vodka on the rocks and Judy and I could not have a care in the world for the next three hours. We were going into 80°F weather. October was the beginning of Brazil's warm winter weather. It was the start of "The Season." And it was "Children's Day" with events popping up in all the cities all over Brazil.

Flying into Galeao International Airport was one of the most stunning sights I had ever witnessed, next to the approach into Hong Kong Harbor and airport. All of a sudden as we started our approach, there, almost in front of us, was "Christ the Redeemer," standing atop the Corcovado Mountain, with his arms spread out. This enormous statue of Christ had been embracing the people of Rio since its inauguration in 1931. One of the Seven Wonders of the World. Even Rita was pointing this out to me and Judy, having been there before. As the pilot gently tipped his wing, we could now see Sugarloaf Mountain, a tall, 395-meter (900 feet) peak rising at the Guanabara Bay in the Atlantic Ocean.

Our lovely flight attendant, Fernada, came over and said, "You must, Mr. Moss, take the cable car to the very top where you will have the chance of your lifetime to take pictures of the sparkling beaches of Rio, and another view of The Christ Statue and the green forests."

Judy said, "We must go tomorrow!"

As our flight started to glide over the coral blue waters to Rio, there was a gentle bump or two as our flight slowly came to a stop at the end of the runway and turned around and headed to our gate.

Within minutes, we came to a stop and the ground crew had wheeled the portable stairs to our cabin door. A very tall and attractive Varig rep walked in, dressed all in white with a Gucci-looking silk scarf blowing in the wind as the sound of Astrud Gilberto singing "The Girl from Ipanema" filled the air. It was the first music I could hear as she came through the door and introduced herself to Rita.

"I am Maria Carmen with Varig, and once you are in the gate area, I will be your escort and take you through immigration and customs and to Mr. Guinle's limo which is waiting to take you to his hotel."

Maria Carmen kept her word since with her help, it was as if we were the most important VIPs to come through Galeao Airport in years.

We were heading for Jorge's white limo waiting with the air conditioning on high.

"Good afternoon, Miss Hayworth," a tall, very dark and very attractive chauffeur bowed and said, as if it were music. "My name is Joao Vitti and I will be at your service while you are with Mr. Guinle." He placed his gold trimmed Porsche sunglasses on.

As we got into the car, there was a frosted silver Dom bucket of ice with a very chilled bottle of Dom Brut Champagne 1962, and a card attached which read, "Welcome home mi vida—JG." The champagne had just been opened.

"We should be at the hotel in about 20 minutes or so, Mr. Moss. Would you like some "Welcome to Rio" music, madam?"

With her famous Rita smile, she nodded as the soft sounds of the samba and the bossa nova started to fill our limo and we waved goodbye to

Maria Carmen.

Rita threw her long, still flaming red hair back as if to think of those romantic memories of her first time in Rio, and the excitement she had when Jorge had brought her to Rio promising her the most thrilling time of her life at Carnival one day.

Rita closed her eyes and took a slow and very long drink from this lovely glass of Dom. You could see her thinking of her first night with Jorge. He would tell people years later that it was "love on the high seas." "We were at a party at the Rio Yacht Club. Rita said, 'It's so hot here. Let take some air!' Guinle recalled. "We went to the shed where they kept the boats and there were steps leading up into one of them. We climbed in and made love for the first time. We later spent two or three months together. It was fantastic, Rita was great in bed."

As the limo came to a sudden stop to avoid hitting a taxi, Rita sat up and realized she was in Jorge's limo pulling up into the driveway at the scandalous Copacabana Palace Hotel.

Chapter Twenty

Rita Returns to Jorge

Within seconds, we were greeted by a very elegant and most charming woman who introduced herself as Madam Fialho, and she would be taking us directly to our suite that Mr. Guinle had reserved for us. "If you would be so kind to give my assistant Nicole your passports, I will have them back in your room later this evening, as Mr. Guinle has requested the pleasure of your company at his customary table at 9:00 this evening for dinner."

There were four other well-dressed helpers to take our luggage up the stairs as quietly as possible. From the moment we walked through the elegant lobby where the desk clerks and managers were all dressed in white, we could see why this hotel was one of the most famous or infamous in the world. It was the Ritz in Paris, the Ville d'Este at Lake Como, the Connaught in London, and the Hassler in Rome, five-star hotels which we had visited over time.

We were taken to the penthouse floor and Madam Fialho explained that there were seven suites on this floor, with a butler and round-the-clock maid service if needed. We could not wait for the doors to open. The minute they opened, a warm, fresh breeze swept across the room, embracing us. You could see the beautiful beach below you with the famous curved sidewalks. It was in the 60's that the whole love of tiles and mosaics came from Portugal, but Rio really made it its own with the famous black and white wave patterns along Copacabana Beach Blvd., supposedly representing the graceful sway of the girls on the beach.

As you can see, that was just the start. I could not wait to put my bathing suit on and go running, not walking, into the warm Atlantic Ocean.

Madam Fialho told us that Mr. Guinle was preparing a special dinner for Ms. Hayworth. "It's one of his favorite meals in your honor: Fogo de Chao, the most famous Brazilian steak dinner." Judy looked at Rita, who seemed to be in some other place. Maybe back in Buenos Aires or with Yasmin, but she sure wasn't with us in Rio at this time.

It was late afternoon as Rita said, "Get me my drink, Judy. I want my vodka," in a tone that bounced back at you like when we were in the hotel in Buenos Aires. You could tell Rita was on edge. "I'll get it for you right away but let's get unpacked, get you ready for your bath and a little rest." I could see Judy was trying to stall and give Rita something else to think about for the time being. Judy gave me a high sign that she was going to close the door to her suite as I started to work my way down the hall to my living quarters for the next few days. I looked at my watch and it was early afternoon in Beverly Hills. I thought this was a perfect time to call my office and see if it was still there. Much to my surprise, it was running along very well without me.

I took a hot shower, put my Nike jogging outfit on, did a few sit ups, and then put my head down on a luxurious silky pillow and closed my eyes, when my wakeup call said in a very British accent, "It is 8:30 p.m., Mr. Moss." I had half an hour to get ready for a very special Brazilian evening.

At five minutes to nine, the doorbell rang and there standing was a beautiful Nicole, all in white, asking if Madam Hayworth was ready for her special dinner.

Judy and Rita were coming down the hallway, Judy with a cigarette in one hand, glancing quickly at Nicole, and Rita in the other hand, a little wobbly but in total control of her senses.

Chapter Twenty-One

The Lovers Meet Again

Within minutes, Nicole had us walking towards the beautiful Pergula Restaurant overlooking a candlelit pool area where our gracious host Jorge, whom we had just left in New York not even a week before, stood in his all-white dinner suit next to his chair with his arms open for his one-time lover to embrace him.

"Hello my beautiful Rita! Welcome home!" Rita gently pulled away so Jorge could greet Judy with a warm hello, too.

"Budd, my friend, I gather from what I read and heard on the news that you had an exciting few days in Buenos Aires with my friend La Mirtha." I think all three of us nodded at the same time as Rita said, "Oh yes, exciting to say the least."

There were four waiters helping us to our seats, and reaching over at the same time with our dinner napkins, placing them on our laps. Suddenly, the sommelier appeared and started to pour our champagne as Jorge reached over and told Rita that in her honor that night he had several special chefs that were going to prepare our dinner right at our table.

After a lovely and romantic toast in Portuguese to Rita, Judy and I, Jorge started to explain about how the Fogo de Chao, which means "fire from the ground," prepared the meats. "We have a large open pit for the 'Churrascaria.' The large pieces of meat are seasoned and roasted in this pit the same way they were done for over three hundred years."

Here we were with one of the last of the millionaire playboys whose free-spending ways and romantic exploits made Jorge a global celebrity from the 1930's onward. Here he was putting together this quiet dinner party for one of his greatest lovers going back to the 40's with probably the greatest sex symbol some twenty-five years later.

As we were getting a history lesson on Fogo de Chao, our Gaucho type waiters in blue shirts with the Fogo de Chao logo printed on them brought a large cart that had hot and cold buffets with veggies, mixed salads and various antipasto meats for us to choose from.

Jorge was interested in knowing more about our few days in Buenos Aires. Was the military everywhere? Were we aware of what became THE DIRTY WAR? How did we find our visit to the American embassy and what had Rita thought of Ambassador Hill, whom he met on various trips to B.A.? And he asked Judy what she thought of the Bosch Palace.

Rita was very talkative as far as B.A. was concerned. She spoke freely about bombings, especially the one that almost blew us off the street when we left the embassy the other night and the bloody mess as we got near the airport with the poor truck driver leaning out the window, with the truck riddled with bullets, bleeding to death. Judy kept looking at me trying to figure out what was going through her mind as she was so relaxed and coherent, even after several drinks.

Jorge started to ask Rita, with all the traveling she had done in her life, would she go back to Buenos Aires to do another TV show? Just then the Gaucho chef came to our table with two additional chefs. They were getting ready to serve in the Rodizio style, bringing swords laden with grilled meat to our table.

Judy and I had never experienced a meal like this. The wines that Jorge picked out were some of the finest Brazilian ones available. Rita and Jorge looked like they were old lovers of the past, being united once again for old time's sake.

Chapter Twenty-Two

A Visit to Sugarloaf

At the end of this beautiful and most unique dinner, Jorge mentioned that he had made arrangements for us tomorrow to go with Mr.Vitti at 11:00 to Sugarloaf Mountain. Needless to say, Judy and I were very excited and asked Rita if she would like to join us. Rita had a long and very trying couple of days and told Jorge that she would rather stay in the hotel with him and rest before her trip back to New York.

"We shall have a quiet lunch by the pool if you wish and maybe you would enjoy the spa for a couple of hours," Jorge said. Rita sat and stared for a minute or two as Judy softly kicked me under the table. Was something happening to Rita? I stood up and reached over to thank Jorge for this most amazing and memorable evening as Judy helped Rita up, seeing she was a little wobbly from a superb two-hour dinner and some of the most amazing "telltale all" from Jorge's unbelievable life.

We slowly walked through the elegant lobby once again, Jorge leading the way and he said, "I will escort you to your suite. I hope you are comfortable there?" I said to myself, "He must be kidding?"

As we came to our suite, Rita was still very quiet as if she did not want to speak to Jorge.

I said to him, "Would you like to come in for a moment?" knowing he was aware of Rita's hazy look. He said to Rita in his most elegant manner, "How thrilled I am to be here with you after all these years. When we were in New York just a week ago, I told you how honored I would be to see you one more time in Rio." He took Rita's hand and in the most elegant manner, and as only this legendary lover would do, gently kissed the inside of her palm and said in his best Portuguese, "I count the hours until we are together again my beautiful lover, Rita," and slowly walked down the hall to his private elevator.

Judy knew it was time to take her to her room, even though Rita pushed Judy's hands away, saying, "Don't touch me, Jorge, go away, damn you! You are not going to fuck me here!" Were we back on our TWA flight to London? I quickly told Judy I would wait for her on the terrace.

I stood there looking at this majestic view and thought of the history of this grand hotel, of how this diminutive Brazilian drank, danced and, of course, slept with dozens of the world's most beautiful and famous women probably in this same suite.

He regaled us with stories about his grandfather, who opened this hotel in 1923. Later, the hotel hosted kings and queens from around the world. Jorge's famous friends included celebrities like Orson Wells, who in a drunken stupor threw everything out of his hotel window. Ironically, years later, Orson married Rita Hayworth.

Guinle served as Rockefeller's representative in Brazil and began going back and forth to the U.S. where Nelson introduced Jorge to the most powerful studio heads such as L.B. Mayer, Jack Warner and Darryl F. Zanuck—which then opened the door to some of the most beautiful stars in Hollywood for him.

Finally Judy came out, having gotten Rita undressed, gave her the meds she needed, washed her the best she could and got her into her night gown and waited with the TV set on for almost a half an hour before she finally dozed off for the night.

"I hope we don't have another night like we did at the steakhouse," Judy said as she lit up her cigarette. "I am sure she will be fine, she is just unwinding. Judy, if you are concerned about leaving her alone tomorrow, I will speak to Jorge in the morning and see if Madam Fialho has an assistant to look after her after the lunch with Jorge."

"Maybe we should cancel Sugarloaf."

"She will be fine, we are only going to be gone a few hours. Want to take a quick swim with me in the morning before we go to Sugarloaf?"

Judy thought for a moment and then said, "I best find our butler when Rita wakes up and get her some breakfast, and see how she is doing before we leave her, and check with Jorge to see what he wants to do about lunch and possibly the spa."

"OK, I will call you after my swim. I need to feel the ocean."

I don't remember going to my room that connected to Judy's. Just a few hours ago we were in B.A. with all of the tension that surrounded us. Now you could hear the waves coming ashore, and in the distance, the romantic sounds of the bossa nova. The music of Antonio Carlos Jobim saturated the evening air all around us.

I could hear the phone ringing down the hall in Judy's room. Later I found out that it was Yasmin calling to check on her mom and to make sure we were on schedule to leave for New York. I shot out of bed. It was almost eight in the morning and I was determined to get on the beach if only for an hour. The sand was almost like powdered snow as I ran towards the water, throwing my towel and shirt on a hotel beach chair. As cold as it was for the first few seconds, I made it. I was there fulfilling one of my many dreams. Copacabana Beach was always one of them.

By the time I got back upstairs, Rita and Judy were on the terrace having their breakfast—lots of juices, fresh fruit and bacon and eggs.

"Hi Roomy," Rita greeted me.

"How was the ocean?" Judy asked.

"Just like in the movies," I said as I headed for my room to shower and get ready for our adventure to climb Sugarloaf.

I was back in the living room as Judy just got off the phone. She was speaking to Madam Fialho, who advised her that she personally would come up to the suite after we left at 11:00 to check on Rita and escort her to the spa first, along with her assistant at noon, for a few hours of relaxation and the world's greatest massage. Rita was looking forward to this and then lunch with Jorge by the pool. She seemed fine and relaxed and told Judy she might come back to the room after lunch and read for a while. I figured that we would be gone two or three hours if we found a place that Mr. Vitti would suggest we have lunch after our journey to the top of Sugarloaf.

Chapter Twenty-Three

Rita and Jorge Alone Together

I personally was very excited about our adventure to Sugarloaf. The phone in Rita's suite rang promptly at 11:00 sharp.

"Good morning Mr. Moss," the operator said in her beautiful Portuguese voice. "Mr. Vitti is waiting for you in the lobby."

Judy grabbed her glasses and purse and we both went over to Rita, who was still on the terrace looking at the morning newspaper in Spanish.

"Are you sure you don't want to come with us?" Judy said one more time, not too sure if Rita was going to change her mind.

"Have fun!" Rita waved as we raced out of the suite, both thinking that all was well and Rita would be right where we left her some three hours later.

"Good morning Ms. Judy. I hope you and Mr. Moss had an enjoyable evening with Madam Hayworth and Mr. Guinle last night," as if it was a song. Mr. Vitti slipped on his gold trimmed Porsche glasses without waiting for an answer as we got into our limo.

"We have a beautiful morning for a journey to Sugarloaf. There is very little traffic so we should be there shortly."

As we drove along passing the various beaches, Mr. Vitti pointed out the different sights and before we knew it we were driving into what looked like a VIP parking area where there were a few other limos and black town cars and a lot of tourists from all over the world heading in the same direction towards the entrance to board the rather large glass cable cars that were going to take us in two stages to the top of Sugarloaf shortly.

Mr. Vitti walked us to what looked like a holding area much like you would see at Disneyland. He then proceeded to go to a window where other people were waiting.

This window looked like a VIP window where there were just three well-dressed people standing there. Finally, Mr. Vitti reached into his jacket pocket and handed a card to the man in the window and within seconds, he came walking back to us with what looked like VIP passes. I looked through my memorabilia files recently for my small ticket that said "Adult" on one side and a photo of Sugarloaf on the other. I remember as we were driving closer to the area, I said to Judy," If you look quickly you could almost see my ol' pal Snoopy who had assumed this 'laid out position' atop of his dog house." Mr. Vitti said that the original cable car was built in 1912 and to date, some forty million visitors had been to the top of Sugarloaf.

We were met by a young lady dressed in all white with a beautiful smile and then escorted to a garden area with tables and chairs to sit and wait until we were ready to be escorted to our all-glass car that had some forty or so people in there waiting for us to enter. The sounds of the wires started to lift us off the ground and slowly into the air from the beginning of our first stage at Praia Vermelha known as Red Beach to Morroda da Urca which was at 220 meters (721 feet), all in three minutes. Within three minutes, after sailing by other trams passing us on both sides, we landed like a swan's feather on a golden pond. It was so smooth. Judy was so excited being there, almost on top of Rio de Janeiro, finally.

We could hear an announcement in different languages telling us that there was an observation area to the right, or we could take the second car on our left. Mr. Vitti smiled and pointed towards the line that was going to the left. As we made our way, we passed a rest area with table and chairs and two pay phones on the wall with rather a long line.

Judy looked at me and said, "Should we call and see how Rita is doing?" I smiled and said she was probably getting her two-hour massage and said not to worry.

Before you knew it, we were in our crowded glass tram again, moving slowly and then faster as we went to the top of the world in three minutes. Mount Olympus could not have been higher. There we were some 528 meters into the air (1,732 feet).

Mr. Vitti removed his gold trimmed Porche glasses and started to point out all of the beaches to us. "There is Flamengo over there. To your right, Ms. Ault, is where Madam Hayworth and Mr. Guinle are probably having lunch overlooking Copacabana Beach, famous Ipanema, Corcovado, Guanabara Bay and 'Dedo de Deus,' God's Fingers—a peak which rises from the Brazil coastal range, Serra do Mar, some fifty miles from Rio."

What was most outstanding and remarkable was the giant statue of Cristo Redentor, Christ the Redeemer, across the bay from us and even higher than the top of Sugarloaf. Had we been able to have another day, I would have suggested we go there by helicopter. What a view! It was Mt. Everest, the top of the Eiffel Tower, the Empire State Building and Niagara Falls all rolled into one giant heart-beating moment. Of the ten largest statues of Christ around the world, this is the most famous and the fifth largest art deco structure in the world.

Judy kept looking at her watch and I finally said to Mr. Vitti, "I think we best go back and see if Ms. Hayworth has finished her lunch," as I wanted to get in one more swim before we worked our way back to New York City and the Carlyle Hotel on top of Madison Avenue.

As we made our way back down Sugarloaf in less than ten minutes and back into our air conditioned limo with Mr. Vitti, both Judy and I,

133

without speaking, became somewhat apprehensive as we were driving back to the Copacabana Palace Hotel.

"If I might suggest Mr. Moss, I know a small, very famous restaurant on the beach that I think you and Ms. Ault would enjoy for lunch." We looked at each other and said to Mr. Vitti almost at the same time, "We best go back to the hotel, please!"

Chapter Twenty-Four

Judy's Concern for Rita

The traffic was getting heavy and we found ourselves moving very slowly along the beachfront. Judy was on her third cigarette as we waved goodbye to what looked like my ol' pal Snoopy hanging out on the beach. Finally, after a lot of horn honking, we pulled back up into the drive way as Mr. Vitti removed his gold trimmed Porsche glasses and quickly opened the door before Judy shot out first.

"What a memorable experience, Mr. Vitti. You are the best tour guide I have ever been with!" I said as I, too, shot into the lobby following Judy up to our suite, without even stopping at the front desk.

Judy fumbled for her key as we got out of the elevator and rushed down the empty hallway towards our suite. Quickly she opened the door and wanted to say, "Hi Rita, we are home!" But we came to a halt as the living room was empty with the exception of the newspaper being spread over the floor, from the wind next to the terrace door that was wide open. Judy and I headed for Rita's room which was empty, save her dressing room closet was open and a few of her dresses were on a chair, and then we looked in Judy's room.

I picked up the phone and asked to speak to Madam Fialho. She was not at her desk, said her assistant Nicole. "Please find her and connect me to Mr. Guinle's apartment. The phone rang and rang and rang and I finally hung up and said to Judy, "Wait here, I am going down to the spa since it is after lunch time and see if she was there earlier."

"Wait, I will go with you!"

As we came around the corner, there was Madam Fialho. "Ahhh Mr. Moss, I was just coming to look for you!"

"Where is Rita?" Judy said almost jumping her.

"We thought she might have gone for a swim since she called my office around noon and told Nicole to cancel her spa and lunch with Mr. Guinle, and that she was going to rest for a while or go to the beach.

"Shit!" Judy said so the bartender could not hear her. "Not the beach alone!"

I did not like the look on Judy's face. "Where is Mr. Guinle?"

"He left the hotel for an appointment shorty after you arrived back with Mr. Vitti." "Fuck," I said to myself softly. Not on the last day!

"Madam Fialho, find me your head of security for the hotel as soon as you can. Judy and I will be in the bar." I was tired from my outing but was getting very hot and needed a couple of Brahma beers as soon as possible. "How about you Judy? A double scotch on the rocks on second thought, hold the ice" as we sat at the bar waiting for Madam Fialho to return with the security. We must have waited ten minutes when Madam Fialho returned with Mr. Spellman, head of hotel security and Mr. Gonzalos, his assistant, both very well dressed for a summer day at the beach. "Do you know how we can find Mr. Guinle?" I asked Madam Fialho again. "Nicole is making numerous calls for us as we speak.

She has already left several messages."

Madam was concerned that Mr. Vitti's car phone was not answering. "When did you last see Ms. Hayworth?" I asked Madam Fialho, trying not to put too much pressure on her.

"I went up to the suite shortly after you left for Sugarloaf, which was around 11:30."

I looked down at my watch and it was almost three in the afternoon.

"What was she doing?" asked Judy in the same way I did. "She had been reading the local paper and seemed to be fine. I asked her if there was anything I could do to make her morning more comfortable and she said, 'No, gracias.' I walked around the suite, trying to fix pillows and make sure everything was in order."

I asked Mr. Spellman if someone was to go for a walk alone from the hotel, where would they go. "Señor Moss, if you walked out the door and turned to the right, the next two streets were very busy streets, with gift shops, dress shops and one jewelry store after another selling priceless stones for thousands of dollars each. A very busy street with tourists from all over the world looking for a special treasure to bring home. A few pickpocket thieves but the police keep an eye on them the best they can..."

"And then after that?" I asked.

"You don't go past the second or third street because you come to the bars and shady clubs and the children pushing dope everywhere you look." Judy looked at me and said, "Where do we start?" I asked Mr. Spellman how many security people he had in the hotel. "Maybe fifty, give or take, which includes some of the waiters that can help out." I said to Madam Fialho that I did not want to have Mr. Spellman contact the police until Mr. Guinle returned. I did not want to draw attention at this time that one of the world's most famous actresses had disappeared or, God forbid, been kidnapped. "How long will it take to get your men together and start a search on the back streets and the beaches as soon as possible?" "Give me a half an hour or so," Mr. Spellman said as he and his partner started to leave. I knew that we had to get a group together and go looking, but where would we start?

Chapter Twenty-Five

Has Rita Been Kidnapped?

Madam Fialho said she was going back to her office briefly. I told her and Judy that we would go with her and wait there for Mr. Spellman to return with some his security force and that she should continue to try and contact Mr. Guinle.

After what seemed like an hour to us, Mr. Gonzalos came back with about ten men and explained that the rest of security were going to be waiting with Mr. Spellman for instructions in the courtyard that leads out to the beach area. I told Madam Fialho to come with us and explain to the head of the group exactly what Rita looked like. She probably had her large dark glasses on and sandals. She always wore her various Pucci caftans even if she had a bathing suit on.

I asked Mr. Spellman to give me about ten of his men and while he decided to have his main security covering the streets in back of the hotel, I wanted to head for the beach. I asked Mr. Spellman to show me which way to go from Copacabana Beach to Ipanema Beach, which was at least a mile or so to the right from our hotel. I cannot begin to tell you how many people there were on the beaches. I knew finding Rita was going to be like finding a needle in a haystack. In this case, it would be like finding a diamond in the sand.

We were minutes away from leaving the courtyard, where from out of nowhere came Jorge and Mr. Vitti. He looked shocked and stunned having just been told by Madam Fialho that Rita was missing. He grabbed Mr. Spellman and said, "You must find her, if you have to call the police tell them to come here right away!" Judy and I took Jorge by the arm and led him off to the side and said to him, "I personally thought even though I might be making a mistake but it would cause an international riot if word got out on the streets that Rita was missing and probably had been kidnapped by a terrorist group or something like that.

"It was still daytime and would remain light for another couple of hours. Let's give it a shot and see how we can do with our security group first." Jorge seemed to have caught his breath and agreed with me.

Mr. Gonzalos started to break them into groups and give them orders. "Some of you men head over to Flamengo and Botafogo Beaches and a group can go with Mr. Moss up to Ipanema. We will have some cars in those areas and some of you will just have to go on foot. The rest of the group that was with Mr. Spellman started very slowly to go into the streets, stopping at stores along the way asking the clerks or owners if they saw this very attractive woman with very red hair that could look like a movie star?

Along the busy streets where there were expensive jewelry stores; Mr. Spellman would personally go in and look around and ask the owners if they saw this mysterious looking lady.

I knew that Jorge was not in good shape over what had taken place. How could this have happened to probably his greatest lover of all the many women he had courted around the world? From the time we were on the beaches, he and Madam Fialho were on the phone along with her staff calling some of the local hospitals, just in case, and some of the other major hotels up and down the beach from the Copacabana Palace Hotel. I said to Madame Fialho and Jorge, "Give us ten minutes to change and we will be ready for the beach."

"Let's do it Judy," I said as I asked Mr. Spellman to have four of his best security men to go with us on the crowded beaches. I needed one that could speak English. Copacabana Beach was almost two miles long and to the south of the hotel is Ipanema Beach, which I was told means "dangerous waters." "I hope not," I said to myself.

Over the next few hours we found ourselves zig-zagging over the hot sand; even though we had our beach sandals on and our shorts and shirts, we could feel that afternoon heat burning into our bodies. No one gave any thought to bringing their Hawaiian Tropic Suntan oil with them. The beaches were crowded in the afternoon. I looked to Sugarloaf where Judy and I had been just two hours before. It was now almost 4:00 in the afternoon and the sun was still hot. I had asked Davi, one young security agent, to go and try and find a phone at one of the local hotels as we got nearer to Ipanema Beach to see if he had any updates from Mr. Spellman's headquarters. He found a stand nearby were we could get some coconut water and try to cool down, and said he would be right back.

I looked into Judy's sweating face. There was pure panic by this time. She could not stop smoking. I was sure if there was a bottle of rum on the table she would drink it straight. It must have been only ten minutes when Davi got back and said he had spoken to Nicole, Madam Fialho's assistant, who said everyone was still either on the beach or on the backstreets with nothing to report, but Mr. Guinle said that he was going to call one of the police captains he knew if he could not find her by sundown.

We were now walking along Arpoador Beach—a small beach wedged in between Copa and Ipanema Beach. It looked like there were more families there than the beautiful bodies on display everywhere you looked. Then one of the security guards said we just passed Post #8 and #9, the famous lifeguard towers that have toilets and changing rooms for a few pennies. It was exciting to finally be there since I wanted to find my girl from Ipanema. Little did I know then that it was going to be a lost Rita Hayworth.

141

There were more people in the water, and kids were all over the place kicking their soccer balls. Our other three security men caught up with us, having gone from vendor to vendor, from selling towels and beach equipment to coco water, asking them if they saw an American-looking woman with red hair and large dark glasses walking along the water.

Some of them nodded with a no head shake and others did not respond at all. The crowds kept getting bigger as we walked along as it got to be later and later. I could see Davi who was ahead of us speaking to one of the lifeguards at his tower. He was in deep conversation and kept pointing up the beach some hundred yards ahead of us. There was a large group of kids flying their kites. Some looked like they were in dog fights going in all different directions as we started to walk towards them. There was one group of about twenty kids surrounding several kite fliers in the middle yelling and cheering as one of the kite's strings had been cut by one of the diving kites. We must have been just twenty yards away when Judy let out a deadly scream, "It's Rita! There she is!" as she started racing towards her with her arms wide open. The kids took their kite strings and backed away from the mysterious lady on the beach, not fully understanding what was taking place as the security agents circled Rita.

Chapter Twenty-Six

Thank God we Found Her

There on Ipanema Beach on a lazy summer afternoon stood one of the world's most famous celebrities in her brown, rust and yellow colored Pucci caftan, with her large dark glasses and her red hair blowing in the wind, flying her kite with some of her new found friends on this famous beach. What I would have given for a camera at that time.

"Quick," I said to Davi, "find a phone and call Jorge and tell him we found Rita; hold off on calling the police and get Mr. Vitti down here as quickly as possible." Judy could not stop crying as Rita kept looking at her, asking what was the matter. The security helped us get Rita back up to the one of the many small cafés along the famous mosaic sidewalk, where if you look carefully at the design, you will notice hundreds of black and white soccer balls in the beautiful pavement on this historic beach at Ipanema.

It was a matter of minutes as we sat there drinking bottles of water and listening to the sounds of "The Girl from Ipanema" playing just for us, I was sure, that we found ourselves surrounded by Mr. Spellman, Mr. Gonzalos and at least ten of his men. Mr. Vitti and Jorge were the first to arrive. Jorge looked like death warmed over as he rushed to put his arms around Rita telling her how worried he was.

Rita could not believe what was happening. I was not quite sure at this time if she really knew what she had been doing these past four hours. I think she just slowly walked out of the hotel and followed the wind and the sea until she found these fun-loving kids of all ages who surround her with their friendship and their wanting to show this stranger how to fly a kite on Ipanema Beach. "Good God," I said to myself. "What a tragedy this would have been after our harrowing week in Buenos Aires, with the bombings, Rita's disastrous dinner party with Mirtha, and the assassination of the poor truck driver on our way to the airport. What else could have happened? And then, to have Rita Hayworth kidnapped and held for a $10-million-dollar ransom by a bunch of terrorists in Brazil, while Judy and I went to the top of Sugarloaf sightseeing." I found it incomprehensible as I sat there collecting my thoughts to think something like this could happen to Rita. To think I could be responsible for Rita being kidnapped or something worse, God forbid. What would have happened if the terrorists decided to kill her if the $10-million-dollar ransom was not paid? I was in a cold sweat thinking I could have been the Hollywood agent that took her to B.A. and Rio and to her untimely death.

Rita was very tranquil most of the evening. Much to Judy's and my great surprise, she drank very little. I watched her and Jorge talk during dinner like they were indeed two old lovers who were given a lovers' gift by Venus being reunited again after many years, just to reflect on their lives now and as they were years ago. It was indeed a special moment to observe, knowing that in the morning, just a week later, it was all going to vanish into thin air and it would only be a fond memory to reach out and touch and reflect on what it was like then, when the world was still very young.

Soon we found ourselves back at the Copacabana Palace Hotel in our majestic suite overlooking the various beaches that we had just been on in search of Rita. Judy had her in the bathtub almost immediately. Jorge was still beside himself saying he should not have left Rita when she cancelled her visit to the spa, let alone their lunch by the pool.

Jorge had planned an elegant dinner party for Rita that night with some twenty of his closest socialite friends, which he had Madam Fialho cancel as soon as we returned to the hotel. He told us that he wanted to have a quiet dinner, just the four of us on the terrace of our suite. It turned out to be one of the most elegant couple of hours, with waiters beautifully dressed in their white tuxedos. In the distance you could hear the music coming from the beach below, the samba, the bossa nova and music of the Gauchos. The dinner was superb. Jorge explained that the various seafood that were served were from the sea and rivers to the north and the south of Brazil, all flown in that morning to the hotel's private airport not too far from the international airport. The white wines were a mixture of the Grand Cru Montrachet from France, a classic Pinot Grigio from Portofino and Rapallo, and of course a beautiful Dom for dessert.

The morning came too quickly and once again, there we were, with the help of two maids putting our bags together as we were racing against the clock to get downstairs to meet Mr. Vitti for our rather brief ride to the airport and back to New York and Yasmin.

As we said our goodbyes to Madame Fialho, her lovely assistant Nicole and her staff, Rita was handed a letter that no one was supposed to notice. She gently slipped it into her Chanel bag as she said her farewells and thanks once again for a very special three days on the beach at the Copacabana Palace Hotel.

We all looked around without making it look too obvious, wondering where Jorge was. Even Mr. Vitti, as he put on his gold Porche glasses to drive, said nothing. As Sugarloaf appeared in our rear view mirror, I noticed Rita holding the note in her hand, and had a smile on her beautiful face. Judy explained to me later on the plane that it was from Jorge, needless to say, telling Rita the joy and the unexpected excitement when she disappeared that afternoon causing him to almost have a heart attack, but thanking her for bringing back the love and fond memories of their three-month love affair in Rio many years ago. Jorge said he could not bear another goodbye.

As we pulled up in front of Vargis, there was our lovely hostess, once again waiting to help us through customs and on to an early pre-board so we could settle down for the next nine hours before we got back to New York, the Carlyle Hotel and Rita's beautiful daughter, waiting this past week, knowing every day that something terrible could, but did not, happen to her mother.

As we travelled back to New York, my mind wandered ever so slowly back to my first trip with Rita to Madrid for the filming of "L Bastiardi" and the three weeks we had together with the fondest of memories. I then had a flashback of our disastrous trip to London and the horrific photo of Rita that went around the world in less than sixty seconds. And now, what had turned out to be a perilous journey to Buenos Aires that was in the midst of a "Dirty War" in Argentina—the bombings that were all around us that we survived. Lastly, now in Rio where Rita walked away from the Copacabana Beach Hotel that had Judy and I fearing the worst. Knowing that after each trip, you could see that something was taking place in that beautiful mind and body of the great Rita Hayworth and there was nothing that anyone could do to stop it. Deep down in my heart of hearts, I had the feeling that sadly, this could be the end of our adventures together.

Finally as we entered the lobby of the Carlyle Hotel, we found Yasmin waiting with open arms for her mother, once again safe for another day. (The following quotes come from Caren Roberts-Frenzel, 2001.)

"From the time that Rita and I returned to the States, she continued her travels despite her problems, but it was evident to all that she couldn't go on in this state. Soon after, a friend checked her into HOAG Memorial Hospital in Newport Beach. Doctors pronounced Rita, 'Gravely Disabled as a result of mental disorder or impairment by chronic alcoholism.'

The Court of Orange County, CA took control over her affairs. But her Lawyer Leonard Monroe stepped in to help Rita. He checked her out of the hospital and informed Yasmin, still under the impression her mother's problem was alcoholism. Yasmin checked Rita into an alcoholic treatment center, The Silver Hill Center in Connecticut. The doctors at the clinic were shocked to find that even without alcohol, Rita's behavior remained the same. She still had problems remembering the simplest things and she often didn't recognize some of her closest friends. On one occasion, she even failed to remember her former husband Orson Welles. 'My blood ran cold,' Orson said when Rita failed to recognize him at a social function. During the following years, Rita told reporters that she had been offered a film role and was considering a comeback.

She seemed to be moving in a positive direction, but friends would later relate the vacant, glazed look in her eyes indicated she was simply going through the motions. The reality was that she was becoming more impaired every day. 'She had to know,' Yasmin later says. "She had to know her mind was being robbed. It was as if she mislaid her life.

In the years that followed. Rita's behavior became increasingly puzzling. Finally in 1980 a doctor named Ronald Fieve, professor of clinical psychiatry at Columba Presbyterian Medical Center, in New York and medical director of the Foundation for Depression and Manic Depression, suspected that Rita was suffering from Alzheimer's disease, a disease that slowly destroys a person's memory and dismantles the mind. Finally in 1981, Rita was finally diagnosed with the disease and the news made headlines all over the world. Yasmin was made conservator of her mother's affairs, and Rita moved to New York to live in an apartment adjoining Yasmin's.

As the years progressed, Rita's physical condition changed very little, and Yasmin continued to do everything she possibly could to make her mother comfortable. Eventually, Rita could not walk nor talk. Her medical team would dress her and put her into a wheelchair and take her to her special chair in the living room. There were brief moments of recognition, and sometimes she would come to life when she heard music. Typical of Alzheimer's sufferers, she would often remember events from her past, perhaps she was recalling many dances she performed onstage as a child and on the screen as the world's Love Goddess.

For Yasmin, the years that followed were torturous and frustrating to witness her mother's suffering. Rita spent her last years in a childlike state. 'All I ever wanted to do was give Rita Hayworth peace in her last years,' Yasmin said simply."

In February of 1987, at her apartment with her daughter Yasmin by her side, she slipped into a coma. She passed away on May 14, 1987 in New York. Yasmin had called me the next day to let me know that she was bringing her mother to Beverly Hills for her funeral services and asked if I would be one of the pallbearers. Needless to say, I was touched and honored. The services were held at the Good Shepherd Church on May 17th with hundreds of her close friends and fans. After the beautiful services, I joined Cesar Romero, Ricardo Montalban, Tony Franciosa, Glenn Ford (who said, "He lost his best friend in the world"), Sidney Guilleroff, Hermes Pan and Don Ameche, and we took our beloved Rita to the Holy Cross Cemetery in Culver City, California for her final resting place.

Hello World – My dad, Louie, and me

1930

My first sport coat with my dad on Butterfield Road

1940

A day with Dominguin at la Real Maestranza with Ruth and Richard and me.
Seville, Spain.

Alfonso XIII Hotel in Seville Spain with Ruth Roman, Dominguin, and me.
1957.

1950

151

Budd Burton Moss – The Actor   Arrivederci – Roma

The cast and crew of "There's Always Julia" Los Angeles City College. 1952

1950

Backstage with Janet Blair and Norma Calderon, cast of South Pacific and airmen from Parks Air Force Base. Curran Theater, San Francisco, CA. 1954

My arrival in Venice, Italy. 1957

1950

Training at the Moss Bull Ranch with Dominguin.

Malibu, CA. 1955

1950

Memorable meeting with Ambassador and Mrs. Guran on the Island of Madeira.
April, 1968

My client Elizabeth Montgomery on the "Bewitched" set with Agnes
Moorehead. Happy Halloween. Columbia Studios 1968

1960

Celebrating Rita's 50th birthday together in Toledo, Spain.
October 17th, 1967

Carolyn Jones and me at the Golden Globes.
Beverly Hilton Hotel, Beverly Hills, CA. 1966

1960

Cocktails with Rita and Bing and the "new Hollywood agent Budd Moss."
Beverly Hills Hotel, 1960

The start of General Artists Corporation with Sidney Poitier, Martin Baum,
agent Don Wolfe, actor John Cassavettes, me, agent Tom Korman, legendary
agent Sue Mengers, and agent Sandy Newman at the home of Sidney Poitier.
1960

1960

Private screening of "The Lost Man" with Sidney and Carolyn, Universal Studios. 1970

Our first Christmas together at Trafalgar Square, London England. December 25th, 1969.

1960

"I now pronounce you man and wife" at the home of legal icon Melvin Belli with Sidney Poitier, me, Carolyn Moss, Joanna Shimkus, and California Supreme Court Justice Stanley Mosk. September 27th, 1970. San Francisco CA

The Royal Wedding Party

1970

California Chief Justice Stanley Mosk and our host for our wedding legal giant
Melvin Belli. September 27th, 1970 San Francisco CA

1970

And they lived happily ever after. At the home of
Melvin Belli, San Francisco, CA

Rita Hayworth and I arrive at Ezeiza International Airport in Buenos Aires.
October 1976

1970

Carolyn and me attending the Oscars. 1975

Parade narrator Tom Bosley at U.S. Bicentennial
in front of The White House.

1970

Maria Felix - Mexico's most beloved
actress with Carolyn and me. Beverly
Wilshire Hotel cocktail party.

Rita Hayworth on Russell Harty
Show. 1976 - 2 days after horrific
picture listed below.

Tragic arrival in London

1970

A day at the beach with Sidney.
Kona Village Resort, Hawaii. 1980.

To the Moss Family – A
memory of a happy meeting.
Coffee with V.P. Bush. White
House Washington DC. 1982

A memorable evening with Ambassador
and Mrs. John Gavin. American
Embassy residence, Mexico City D.F.,
Christmas 1980

1980

Rita Hayworth's funeral. Church of Good Shepard with daughters Princess Yasmin and Rebecca Wells. Internment Holy Cross Cemetery, Culver City CA. Pallbearers Anthony Franciosa, Glenn Ford, Ricardo Montalban, Cesar Romero, Hermes Pans, and me on the far right. A sad farewell to my beloved friend.

My first day in space at the San Diego Naval Station with Lt. John Virden

1980

Cocktails with Prime Minister of Canada Pierre Trudeau, William Shatner, Sy Marsh and me. Beverly Hills, CA. 1970

At the Vatican with actor John James ("Dynasty"), singer Marie Osmond, and me. 1980

1980

An evening with the Reagans and actor Gary Coleman. Century Plaza
Hotel Los Angeles, CA.

Christmas at the American Embassy Residence In Mexico D.F. with
U.S.Ambassador John Gavin, Mrs. Constance Towers Gavin, Carolyn,
Geoff and Budd Moss , Miguel De La Madrid and Actress Apollonia
Mexico D.F. December 1986

1980

To Carolyn and Budd Moss
with best wishes, Ronald Reagan

President Ronald Reagan welcomes everybody to the White House,
Kennedy Center Honors. Carolyn and me with Patricia and Tom Bosley.

My son Geoffrey and me with Buzz Aldrin. Monte Carlo, Monaco. 1984

1980

Signed picture of Edwin "Buzz" Aldrin received 1994.

A memorable week at the Canary Islands Musical Festival with actress
Jacqueline Bisset. 1994

1990

Ladies and gentlemen start your engines! Actor Robert Vaughn, me, actor
Norman Fell and guest at the Indy 500 May 27th, 1979

Jack Valenti and me at the Polo Lounge Beverly Hills Hotel.

1990

Me at my office. Beverly Hills, CA. 1990

Somebody had to be the judge! Hawaiian Tropic International Beauty Contest.
Turtle Bay, Hawaii.

1990

French producer Laura Pels and Jack Valenti signing "Protect and Defend"
contract. Office of Jack Valenti's Motion Picture of America, Washington DC
Agent Budd Burton Moss

1990

President George and Laura Bush with Cyd Charisse receiving the National Endowment of the Arts Medal, and me. Oval Office, White House November 2002

Lunch at Fouquet's. Paris, France 2002 with actress and dancer, Cyd Charisse

2000

Carole Bouquet and me having lunch at Sardi's Restaurant. New York City,
New York. 2002

Royal Shakespeare Company actress Dame Jane Suzman and me.
London, England 2002 "Nicholas And Alexandra"
Oscar Nomination - 2002

2000

Anthony Quinn, wife Kathy, daughter Antonia, and son Ryan. Bristol, Rhode
Island 2000. "To Budd, My best life"

UCLA track star and actress Carolyn Shea, host Bob Barker, and me. CBS
Studios 2004

2000

Left to Right, Front Row: Songwriter/Composer Hal David, Shawn and Larry King, Motown founder Berry Gordy, back row: Mrs. Hal David, Ron Rosen, Director Walter Grauman and me at Hillcrest 90th Anniversary Luncheon Party. 2010

Legendary Broadway talent agent Dolores Sancetta and me. Westwood Village, CA. 1980

2000

Legendary journalist Larry King and me on our way to Nate 'N Al's to get our morning bagel. 2015

2010

Juliet and me on the set of "Hot in Cleveland." January 2015

2010

Carolyn and me with Sidney and Joanna back together again to celebrate
Hillcrest Country Club's 90th Anniversary. 2010

Me, Addy Fleming, client Juliet Mills, actor Stacy Keach,
and cast of "Hot in Cleveland." January 2015

2010

One of the discoverers of the model of DNA – Nobel Peace Prize winner Dr. James D. Watson with me discussing a major motion picture of his life. Oyster Bay Long Island, NY. 2013.

2010

Chapter Twenty-Seven

Jack Valenti / Milos Forman / Robby Lantz "Protect and Defend" 1992

Little did I know that when Jack Valenti invited me to attend a very private cocktail party at the plush L'Orangerie restaurant on famed La Cienega Blvd. in Beverly Hills that my life was going to change as quickly as the space shuttle being launched from Cape Canaveral.

Anne and Kirk Douglas were hosting a press party along with Warren Cowan to introduce to the exclusive Hollywood crowd Jack Valenti's new novel "Protect and Defend." Kirk announced at the beginning of the party, "Valenti blows the dome off the capitol—as only an insider can."

Edie and Lew Wasserman were there to cheer Valenti on as were Bernice and Sidney Korshak and all of the Valenti family—Mary Margaret, Courtenay, Alexandra and son John. Also in attendance were Sidney Sheldon, Angie Dickerson, Jolene and George Schlatter, Suzanne Pleshette, Bob Evans, George Stevens Jr., Irving "Swifty" Lazar, Bethlyn Hand and other top executives from the Motion Picture Association of America.

I was first in line to have Jack sign my personal copy and could not wait to take it home and read it cover to cover over the weekend as quickly as I could. I felt from the first page that I had my own personal key to the oval office. Sidney Sheldon said that the book was "A suspenseful blockbuster of a novel, filled with twists and surprises and brilliantly told. Not to be missed."

Ann W. Richards, former governor of Texas wrote, "Jack Valenti has written a powerful morality play about the presidency of the United States. He takes us behind the evening news sound bites to show us the flawed and the inspiring, the dangerous and the hopeful. And who better to instruct us on the ways of the capitol than this knowledgeable and erudite observer."

I couldn't help think to myself at that time, what I wouldn't give to represent the book for a feature and or a movie for TV. (Be careful what you wish for…you just might get it!)

Ann Grimes from The Washington Post Book World wrote, "Jack Valenti—Hollywood's man in Washington and president of the Motion Picture Association of America (MPAA) has written a political thriller that reads like a made for TV script. Fast paced with neat chapter breaks for commercials. *Protect and Defend* shimmers with glittery people who run back and forth between the oval office and the Russian embassy, the parlors of Washington cave-dwelling matrons and campaign planes, all the while making time for that randy late-night page-turning twist in the sheets."

It wasn't until September of that year, 1992, when I told Valenti that I had merged my talent agency with Shapiro-Lichtman Literary Agency giving them, after many years, a full service agency. At that time I told him I was so excited about the success of his book and I would like to speak with him on his next trip to LA to possibly let Shapiro-Lichtman and Budd Burton Moss have a shot at representing the novel as a possible major feature or an HBO feature for TV.

We had several conversations about the book and suggested that I possibly meet with Swifty Lazar, who had put Jack's deal together with Jackie Kennedy Onassis when she was the senior editor at Doubleday.

It was late in October when I received a call from Swifty asking me if I was available on Friday to come over to the house. Later that day, Valenti called to see if Swifty had checked in. "I am seeing him on

Friday," I reported to Jack.

My mind flashed back to the first time I think I heard the name "Swifty Lazar." My first wife, Ruth Roman, was under contract at Warner Brothers in the 40's and had heard from her weekend sailing buddy, Humphrey Bogart, that Swifty had made three major feature deals at Warner Brothers for him in one day. Bogart gave him the nickname, but it was a name that Irving disliked.

In addition to Bogart, Swifty, after leaving MCA years later, represented the top tier of the Hollywood elite; Lauren Bacall, Truman Capote, Cher, Noel Coward, Ira Gershwin, Cary Grant and on and on. He even represented President Richard Nixon, Tennessee Williams and Cole Porter. Swifty's power became such that he could negotiate a deal for someone who was not his client and then collect a fee from that person's agent.

As brief as it was, I first encountered Swifty, of all places, in Tijuana, Mexico with Tony Quinn. We had taken Spain's greatest bullfighter, Luis Miguel Dominguin, across the border to see his close friend, Alfonso Calesero, fight at the Plaza de Toros after getting clearance from the local authorities. However, after a fuck up, word got out to the higher up police who knew that Carlos Arruza, Mexico's greatest torero, had put a price on Dominguin's head some ten years before for sleeping with his then mistress, Miraslava, who ultimately committed suicide by jumping out the window of her hotel. Dominguin was to be arrested on sight and taken to the infamous Tijuana jail.

It was a great afternoon at the bullfights and Dominguin's friend, Calesero, dedicated the first bull of the day to Dominguin, as did the other two bullfighters that afternoon. Luis Miguel smiled at me and started to thank me for bringing him to the fights. Now he wanted to go back to the Caesar Hotel to see Calesero.

As the bullring started to empty through all the exits, two or three armed soldiers entered the ring and made their way to our front row seats. Needless to say, Tony Quinn tried his hardest to tell the police and soldiers they were making a great mistake, but out came the handcuffs and with a know it all smile, Dominguin was lead off. Tony and his group followed behind. "Where are you taking him?' Tony yelled in Spanish. "The Tijuana jail of course!" they yelled back in English.

We all sat at the smelly jail for hours. Tony had been on the pay phone most of the time. He was calling everyone he knew in Hollywood to get Dominguin out of jail. We all took turns letting the police know we were protesting this arrest. Around 10:30 pm., a police officer came out and said to Tony in Spanish, "Please come into the office. El Capitan would like to speak with you."

It seemed that the captain got a call from Mexico City from a very high source that some VIP from Hollywood was flying down to San Diego, where a limo was bringing him across the border to meet with the chief of police and the local commanding officer of the army in Tijuana.

We were all standing around the jail, some five hours later, when a long, black limo pulled up and a small, rotund man with larger than life black ringed glasses pushed his way thru the crowd. It was Swifty Lazar. At the same time, three military jeeps pulled up, with machine guns in hand. All headed into the jail and then they waited for the official word from Mexico City to free Dominguin and escort him across the border as soon as possible.

It is strange how the mind works, I thought, as I was driving up Loma Vista to the top of the hill in Truesdale. I had attended dinners and galas with Valenti over the years that Swifty hosted, and now I was on my way to his home for a private visit with one of the truly great agents and dealmakers in show business.

I was greeted at the door by his personal secretary, Teresa Sohn, and escorted into the living room. "Mr. Lazar will be with you in a moment, Mr. Moss."

"Thank you," I said. I looked around the spacious living room that had a feeling of a 19th century English home, with beautiful antiques, 20th century art, a wall of shelves laden with leather bound books and photographs with his beautiful wife, Mary, who was 25 years younger, photos with various presidents, clients like Irwin Shaw, and much to my great surprise, a photo of Swifty with Luis Miguel Dominguin in Spain, alongside a photo of Noel Coward, Cary Grant and Laurence Olivier with Irving, Bogart, Bacall, Sinatra, Ingrid Bergman and on and on and on.

I sat there in shock for a moment or two. This solved the great mystery of how Dominguin was released from the Tijuana jail with Tony Quinn, some 40 years earlier, which when I shared this with Irving later on, we both were amazed over that brief moment in time and that our paths crossed for one one-hundredth of a second. I shared with him my years in Spain when Ruth and I were married and our travels with Luis Miguel and his wife Lucia Bose for almost two years. Dominguin returned to the Plaza de Toros in Madrid in 1957, after a serious goring causing a long retirement, and dedicated his first bull, Cara de Rosa, to Ruth and me.

As Irving walked into the room he said: "Budd, thanks for coming up. It was easier than trying to meet you at the Bistro. Besides, I wanted to share with you a few private things. Let's go into my study."

I sat alone with Irving in the same room that every great Hollywood star sat at one time or another. Presidents, kings and queens, I am sure were there also.

"Sit here next to me. What would you like to drink?" he asked.

"Just some hot tea would be fine," I said. Irving reached over and said into the voice box, "Teresa, have Edna bring us some hot tea please." He asked me how I met Jack and I told him I was at his "Coming out Luncheon" at the Beverly Hills Hotel and he asked me afterwards "how I was on 7:00 a.m. breakfasts." And that started this long and loving relationship. "Well, he certainly thinks well of you and said he would rather have you represent his novel 'Protect and Defend' than the Morris office or CAA or MCA." I thanked him for the compliment.

Irving then proceeded to tell me that he has been slowing down and that he planned by next year to try and retire and spend more time with his wife, Mary. "I will send Jack a note in the next few days telling him that I am giving you the motion picture and TV rights to represent his novel." Needless to say, I felt like I had been anointed by one of the great "Kings of Hollywood."

Much to my surprise, Jack Valenti faxed me a copy the very next day of a brief letter on Irving Paul Lazar stationary, dated October 28, 1992:

"Dear Jack, I received your fax about Budd Moss, who is a friend of mine, as well as yours. If he has an idea about a Made-for-TV movie for your book, I don't think anything should stand in his way, because I am more interested in your having a personal success than I am in the money.

So, give him everything with my best wishes. I will see you when I get back to California. Much love to you and Mary Margaret. Sincerely, Irving"

Little did I know that Mary was very ill with bone cancer (some reports were she had liver cancer) and that she passed away in January of the following year. Irving, too, was ill with diabetes—that was a very well-kept secret in Hollywood, which was hard to do.

Irving had slowly closed things down after Mary passed away. Here was an icon that had done everything there was to do in his lifetime. From the streets of Brooklyn to the homes of kings and queen, presidents and the biggest Hollywood stars that belonged in the Heavens. They were all Swifty's pals. Sadly, as the months passed on, he became very lonely and took to himself.

Finally, as December 30th 1993 approached, it was reported that "his right foot was starting to turn blue—a sign that he'd need another operation. A few members of his inner circle tried to encourage him to take the chance. With his beloved Mary gone, he decided to take himself off his dialysis for three days and surround himself with his staff, Teresa Sohn, and Gene and Patricia Kelly. Irving did not have the luxury of dying painlessly. Once the decision was made, he was scared. His body convulsed from pain and medication; he did not want to die alone. Like a child, he asked Patricia Kelly to cradle him in her arms."

The end came in the late afternoon of December 30th, sixteen days short of the one-year anniversary of Mary's death.

Chapter Twenty-Eight

Jack Valenti's "Protect & Defend"—How the Adventure Started

In 2007, a great opportunity presented itself from a dear friend, Karen Cadle. She felt that "Director's Choice," a talk show she had written, would be perfect for Jack Valenti to host. The idea was that each week an acclaimed director would be interviewed about the making of his Oscar-winning film—in particular, the casting. For example, Sydney Pollack would discuss "Out of Africa," showing plenty of clips and b-rolls from the film, and discuss his choice to go with Meryl Streep over probably 10 other actresses. In the second half of the hour-long show Meryl would join Jack and Sydney to talk about her experience filming. There were all kinds of great possibilities: Garry Marshall on the making of "Pretty Woman" and the casting of Julia Roberts. Jack was very excited about the concept.

He envisioned an empty stage with the screen director's logo hanging behind three empty directors' chairs, with names such as Sydney Pollack, Garry Marshall, etc. The possibilities were endless. The plan was to put the show together with George Schlatter directing and Larry King's company, Brooklyn Boys Productions, producing the series. On Oscar weekend February 25th and 26th when Jack, Larry King and I met for lunch on Saturday at the Peninsula Hotel in Beverly Hills, Jack told Larry that this was the kind of series he would love to do. During our lunch, Jack also told Larry that his new book, an autobiography called "This Time, This Place," would be coming out in June and thought that Larry King Live should be the first stop for this book.

Needless to say, Larry was the first to agree. Larry wanted George Schlatter to join us, but he was in Palm Springs that day filming the Frank Sinatra golf tournament with Barbara Sinatra. We met in the bar of the Peninsula Hotel the next day and sat by the fireplace and George went over the concept of the show for Jack.

Jack was just as excited as he'd been the previous day as George laid out the format of the show and listed some of the names of the directors and stars for the first 13 episodes. All Jack kept saying as he looked over at me, "Let's do it. Can't wait. What a great show this is going to be!" Little did I know as I put my arms around Valenti as we always did and kissed, sometimes on the lips, that this was going to be the last time I would see him alive. None of us could have known what tragedies lay ahead for Jack and his family.

As planned, Jack and Mary Margaret attended the Oscars, spent a few days in New York with Kirk and Anne Douglas, for Kirk's latest book party, and then took the train down to their hometown of Washington, D.C. Jack told his wife that he wanted to go over to Johns Hopkins now that he was home to check on some eye problems he'd been having. While Jack was going through various tests at the hospital, he became ill and out of nowhere, had a major stroke. Fortunately, as he was already in the hospital, he was rushed into surgery without delay. The days and weeks that followed were agonizing and painful to both the Valenti family and all those who had been so close to Jack over the years. During the time that Jack was in ICU, I called every day to get an update from Courtenay. When Jack was able to communicate with both Mary Margaret and Courtenay, he had said to them, "If I am going to die, I want to die in my own bed."

Shortly thereafter, they took him home and after a brief amount of time, my dear loving friend passed away on April 26, 2007. We were all in shock that this could have happened to Jack Valenti, who was supposed to have been made from the finest steel in the world. We thought he was unbreakable!

Following Jack's death, it took weeks before we realized that he was gone. At the end of April, I found myself flying into New York City with Larry King on the CNN jet heading for Teterboro Airport in New Jersey, a small airport seldom used by the public, located only a few minutes from downtown New York. I was one of many on the way to attend Jack's funeral, along with a better part of the members of the Hollywood MPAA and numerous loyal friends spanning a 40-year period.

As our Lear jet slowly worked its way down, with a few bumps here and there, we came out of the clouds and I started to rewind sixteen years of meetings, contracts, faxes and emails on the "Protect and Defend" project. A long journey that ended here on this late April afternoon as the plane came to a silky smooth landing finally stopped at a private hanger, where Larry's limo and driver were waiting to take him and his staff to the Regency Hotel on Park Avenue.

I was looking forward to spending a day with my dear friend Robby Lantz prior to my taking the train to Washington D.C. the next day. Robby, my special friend and legendary Broadway agent, worked with me and tried to help put together a deal for Jack's book "Protect and Defend" for sixteen years with his client, director Milos Forman. It had been a tortuous and complicated journey in so many ways with so many people involved.

How did this all start, I asked myself? Looking back to how this adventure first began, Robby originally planned to take Jack's book to producer and now head of Tristar, Mike Medavoy. Milos had done two very successful films with Mike: "One Flew Over The Cuckoo's Nest," and "Amadeus," both Oscar winning films. Milos and Jack had just spent four days at his farm in Connecticut. Milos asked Robby to call Mike and get him a copy of Jack's book along with the ten-page outline they had just carved out.

Having had a long relationship with Mike when he was an agent, I received a call from him. "Hey putz (his favorite word for most of his friends), I see you got involved with Robby, Milos and Valenti."

"If you mean do I represent Jack Valenti, yes I do!"

"Robby thinks that Milos wants to do 'Protect and Defend' with Jack. Send over the book and I will call you next week." Outlines, drafts, phone calls between Medavoy and Jack, Milos and Robby went back and forth for months. I met with Medavoy, and discussed Tristar buying the book. Mike wanted some names of some good writers. He was going to give this a lot of thought and get back to me after he spoke again to Jack, Robby and Milos. (Boy, was he stalling. I soon found out why.)

Little did any of us in Hollywood know what was happening behind the walls of the Thalberg Building. When we opened the morning LA Times on March 15th 1993, it read like a movie script: "The Dance At Tristar; Who's Leading Movies; Hollywood wags interpret the interest of Peter Guber as a no-confidence in Mike Medavoy." Mike was fired and our dance with Jack and Milos and Tristar came to an abrupt end. The putz was out!

Tony Randall had just started filming "7 Faces of Dr. Lao" with Barbara Eden and Arthur O'Connell in 1964. Like all good agents in those days, you made it a point to visit the set once if not twice a week just to let your clients know that you care about them and want the other actors whose agents might not have come out to see them to notice.

I loved Tony and knew even in those early days he would go on to be a major star in films; little did I know that he and Jack Klugman would move in together and be known as "The Odd Couple. "

It wasn't until 1991 when I was back in New York, having lunch at the Russian Tea Room with Michele Herbert, my longtime friend, actress, supporter of the dance world and New York's most respected and admired socialite, when Tony came walking to his table with his newest supporter and philanthropist, Laura Pels, who had just donated one million dollars to help get Tony's new National Actors Theatre open. It was a quick hello and, "Come and see me at the Belasco. It's my new home when you have time." Tony had not changed since I first knew him when Barbara co-starred with him in "Dr. Lao," and over the years when I had clients on "The Odd Couple," I would stop by and say hello. I would even bump into Penny Marshall and Al Molinaro on the set from time to time.

On numerous occasions when I was in the city, I made it a point to visit Tony. Laura was usually there especially during rehearsals. It wasn't too long before I had Michele Herbert meet Tony again, and she read for one or two plays for him; and at the time she was not right for those roles but he asked her if she would like to be a part of his theatre group both as an actress and part of the production company. I was sure she would be a welcomed supporter of Tony's theatre group.

The following year, out of nowhere, I received a call from Jack Valenti asking me if I could be of help to the State Department as they were looking for a few Hollywood celebrities to hang out at the U.S. Pavilion in Sevilla with Peter Max, who designed the U.S. Pavilion, along with a few of his friends.

I spent a week making calls to various agents and friends and finally I came up with my dear client, Barbara Eden and Tony. It was a week in my beloved Sevilla where I spent many happy days with my former wife, Ruth Roman and her son, Richard, Spain's greatest matador, Dominguin, and my bullfighting crowd, but now as a VIP with Tony, his close friend and PR man, John Springer. It was an amazing experience to visit the various Pavilions as a USA dignitary of sorts. We even got a chance to say a quick hello to Prince Charles and Lady Diana at the British Pavilion. The highlight of our trip was when Barbara and I got to take a balloon ride over the historic Palace in Sevilla at sunset, a twenty-minute ride floating over the city and countryside. Tony, at the last minute, had backed out. It turned out he was very wise as when we started to head for our landing place, we got caught in a severe wind draft and found ourselves miles from where we were supposed to land. Our spotters lost us for a while and as our pilot decided to land in an open bean field, just as our basket with the three of us touched down, another gust of wind hit us and our basket turned over on its side and Barbara and the pilot fell on top of me, as we were dragged over a hundred yards with the dirt flying in to our basket being pulled along, not able to stop for what seemed forever. Finally, the pilot managed to cut our basket loose from the balloon, which was slowly deflating, and the dirt-filled basket came to an abrupt stop.

I could hardly catch my breath as I looked at Barbara who was recovering from this near-death experience. The pilot too was slowly recovering and he tried so hard to tell us that this had never happened to him and kept asking us if we were okay and what he could do to help as we pulled ourselves out of the basket and sat on the ground hoping that the spotter would find us soon.

I think we sat in the bean field for maybe twenty minutes before we saw two white vans driving our way with their lights blinking on and off and their horns honking loudly. Barbara and I were still a little shaky and I was sure we were going to be bruised the next day, but with the exception of washing out two tons of dirt off our hair and bodies after an hour in the showers; we all met in the lobby of our hotel with Tony, John and our American hosts, waiting eagerly to hear our adventures over dinner that night.

The week at the expo shot by so fast. We were wined and dined and taken to some of the top ten expos from around the world and needless to say, wherever we went, there was Jeannie looking just like she came out of her bottle, signing autographs and taking photos with Tony who was also recognized as an American movie star.

We returned to the States feeling that Barbara and Tony were a great success and that the USA was properly represented in Spain.

Chapter Twenty-Nine

From Jacqueline Bisset to Laura Pels to Jack Valenti

I had arranged for my longtime friend and actress, Jacqueline Bisset, to host an exciting musical festival in the Canary Islands. It was a glorious week and I was with one of my very special actresses whom I had first met in London when she was an aspiring model, having just turned eighteen. We got to Paris the following week and Robert Kuperberg, a talented film writer and producer, contacted me. He had heard that I was there with Jackie and had a screenplay called "A Way of Desire" that he thought Ms. Bisset would be right for the leading role. It was a charming adult comedy and he and his partner, Bernard Verley, asked if I could get a meeting with producer, Laura Pels, whom he knew and was now in the States and had just put a production company together with Peter Bogdanovich.

I told Robert that I had recently met her with Tony Randall in New York and would contact her when I returned assuming that Ms. Bisset liked the script. I called my office the next day and had my assistant contact Laura's office in New York and she remembered me and told Nicole that she was planning on being in Los Angeles in two weeks, and would Jackie and I meet her for lunch at the Hotel Bel-Air with Peter.

I suggested to Robert and his partner Bernard that we meet the next day for lunch and see if we could work out an arrangement on behalf of Shapiro-Lichtman to represent them worldwide for this project. We met at the Ritz Hotel in Place Vendome to make our deal—the only place to have lunch and make a deal. They were pleased to know that I would be looking after them in the States.

I went back to my hotel, just as Jackie was leaving to meet her "then" boyfriend who was coming in from Italy and was then heading to London for the week. I asked if she liked "A Way of Desire" and like all good actors she said, "Yes, but it needs some work!" I told her of my meeting with Robert and Bernard and that we were going to meet for lunch with Laura Pels in two weeks at the Hotel Bel-Air with Peter Bogdanovich, which pleased her very much.

People over the years always said about Laura Pels, "She was one of the best kept secrets." She was a fabulously rich divorcee who spent millions supporting the theatre in London, Paris and New York.

In the early '90's she was married to Donald Pels, an American media mogul and multimillionaire and found herself commuting between Barbados, New York and Martha's Vineyard.

Due to a rather large divorce settlement, she soon became a high roller in the theatre. Needless to say, I was looking forward with great expectation to seeing her and Ms. Bisset for lunch at the Hotel Bel-Air at the end of March.

Lunch at the Bel-Air was always a treat. I met Jackie in the lobby at exactly 1:00 p.m. and asked the lovely receptionist to ring Ms. Pels' apartment.

"Mr. Moss, she left a message that she was already at her booth waiting for you and Ms. Bisset," she graciously announced.

I brought Robert Kuperberg's screenplay "A Way of Desire" with me all the way from Paris for Ms. Pels. The hostess was kind enough to recognize me and said; "Ah yes, Mr. Moss, Ms. Pels is expecting you. This way please!"

There was Laura Pels dressed in a beautiful all-white Chanel suit with what looked like a Hermes scarf hanging loosely around her neck with a stunning collection of pearls that resembled some my wife had that we purchased in Japan from Lake Biwa many years ago.

As we started to sit down, Laura started to say in French, "Jacqueline, how lovely you look. I am so pleased you could join us for lunch. Do you like to be called Jacqueline or Jackie?" "Whatever pleases you, Ms. Pels" she said. "It's Laura."

"Then it is Jacqueline, please," she responded in French. "Bon! What would you like to drink? As you can see I am having my morning glass of champagne." I thought to myself how charming she was and how powerful she must be sitting behind a desk, doing business her way.

Over the next few hours, we spoke about Robert Kuperberg and Bernard Verley, both as very good actors and writers. Laura had known their work over the years. She freely expressed herself about the love story and also what she thought could be done to improve the script.

"I look forward to reading the script over the weekend and hopefully if time permits, Jacqueline, you will join me one night for dinner." She said in French, which Jackie responded to with a gentle nod and smile," Of course, Cher Laura."

Chapter Thirty

"You Represent Jack Valenti?"

As Laura started to order coffee, she asked me what else I was working on at this time and I told her that I was off to MGM that afternoon for a meeting on a Jack Valenti book that I represented. Laura's eyes lit up. "You represent Jack Valenti?"

"Yes, he recently wrote an excellent novel called "Protect and Defend." Jack calls it a White House thriller that Jackie Onassis published for Jack at Doubleday."

"Yes," Laura said," I had heard she was now over there. As you know, Peter Bogdanovich and I are going into partnership to make some movie next year. Peter is due here shortly, can you wait and meet him?" I looked over at Jackie and she nodded yes and said to the captain, "I'll have some tea. Earl Grey, please."

Peter and I had bumped into each other over the years that I had been an agent. We greeted each other warmly and he leaned over and kissed the air next to Jackie with a "Lovely to see you again and as always, so beautiful" greeting.

Laura said, "Budd represents Jack Valenti and he has a new book that just came out called "Protect and Defend." I think we should read it as soon as possible as I am a great fan and admirer of his. What he has done with the Motion Picture Association of America (MPAA) and our industry in just a few years has been very exciting."

"I will have a couple of copies sent to your office in New York over the weekend," I promised.

After reading "A Way of Desire," she called Marty Shapiro and said that with a good director and significant rewriting, she wanted to take an option on it.

It was not too much longer when I went to New York the following month that I had dinner with Laura Pels at the famous Riverhouse overlooking the East River. Her apartment was stunning and had the feeling of what her home in Paris must be like. We were able to speak candidly about "A Way of Desire" and how she hoped to put that project together with Ms. Bisset, Kuperberg and Verely.

She then, with a touch of drama, leaned over and touched my hand and said, "Budd, Peter loved the Valenti book. It indeed was a White House thriller. He had trouble putting it down at times. I am going to read the book on the plane to Paris next week but I want you to meet Gil Donaldson, my partner and head of production of our company tomorrow afternoon at my office."

What a historic evening for me as an agent and for Jack whom I know will be thrilled! Laura and I toasted to our new relationship over a glass of fine champagne and I found myself slowly saying good night and heading for the Lombardy Hotel and giving my wife, Carolyn, the good news. I decided to wait to give Marty and Mark a call in the morning.

My meeting with Gil Donaldson was very cordial and most productive. We managed to get a few optioned points put together with a simple step deal that would fall into place as we moved along. I told Gil and Laura that I would go over the figures with Marty that night. We also continued to speak about "A Way of Desire" and Gil all of a sudden asked if I could be of some help in trying to find out about the rights to the W. Somerset Maugham novel "The Hour Before Dawn" which was owned by Universal.

Laura had to excuse herself to take a call from Paris. I asked Gil, since this was a great opportunity to put all of our cards on the table regarding our new relationship, if "A Way of Desire" were to move ahead and since this would be a Laura Pels Production, that Shapiro-Lichtman could not only represent Ms. Pels there, but could also work to place her as executive producer for "Protect and Defend."

Gil said he would discuss this with Ms. Pels and definitely felt that this would be an excellent way to start working together. I said to Gil at that time, that if I could help open the door with the Maugham novel, I would like to get involved in working with Laura on this also.

From that time on, through the first of May, when the Valenti deal was finalized on "Protect and Defend," there was never a time when I would ask Gil for a simple piece of paper confirming that Shapiro-Lichtman was going to be the agents for Laura Pels. Gil kept saying it was confirmed and that the paperwork would be coming from Laura's attorney, Allen Arrow, Esq.

Jack was beside himself at this point after the Medavoy debacle. He was eagerly looking forward to sitting down with Laura and Gil when they came to Washington. They had several meetings at that time. I told Jack that I was going to represent Laura and that Marty Shapiro had an idea about a writer for her, David Milton. David Scott Milton was a personal friend of Peter's and they had worked well together in the past.

It was towards the end of April that Jack came to LA and we started to spend a lot of time at the Peninsula, with Bogdanovich and David talking about the book and to layout the direction of the screenplay. Throughout early May, discussions were going back and forth between David Scott Milton, Peter and Valenti. It was at this time that Jack suggested a "HANDS ON TOUR" of the White House and that he personally would arrange this tour for them on July 10th, as President Clinton was in Europe for "G-7" and the White House was going to be empty. Jack could then take Laura, Peter and David by the hand into key areas that would normally be off limits.

Chapter Thirty-One

Valenti, Laura Pels and Moss Go to Cannes Film Festival

It was during this very exciting period when Laura announced that she was planning on going to Cannes with Jack and Peter and do a grand announcement that Laura Pels and Peter Bogdanovich had purchased the Jack Valenti White House thriller "Protect and Defend."

For me, this was the end, I thought at the time of a two-year journey fulfilling my promise to my loving friend Jack, to take his exciting novel and put it in the hands of some exciting filmmakers like Peter Bogdanovich, who was at the top of his game at that time.

The public relation machinery of Rogers and Cowan went into overtime. My longtime friend Warren Cowan and I started to put all the pieces together for a gala press party at the Majestic Hotel where for years, it was a tradition that all major press announcements be done, or at the Carlton or at the legendary Hotel Du Cap-Eden-Roc at Cap d'Antibes. I will never forget that when I checked into the hotel the first time with my former wife, Ruth Roman and her son Richard, there on the reservation desk sat a small leather card engraved in gold, "Cash only." It is truly one of the grand Five-Star hotels in Europe, if not in the world.

In just a few days, Warren and his partner, Henry Rogers, started the releases in the Hollywood Reporter, Variety, The New York Times, etc:

"Newly-formed Laura Pels/Peter Bogdanavich Productions has purchased the film rights to Jack Valenti's highly-acclaimed political page-turning novel, *Protect and Defend.*

"Noted film director Peter Bogdanovich, whose film credits include 'Paper Moon,' 'The Last Picture Show,' 'Daisy Miller' and 'The Mask,' has joined Broadway producer Laura Pels, to produce and direct Valenti's fourth book and first novel. Valenti, who is President and CEO of the Motion Picture Association of America, will act as consultant on the script, bringing to the screenplay his long years of intimate knowledge of both the workings of the White House and the Washington political environment.

"*Protect and Defend*, a White House-based suspense story, is set in 1996, and moves from the Oval Office, to the Senate, to Moscow and Mexico City. Much of what has happened in real life news since the break-up of the Soviet Union and the unveiling of the Ames spy case are eerily forecast in the novel. The deal was structured by Valenti's agents, Budd Burton Moss and Martin Shapiro of the Shapiro-Lichtman Agency."

The release went on to say that the newly formed production company that was announced by Laura Pels stated "that they will launch an impressive slate of eight major motion pictures of varied genres, having broad appeal for both U.S. and international audiences. Bogdanovich will direct a number of projects over the next three years."

Ms. Pels said, "On Peter Bogdanovich, I have a partner of remarkable experience and talent. I look forward to a fruitful and rewarding relationship." Peter went on to say, "Forming this company is a dream come true. Laura Pels is a person of rare perception and exceptional taste, with a theatre-trained artist's eyes."

The press release went on to announce their additional projects which included "Unhook The Stars," a character study starring Gena

Rowlands, Gerard Depardieu and Gary Oldman. The screenplay was written by actor/ director and son of Gena and the late John Cassavetes, Nick. Both were clients of ours when I was with General Artist Agency in the early 60's.

A second project that had just begun casting was "The Cards Are Wild," written by Nick and his late father John Cassavetes. This was one of the last works by the Academy Award nominated veteran actor/director. Bogdanovich was set to direct and Ms. Pels would executive produce.

The article finished with the listing of several other films in development, including "Passion Play" by English playwright Peter Nichols based on his own successful play of the same name and "The Dreamers," by Orson Welles and Oja Kodar, a romantic adventure story that was based on two short stories.

It was very exciting for me at this point in my career to have brought Jack and his novel into this new and aggressive production company and to be a part of Laura and Peter's new production company. Both my partners, Marty and Mark, could not have been happier since my joining their offices in 1992 and bringing with me not only Jack, but to add to their agency that for years just represented some of the finest writers, now producers and directors. This deal for Jack opened the door for Mark and Marty to have entrée to Laura and Peter in hopes that if their production company proved to be successful, they could bring new writers, producers and directors and exciting projects for their future development.

Tony winner Tom Bosley, soap star Hunter Tylo, John James from the "Dynasty" series, and Constance Towers to mention a few others, were now a part of this prestigious talent agency.

Chapter Thirty-Two

A Historic Week for Valenti and Moss

The long awaited day had come. We all arrived at the Majestic Hotel at 8:00 a.m. for a quick review of what was going to happen at the press conference. Jack was at his best working the room as only he could. Between the press, whom he knew like the back of his hand, to many of his business associates and film producers that included, of all people, Mike Meadvoy, who could not have been happier (and I am sure disappointed) that I made this deal work for Jack. This time, going back with Medavoy when he was playing "go-fer" for agent Bill Robinson in the late 60s, there was no "Hey putz!" It was, "I knew Jack that this was going to work for you. It was just a matter of time. Good job, Budd!"

I could see over Jack's left shoulder Marty standing there with a big smile on his face. Standing off to the side in this overcrowded press room, next to Laura and Peter, was Harvey Weinstein, Peter Hoffman, Mike's partners and Arnie Messer, longtime friend Jeffrey Konvitz from Odyssey, and many others congratulating Valenti on the sale of his novel to Pels/Bogdanovich Productions.

There was an ironic twist that very few people knew about at that press party, and even today, and that was Jack did not know Jackie Kennedy well over the years during the Kennedy administration. But it was almost thirty years later when she was senior editor at Doubleday, through a girlfriend of Jack's daughter Courtenay, she heard that Jack was writing a political thriller. Jackie called Jack and asked to see a few of the chapters and after numerous meetings together agreed in 1991 to publish "Protect and Defend."

On this day, May 19th, as Jack was thanking everyone for attending this memorable moment in his career as president of the Motion Picture Association and now going to work as an consultant on his new film that he hoped to have in production in 1994, Jacqueline Kennedy Onassis quietly passed away in her apartment on the Upper East Side of New York from a form of cancer of the lymphatic system at the age of 64. Some three thousand miles away from her, a writer by the name of Jack Valenti was quietly thinking of her and the success of his new book being made into a major motion picture.

Over the previous months since my first meeting with Laura Pels and Jackie Bisset regarding "A Way of Desire," a lot of things had been transpiring. Some for the good and some for the bad.

After the warm glow of Cannes had diminished, a meeting had been set up for Laura, Gil, Robert, Bernard and me on May 24th at the Plaza Athenee in Paris to finally decide what course of action should take place prior to our going back to Cannes.

There was a conference call with Marty, Gil and Robert that I attended where Laura wanted to make the following offer: Robert would have to bring in a writer (approved by Pels) to work with and do a rewrite and direct the film in Paris, or that a buyout of one million francs (at the time $200,000.00 U.S.) would buy the rights and Robert and Bernard would be out.

Unfortunately, at the last minute, my wife Carolyn's mother had taken ill and had to be rushed to the hospital and I was needed at home. Robert had told Marty that Laura would probably want to buy him out which was the easier way. Gil confirmed that he needed a formula to work out the options. Marty suggested, based on a $200,000.00 deal, three payments should be made; 1/3 at the signing of the contract, 1/3 on the start of principle photography and the final payment when principal photography was completed.

Once again, at no time did Gil disagree with this but needed to get back to Marty. He had asked Gil when he might get the paperwork back to him both regarding the representation paperwork that had been dragging on and the buyout paperwork for Robert. All he could say at that time was he was behind in getting things out but would take care of it right away.

Both prior to our trip to Cannes and afterwards, discussions continued with Laura about additional casting for "A Way of Desire," including Donald Sutherland to play the husband of Jackie Bisset. Laura asked me to contact CAA to find out his availability, as at one time there were talks of trying to start as early as September or October, subject to a rewrite.

During this time, new meetings were set up for Jack, Peter and David Scott Milton and me at The Peninsula Hotel. Once again it was at this time that Jack wanted to set up a hands-on tour of the White House on July 10th when President Clinton was in Europe for "G-7." When Laura advised Valenti that she and Peter were not going to be available, Jack suggested that if at all possible, I could go with David, since apart from the White House, I knew Washington D.C. very well having been going there for over 25 years and had numerous contacts there on both sides of the Hill, Congress and the Senate, and he could also plan an extensive "tour' for David to help him get used to D.C. and find ideas for location sights.

Laura notified Jack that the date would have to be changed and that she did not feel that my going with David would be a "profitable exercise." And she wanted to attend the tour with Peter and David, which I had no problem with.

Discussions regarding "A Way of Desire" continued and I said to Laura that I thought my longtime friend and former client Sidney Poitier, when I was with Marty Baum, who was now at CAA, might be interested in reading the script and possibly directing the film in Paris. This idea needless to say, had Laura very excited once again.

I called Cedric Scott, Sidney's partner at Verdon Productions and quickly brought him up to date on the script and asked him to read it and if he liked it to pass it on to Sidney. A couple of days later Cedric called and said as all producers say, "I enjoyed reading the script but it could use a rewrite, but I am going to send it to Sidney with my recommendation." That was all I wanted to hear at that time.

Laura had just gotten back from Paris and I suggested that she join Marty and me for lunch at the Ivy, our local watering hole on Robertson Blvd., just around the corner from our agency on Beverly Blvd., and continue our discussions on "Protect and Defend" and "A Way of Desire" as well as how we all felt about our great success in Cannes at the film festival.

Marty spoke about putting "A Way of Desire" together and I assured her that we would find a way to structure the option monies. I also told her that I had arranged for her to meet the noted English director, Trevor Nunn, for *"An Hour Before Dawn,"* who had two major successes in his early career, "Cats" and "Les Miserables" along with directing some of the greatest Shakespeare plays at the Royal Shakespeare Company, many of them with his wife, one of the RSC's most important actresses, Janet Suzman. Please note that both of them went on to be knighted separately by H.R.H. Queen Elizabeth, years later.

Marty had told Laura that he had been in contact with Universal studios regarding the project. The next day, I spoke with Gil Donaldson and brought him up to date and once again asked him for a formula for "A Way of Desire" and he said the first option monies that Marty had put on the table were too high and once again, he would have to speak with Laura. I also told him at that time of the Poitier interest and that I had scheduled the Trevor Nunn meeting on June 24th and that Marty once again had requested a "simple brief one-page agreement." He asked at that time if Marty would send something to show to Allen Arrow,

Laura's attorney.

The letter that Marty sent a couple of days later was a short form to cover the three projects and that Shapiro-Lichtman would represent Laura Pels for these projects. Once again, Gil said at the time "this would probably be fine and would review them with Laura and Allen Arrow."

The following week, I went to see Laura's brand new offices on Wilshire Blvd. and Glendon Ave., in Westwood Village. They were beautiful, with flowers everywhere in lovely French vases, not overly stated. The furniture looked like it belonged at the Ritz Hotel in Paris. I said to myself, knowing Laura, she probably had her furniture flown over from her home in France.

Gil was there to greet me having just come in from New York. We sat in Laura's sitting room and sipped tea from what looked like Limoges tea cups topped with a touch of crème. Once again, at no time was there any discussions that the monies were too high for Robert, other than they wanted to find a different formula and would get back to me. As far as the Maugham project was concerned, it was agreed in principal that we would represent the "project" but first Gil was going to meet with Merchant and Ivory as a possible idea and would get back to us after he and Laura returned from Europe.

I had made a date with Laura to go and see the new Mia Farrow film, "Widow's Peak," in Westwood Village before she left for London. I thought Mia would be great casting for her "Cards Are Wild" film with Charlie Sheen. Even at that time Laura said she would only go ahead with the deal with Robert if we could work an option for very short monies. And much to my great disappointment after a heated discussion between Robert and Laura, it was decided on Monday that she wanted to forget about the film. How was I going to tell Bisset after all this time and effort? This was all I could think about at this time.

Was it the great Gloria Swanson who once said (and so articulately), "Who do I fuck to get 'out' of this business?"

Chapter Thirty-Three

As the Storm Clouds Started to Gather Over Beverly Hills

After several calls and a fax that was dated June 22nd, as much as I hated to do it, I had to cancel the Trevor Nunn meeting because Gil would not return my calls or send me the authorization I had requested.

The following week, I called my old boss Marty Baum and went over to CAA to see "Big Red," as all the guys used to call him with love and affection. Marty was Marty in his London handmade Saville Row suit. It was grey flannel with a light grey shirt and an almost black Gucci tie and black suede Gucci shoes. I was sure the next day Marty would probably do it all over again in his brown silk suit that he had made the year before in Hong Kong.

Marty was at the door when I came in and we embraced almost as father and son would after all the years we shared together when Ruth and I first came to New York to meet him at the Baum and Newborn agency in 1958. "Sit here Budd next to me" he said as I sat on the leather couch near his beautiful English desk that never had a piece of paper on it when he had a guest in his office. Marty enjoyed his office that looked out on little Santa Monica Blvd., right across the street from The Peninsula Hotel. Sitting next to him at all times in a beautiful glass case was the Oscar that his client and longtime friend Gig Young won for his performance in Sydney Pollack's great film, "They Shoot Horses Don't

They?" Tragically, Gig committed suicide in 1978 after killing his new bride of three weeks and leaving the bulk of his estate to Marty along with his treasured Oscar. "How is Carolyn these days, and your son?" Marty asked.

"It's hard to believe but he is going to be 21 in September. He is our greatest joy I must tell you, Marty," knowing that he had two lovely kids, Fern and Richard.

Marty then asked me about Laura Pels and how we met. Marty was very aware of my representing Jack and that Laura was going to produce "Protect and Defend" with Peter Bogdanovich. Marty said he enjoyed reading about our press party in Cannes with Valenti. We then spoke about Mia Farrow and Laura Pels. Marty and I both had a relationship with Mia Farrow, my having placed her in the TV series, "Peyton Place," which launched her into stardom.

I told Marty that I had taken Laura to see Mia's new film "Widow's Peak" recently and she thought that Mia would be perfect to star opposite Charlie Sheen in "Cards Are Wild." Marty said he would be happy to be of help and to keep him up to date as to how the project moved along. "Keep up the good work, Budd" Marty said as explained he had to go down the hall to a meeting with Ovitz and Ron Meyer. I replied, "Give them my best. Maybe when we start filming at the White House, you will come and visit."

Laura called me the following week and asked if I would join her for lunch across the street at the Hamlet Gardens as she wanted me to meet one of her new helpers by the name of Alex Hyde-White, who was going to be the "Point Person" from her office for "Protect and Defend." I knew that his father was one of England's most distinguished actors, Wilfrid Hyde-White. Probably he or someone close to him suggested to young Alex, who seemed to have a budding acting career, that in between acting jobs, he could be one of Laura's "helpers" as she called him. (This was all an assumption on my part at the time.) It was at this time that Alex called me after lunch and advised me to have Marty finally prepare the paperwork to represent Ms. Pels for "Protect and Defend." He also confided in me that Allen Arrow was not in favor of it but he felt he could "push it through" and send the paperwork over to his office and he would forward it on to Ms. Pels in Paris.

From that point on, Alex did not tell Marty and me the truth and he was actually sending the paperwork to Allen Arrow and not to Laura in Paris. That was when all communications started to breakdown between Shapiro-Lichtman and Laura Pels. I explained that Gil had agreed in writing that Shapiro-Lichtman would represent Pels. Arrow said he would speak with Pels but he personally was against it.

The following week, Marty and I received a fax re-confirming his position that the paperwork was not acceptable. It was at that time I suggested to him that the two of them speak to find out what would be acceptable to both Shapiro-Lichtman and Laura Pels.

It was now the July 4th weekend and I found myself locked in my office. This was a time that I was supposed to savor and enjoy my greatest victory with Jack. The first $15,000.00 had come in from Pels/ Bogdanovich to take the official option on the book while we were all in Cannes celebrating. The representation paperwork for Laura had gone to her lawyers.

However, my frustrations were mounting every day. I decided to sit down and send Laura a "personal fax," with no copies, to her in Paris. I told her that I wanted to speak with her on a personal level like we used to before her world became so "crazy."

We were all supposed to go to Washington the next week for a fact finding trip while President Clinton was in Europe for "G-7." Jack had personal clearance from the White House to take Laura, Peter, Gil, David et al to the Oval Office. At the last minute, she had to cancel the trip after all the planning I did with Valenti. "It must be re–scheduled," she said.

Chapter Thirty-Four

Finally Valenti's First Check Arrived

When Laura and I had lunch with Alex, I thought it was decided that we were going to forget about "A Way of Desire" and "The Hour Before Dawn." We were going to put all of our efforts on getting "Protect and Defend" made the following year. I remember telling her that I had planned on going into New York with her after the D.C. tour and arrange a lunch meeting with Robby Lantz and Milos Forman.

When I spoke to Allen Arrow before the holiday I told him "I had a feeling that no one knew what the other person was doing half the time." Gil would tell me that the paperwork I was waiting for was with Allen and then when I spoke with Allen, he said, "I know nothing about it." Ms. Perino said to me that she did not have signed contracts from David Scott Milton and then all of a sudden his contracts were faxed to me.

I spoke with Alex one morning about the pending D.C. trip that was scrubbed, and he said he had just picked up a copy of the fax I sent him on Monday of the prior week. I asked him when he was due back from Paris and he thought in a week. I then spoke with Allen and he told me Alex had come in the day before and was going to meet with me to discuss the issue of Shapiro-Lichtman representing Laura as the executive producer for the film, but he added that the paperwork Marty had sent was not acceptable to him, even after Gil and I had already agreed that we would be Laura's agents for "Protect and Defend."

I wrote Laura in my fax, "I remember walking with you from your beautiful apartment building one night on the East River over to First Avenue, where you introduced me to a charming Thai restaurant where we sat for almost two hours talking about your world, your daughter, my family and background in the film industry, my travels with Rita Hayworth and your interests in wanting to know more about this legendary actress. I had told you that Jack wanted me to co-produce the film with you and Peter but I had explained to him that I did not have the time and that I would rather be your point person and work with you every day. My seeing that this film made was the most important project in my career.

"There was a lot of friction and disharmony amongst all of us at this time. It was vital that we speak next week. We have to have a serious talk about your direction and what you wanted to do at this time. If not, I suggest that we put "Protect and Defend" on the back burner along with five or 10 other projects that are now sitting there, and let Gil, Alex and Peter decide what should be done with it when the option comes up next year.

I am still making the same promise and commitment that I did before. I will help you get this movie made. I will put eight days a week into our project until they say, "It's a wrap." But you must allow me to work directly with you and you must trust me and my judgment and that of Marty Shapiro. If not, I will gladly withdraw and continue to be available to you whenever you need help.

I look forward to speaking with you on Monday. Fondly, Budd."

When I returned to the office, there waiting for me was a fax from Laura and Gil, which simply read:

"Dear Budd, Thank you for your fax of July 7th, 1994. We all appreciate your work as agent for the sale of 'Protect and Defend' and the writing services of David Scott Milton. We intend to commence pre-production of 'Protect and Defend' in the near future— after we have a completed screenplay and at a time that makes sense to Pels/Bogdanovich.

As you can see from the attached fax, we have made contact with David Milton and he will serve as liaison to Peter."

There was no "Kindest regards" or even "Sincerely." A storm cloud hung over our building.

The following month, I met with Marty Shapiro. I was very upset after spending almost two years trying to sell Jack's book (now optioned) and Laura now felt that she did not want me to be the point person for her on the film. I told Marty that part of the failure was that I might have pushed too hard with Gil and part of it was due to his being "new" in the business and not understanding what it means to tell the truth. He and Laura had made promises they never meant to keep.

Marty being the wise old agent, agreed with me and said, "Just leave it all alone for now and just stay with David and get the fucking script finished."

It wasn't until the end of September when Marty got a fax from Allen Arrow once again stating that he had advised Shapiro-Lichtman in early July that on behalf of his client, Laura Pels, there was no agency relationship between the respective companies at all other than "your offices represent both Jack Valenti and David Scott Milton in association with Pels/Bogdanovich and 'Protect and Defend.'"

It wasn't until November that I finally heard from Diane Kramer, Laura's production assistant, that the long awaited script meeting was finally taking place. It was now time for Jack, David and Al Ruban, Laura's line producer, to start on the re-writes of the first draft.

To my surprise, I had received a call from Laura's office a few days

217

before David went to D.C. Laura asked that I meet her at her new home on Moraga Drive in Bel-Air. On a good day, I could have jogged over to her home. She now lived so close to our house just a few blocks off Sunset Blvd., across the street from UCLA. Many of the residents in our neighborhood called it "The Slums of Bel-Air." (Hardly!)

Laura was very warm after all the time I had been put on hold. It was lovely to see her again and it felt like two old war heroes from opposite sides, trying to shake hands and let bygones be bygones up until she started talking about David's first draft for the next two hours. She told me, reading from notes, why she did not like what David had done. "It was awful," were her final words. When Valenti was asked what his thoughts were when he read the script? "It was a terrific script, but it was not my book," Jack said. David Scott Milton said, "I thought I made it clear to everyone what kind of script I was going to write."

Chapter Thirty-Five

The Storm Clouds Got Darker and Darker

Here we were, six months later after our victorious party at the Cannes Film Festival with a script that needed a major overhaul to make it work as far as Laura was concerned. I had sensed that "There was something rotten in the state of Denmark" these past months. There are times as an agent you can smell it from afar.

Laura looked at me with her beautiful and commanding face and quietly advised me that "the Pels/Bogdanovich Company was in a holding pattern." I sat still for a moment and started to say something like I am sorry. Just then she said to me, "Peter is no longer active in bringing in new projects." Laura held off for a second and then said that she and she alone would be responsible for making any and all decisions regarding "Protect and Defend."

I finally took a deep breath and started talking about us and Shapiro-Lichtman coming back on board as agents for the film and I could feel that she had felt bad when everything fell apart in July. Laura said she would like to see the new script first and then sit down and talk about our relationship.

I called Jack the next day as he was working on his notes for the pending meeting and I shared with him my conversation with Laura at her beautiful new home. The news about Peter came as a surprise to

219

him at first, and then he said, "I felt it coming!" I suggested to Jack that we try to stay very close to David at this time to insure the proper development of the screenplay.

I vividly remember when I sat with Jack, Peter and David at The Peninsula that Peter, who had a longtime relationship with David, and had worked together on several successful projects together over the years, said, "Don't worry David, I will stay very close to you and be available at all times. Write some thirty pages at a time and then we can go over those pages together and then on to the next thirty." I remember getting calls from David saying, "I have been trying to reach Peter but his assistant would say he is traveling and will call you as soon as he can." This went on for weeks and when they finally spoke they would try and go over the pages on the phone with very little success. Finally, David gave up and just finished the draft without any help from Peter.

Phone calls and faxes went back and forth over the following days and Laura wanted to set up a power meeting for four to six hours with Jack, Gil, Al Ruban, David and herself at The Peninsula on November 10th. Due to Valenti's heavy workload he requested that the meeting be scheduled at his office in D.C. on November 14th instead.

From my various conversations I had with David and Jack, the power meeting in D.C. at Jack's office went better than anyone anticipated and it was agreed, after Christmas and New Year wishes were extended, that a "Working Lunch" be arranged on January 4th 1995 subject to any last minute cancellations. It was Laura's hope at that time that David write a ten-page short story line to work with.

Laura was planning on being at home in Paris for the holidays and returning to Hollywood the week after to pick up where David and Al had left off in continuing the re-writes.

I had sent Laura a "Happy New Year" fax, with an Irving Thalberg quote; "He knew what he wanted and he knew how to turn a bad film into a good one and a good one into a triumph." I told her how Jack and

I were looking forward to seeing her and moving ahead with "Protect and Defend" and putting it into production that year.

It was just a few days later when I learned that Laura had still not yet made a decision to go ahead with David doing his re-writes. Laura was due back the next week and I followed up with my last fax to her with the suggestion of planning on meeting Milos Forman when she was in New York. I had told her how much Milos liked Jack's book and had tried for weeks to find a way to work together. She expressed interest in meeting Milos when he returned to the States at the end of the month.

I had suggested to Jack that he send Laura a fax in Paris. "Tell her of your relationship with Milos and that at this time, he is available according to his agent Robby Lantz. Since Milos and David have been good friends, have Laura send Robby a copy of David's script for Milos to read."

Laura responded with interest to Valenti's fax and he sent a copy of David's script to Milos and Robby. When she returned to her office in New York, I spoke to her for a long time without any interruptions. I reviewed Milos' relationship with her, Robby and our agency. I also made her aware of the long friendship between David and Milos. "Tell Milos when you speak with him that everyone was disappointed with the first draft but it was due to the lack of guidance that Peter promised David."

I felt that Laura was close to letting David do the re-write but I thought she was going to wait to press the green light when she knew what Milos thought after he reads the first draft. Towards the end of the month, I told Robby that Jack was anxious to speak with Milos. What Jack would like to convey to Milos was that David Scott Milton would like to be a part of the conversation. Valenti felt that between the three of them, there was a way of structuring the rewrite or second draft.

I know that Milos wanted Jack to move in with him to get the screenplay into place the first time around. It was my hope that David could go to Milos for a couple of weeks to complete his rewrite. Al

Ruban, the line producer, had asked Laura before the holiday if he could take a crack at the outline. Gil Donaldson had sent Jack and me a note along with his finished outline asking us to read it as soon as possible, which we did. Jack sent Al a note telling him that "Al's latest outline was far more congenial to me than anything we have done. I have some suggestions but generally speaking, I think we are on course. I am so hopeful that Milos Forman will renew his once avid interest in this project. If so, we have a bankable director on our hands."

During the next couple of days, Robby, Jack and I were going in circles waiting for Laura to make up her mind. Robby wanted to take Al's paperwork along with Jack's five pages to Milos. Milos was also aware that Laura had to let David finish the re-write, which he owed to her. I tried to tell Laura that with Milos aboard we had a bankable director that any major studio would make a deal with in a hurry.

Finally, a week later we were all notified that Laura was putting a hold on the script, even after my numerous conversations with her. We had spoken about Laura getting on the phone with Jack, David or Al and Milos and agree to do a second draft. Robby had all the players in place and then on February 12th, the whole project was put on hold.

I told Laura that it was over two months since David had turned in his first draft. For two months, the screenplay sat in a dark corner, collecting dust. I said to her that Jack wrote a brief five-page outline trying to move things along from his end. Al Ruban wrote an excellent outline from his p.o.v. to add to Valenti's thoughts. We could be very close to putting the second draft together but she elected to shut it down. I said to Jack and Robby that "someone is giving Laura bad advice."

For several days, Marty, his partner Mark and I had numerous meetings trying to solve this stalemate. I explained to Laura that I finally called Allen Arrow and suggested "that if you are not going to do anything with the script, and since you had only 12 weeks left on your option, to allow us to move elsewhere with the property." I believed there were a lot of producers out there that would be interested due to all the press our project had received that past year.

I also said, "Allen did mention you had been discussing that Peter might come back into the picture and direct the film which Jack and I thought would be excellent." I told Laura that I was still planning on coming to New York during the next month and would like to see her and for her to meet Robby before I went on to Paris with my client actress/dancer, Cyd Charisse.

Once again, I received a fax from Gil advising Jack, Marty, Allen Arrow and me that there should be no additional letters to Laura for the time being, until she determined how to proceed with the project. I had told Laura how deeply saddened I was over what had transpired. I told Jack and Marty that after almost two years, I felt the end was near to saying goodbye to Laura Pels and her production company.

Chapter Thirty-Six

A Sad Farewell to Laura Pels

Not giving a shit about what Gil had to say, I saw an interesting article about Wendy Finerman and the ten year battle she had putting "Forrest Gump" on the screen and sent it to Laura. I had reminded her when we first started to work together that Freddie Fields, one of Hollywood's greatest agents and wheeler dealers when he was with the MCA agency, once said, "You can walk into the Polo Lounge at the Beverly Hills Hotel on any given Friday night and put a movie together in five minutes or it can take you five years." I thought Laura would enjoy the adventure.

Just three days later, Laura sent Jack a fax telling him that his most recent fax had been forwarded to her while she was in Europe.

"This last trip to Europe turned out to be very successful on all counts, but partially for 'Protect and Defend.' There are at least two French motion picture companies interested in the project. Ideally what we would like to see happen would be for Laura Pels Productions to co-produce the film with one of these highly reputable French companies. As we get more information as to their respective levels of interest, I will let you know.

"As you can see, my determination to adapt 'Protect and Defend' into a feature has not abated. It does appear, however, that the film will be

225

structured in a more international way—which would speak well for our desire to cooperate with the European Community and its cultural entities.

My very best, Laura."

That fax to Valenti dated March 14th was the last I had heard from Laura Pels, via Jack's copy to me. My mind had gotten cloudy and when that happened and I had a couple of hours to try and search my mind and do a post-mortem, I would drive up the coast to Malibu and then into the canyon to my folk's ranch they had bought back in the late 40s, off Cold Canyon Road in Calabasas.

Growing up, whenever I needed help, needed some soul searching, I used to grab my old collie, Cyrano, and take a long walk through the ranch. Even years later after we sold the ranch and my folks passed away, I had my own secret passage way off the road to get down to the creek that Cyrano and I used to play in—the cold water, as it moved over the rocks that had been there for probably hundreds of years.

Where did "Protect and Defend" go wrong? Was it me and my daily faxes to Laura Pels, trying to guide her through each day moving along until she agreed to take an option on Valenti's novel? Who was the villain? Could it have been John Gilbert Donaldson Jr., who was ill advised and ill equipped in his new position at Laura Pels Production having just been a Wall Street analyst for E.F. Hutton and had gone to work with Laura in 1994? As far as I was concerned he had no knowledge whatsoever of being a film maker and was way over his head as far as dealing with the film industry on a daily basis. Was it Peter Bogdanovich, who made promise after promise and then was never around when we needed his help with David Scott Milton and the screenplay? Was it me? I was determined to put this film together for Valenti.

I said to myself, look at the people I had brought to Laura and for one reason or another, she was talked out of using them by her associates, let alone meeting them. Trevor Nunn, one of England's most honored and respected directors. "Cats" and "Les Miserables" was on his business card. Sidney Poitier was ready to meet with Laura. So was Mia Farrow and Milos Forman. Little did any of us know, and there was no reason for Robby to tell us, that he and Milos were in discussions with Columbia and Oliver Stone to direct "The People vs. Larry Flynt"— the biopic about the controversial publisher of Hustler magazine. Laura still had until May 12th before the option expired.

March and April came and went with a gust of wind down Beverly Blvd. I had told Jack that I was in the process of putting a list together of those producers and studio executives that I planned to contact as Laura's option was about to expire, not hearing word one from her.

Do you, my friendly reader, believe in right place at the right time? Over the years that I've been an agent, I have grown to accept the fact that when you find yourself at a certain meeting or event or getting on a plane, there was a reason for it. I had spent the last several months knowing that Laura's option was almost over and I wanted to keep the momentum going.

I had just come back to the office with Mark from a quick lunch down the street at our local pasta house, Maddeo's, in the old ICM building owned by the legendary Pierre Cossette, producer extraordinaire, when I was handed my messages from our trusty receptionist, April Rocha: "The call from Mark Diamond's office from Palm Beach regarding Cyd Charisse sounded important." Mark always had that dangerous smile and said, "Hmmm, Palm Beach? Cyd Charisse?"

I walked down the hall to my office in back of our building and picked up the phone and called Mark. "Thanks for getting back to me so promptly, Mr. Moss. I understand you are Cyd's agent. How is she feeling these days? Is she interested in coming to Palm Beach in a couple of weeks? I am putting together a new, very chic, elegant and classy film festival here and the theme of the first festival is a 'salute to the glory days of MGM' with a special tribute to the late Gene Kelly. We would be honored if Ms. Charisse would join us."

I found myself asking the standard questions about honorariums, who else is going, how many days, dress, transportation, etc.?

"My office has been in contact with MGM directly, and with several top PR firms in Beverly Hills, and with the agents for many MGM stars that would enjoy this first class trip and most importantly, the international press coverage that the first Palm Beach Film Festival will receive. Of course you would be our guest along with Tony Martin, Ms. Charisse's husband, if he would join us too having appeared in several MGM musicals. My favorite was 'Hit the Deck.'" I was caught off guard when he said that because in my other life of wanting to be an actor, I worked as an extra on this film with Tony, Debbie Reynolds, Vic Damone, Russ Tamblyn and a cast of some two hundred extras and me, dressed in Navy uniforms for almost three weeks. What a memorable time was had by all and for those who enjoy Hollywood trivia, it was on stage 18, I believe, where Vic Damone brought his singing pal Eddie Fisher to come and spend some time on the set—I was right there when Vic introduced Debbie to Eddie. The rest became Hollywood history for those who remember that they fell in love, got married and were supposed to live happily ever after. And then along came Elizabeth Taylor.

Within days, Cyd and Tony were set to go. The studio and Mark's team had rounded up most of the MGM greats that were still up to going to "another film festival." A very trim looking Donald O'Connor was going to serve as M.C. Van Johnson, Kathryn Grayson, Cyd, Tony, my special pal and former client June Allyson, her special sidekick Gloria DeHaven and Esther Williams rounded out the Starlight Gala.

The opening night soiree was at the Boca Raton Hotel and Club. With the golden lamé drapes and palm tree silhouettes, the hotel's convention hall became the glamorous setting for this $500-per-plate black-tie dinner. As Cyd, Tony and I made our way to the grand ballroom with Mark's black-tie helpers that came to our suite promptly at 8:00 pm, we were taken to table 112 in the golden circle. There at the table I found myself catching my breath as there seated, waiting for our arrival, was the beautiful actress and heiress and former client Dina

Merrill and her new husband, Ted Hartley, who also was a client many years ago at my old agency, General Artist. "What a delightful surprise!" I said to Dina, leaning over and kissing the air around her.

"I trust you all know one another?" as Tony and Cyd found their table cards and sat down next to three other guests who gladly paid their $500.00 to sit at one of the tables with true Hollywood royalty. Dina was the daughter of E. F. Hutton and Marjorie Merriweather Post, of the Post cereal family, and had a home in Palm Beach and had come down to see what Donald Trump had done to Mar-A-Lago, the famous pale pink magnificent mansion that her mother had built in 1927 and where Dina spent a lot of her childhood. Trump had transformed it into a private club with a $100,000 initiation fee.

Chapter Thirty-Seven

"Protect and Defend" Meets RKO

Donald O Connor started the evening with a tribute to MGM and their legendary musicals—the special guests attending had appeared in many of them. Van Johnson and Kathryn Grayson had a few words of welcome as they tried to read from the teleprompter with little success. Cyd was asked to come up on the stage with Tony so all of the high rollers got their monies worth staring at these stars. Cyd looked divine. Cyd was wearing a sea-green silk pant suit by Bob Mackie and Ray Aghayan that put all the ladies to shame.

I had first met Dina when I was covering MGM Studios as an agent and had booked her on one of her early TV shows, "Dr. Kildare," as the guest star. She had recently starred in two very good films, "Operation Pettycoat" with Cary Grant and "Butterfield 8" with Liz Taylor. Dina had a very promising career as an actress and she was probably the most prominent socialite of her time. She was being developed as the new Grace Kelly in the 60s.

Dina had been married to Stanley Rumbough, Jr., the heir to the Colgate-Palmolive toothpaste fortune, and they had three children together. They divorced in the mid-sixties and she married Oscar winner Cliff Robertson, whom during the years that I was at General Artists was one of our favorite clients. I remember one of the last deals I put together before I quit to open the Burton Moss Agency was booking them together on the TV show "Batman," because his daughter Heather loved the show and wanted her dad to be on it.

Cliff and Dina were Hollywood's most beautiful and successful couple. Nobody expected after a 20-year marriage and a daughter, Heather, that they would divorce. People were always curious how Ted and Dina met. It seems he was a White House aide at the time he first met Dina with Stanley Rumbough, Jr. Years later, when Dina was working on "Operation Petticoat" with Cary Grant, Ted was a naval attaché.

It was in 1961 when Ted was flying a navy plane, he crashed and broke his back and was discharged from the Navy. So he decided to try his luck at acting and did rather well over the years. Finally, in 1966 when Dina and Cliff broke up, Ted started to see Dina and finally married her, some forty years later after they first met.

The gala was filled by 8:30 and dinner was being served. As the band played on even Tony and Cyd were out there dancing very close, which was a crowd pleaser.

By then, they started to clear the tables when Donald came back on stage to find out how everyone was enjoying the evening. He also brought Esther Williams on stage, to a very big round of applause.

Cyd looked at Tony and said softly, "I hope they don't let her stay up there too long." Esther was known, with a drink or two, to get a little X-rated at times. Esther got on stage with Donald, looked out into the audience and became an instant hit with her amusingly frank recollections. "Turn off the teleprompter, I'm not through," Esther warned. She proceeded to tell how her talent for staying afloat helped her escape a $75.00 a-week job at I. Magnins in Beverly Hills. It all started when MGM decided "to melt the ice from Sonja Henie (the ice-skating movie queen at 20th Century Fox studios) and throw me in." In her first meeting with studio chief Louis B. Mayer, Esther asked if she thought she could change her name since she didn't think Esther sounded right for a future movie star.

"Don't you say anything against Esther," Mayer quickly said, "My mother was named Esther." So much for that idea.

Esther then explained how she, of all the MGM stars, found herself cast opposite Gene Kelly in "Ziegfeld Follies." June Allyson, Esther called her "Little Junie," had turned down the leading role because she was pregnant. Ann Miller was, in Esther's words, "dancing God knows where." And so "a swimmer" who described her feet as "flippers" became Kelly's most reluctant dance partner.

As the audience started to make their way to the various exits, Dina and Ted started to stand up. She said to me, "So nice seeing you Budd. What are you doing now?" "I had merged my talent agency with two old buddies of mine, Marty Shapiro and Mark Lichtman in '92 and have been working with Jack Valenti and his new book, 'Protect and Defend.'" Ted jumped in, "Jack is one of my best friends, Budd. I did not know he wrote a book? I would love to read it. I am going to give Jack a call next week!" Dina quickly added, "You know, Ted and I have taken over RKO. Please send me the book on Monday. We are eagerly looking for good material."

"It's on its way," I said as Ted and Dina said goodnight to Cyd and Tony and our three other guests who had sat at our table for over two and a half hours and did not say a word to any of us.

As Mark Diamond's handy helper appeared from out of nowhere to take us back to our suite, I said to myself, now, in the middle of trying to put "Protect and Defend" together with a new producer, Dick Berg, Chuck Heston and Jimmy Woods, when all of a sudden there was RKO, Dina Merrill and Ted Hartley staring me right in the face. Little did I know what lay in front of me and Valenti in the months to come.

Chapter Thirty-Eight

Valenti, Milos Meet Dina and Ted and RKO

I must tell you that getting away from Hollywood and enjoying that brief respite from all the weeks and months of dealing with "Protect and Defend" and Laura Pels came at a very special time and was well needed. I did have to smile on my face as I headed home to think that I went all the way to Palm Beach to run into two old friends, especially Dina Merrill. I had made a note to call Valenti and get copy of the book over to her and Ted when I got into the office.

In the weeks that followed, we were still waiting to get our meeting with Jimmy Woods. I bumped into Sid Sheinberg one afternoon walking along on Beverly Blvd. At one time, he was the third most powerful executive at Universal Studios, next to Dr. Jules Stein and Lew Wasserman. Sid and Jack were very close in those days so I told him about Jack's book and had hoped to set up a meeting with the two of them. "Call me, Budd. I am at the Bubble Factory on Wilshire Blvd., as you know, and we will set it up." I thought, as easy as that?

I tried to call several times but when I did, his assistant said he was out of town and when he returned on Friday, he was too busy at that time to meet. We moved on. G.A.C. agent Jack Gilardi was trying to set up a Chuck Heston, Jack Valenti, Robert Halmi, Dick Berg meeting as soon as he could get him, or someone in his office to read the book.

Berg was off to Europe the next month so all of a sudden it was now mid-June. Once again there was a lot of excitement in the air. Halmi, after reading the novel, suggested that Dick Berg take the screenplay into the next century giving the writer the freedom of bringing in a lot of modern technology that was not in the 80's, like a handheld computer and a small phone that you could call from anyplace around the world, even instant text messages to someone with an instant reply. It was too Buck Rogers for me at the time and beyond most people's comprehension, even in 1996.

During this time, I checked in on Dina and Ted, hoping they had the time to read Jack's novel and get some coverage on the outline. I also reminded her about Milos Forman and Peter Bogdanovich being available. And now that we had Dick Berg aboard, who she liked very much personally, she thought we had a good working team in place. I told Dina and Ted that as soon as I had Valenti's schedule he was looking forward to meeting with them during the next month.

Before you knew it and after Jack, Dina, Ted and Dick Berg got together, they started discussing possible writers again. Marty and Dick suggested they all meet with Erik Tarloff. It was on November 18th, just four months later, after we met in Palm Beach at the film festival's MGM dinner party that a top level meeting was set up in Jack's presidential suite at The Peninsula Hotel, at 9:00 a.m.

The whole RKO team including Ted Hartley, chairman and CEO, Dina Merrill, vice chairman, Robert O'Connor, president and head of production, Marty Shapiro, Dick Berg, Erik Tarloff, Jack Valenti and I met to discuss "Protect and Defend" for over two hours. Finally Ted got up and walked over to Dina and Robert and said, putting his hand on Erik's shoulder, "I think we should move ahead as quickly as possible and let Erik and Dick get started on his screenplay."

I could see, out of the corner of my left eye, Jack smiling and shaking Ted's hand. "Just think," Jack said, "Budd had to go all the way to Florida to bring Dina and Ted a copy of my book. Now that is what I call an aggressive agent."

Over the next couple of weeks, Marty and I started to put our deal together with Robert O' Connor and Arthur Horan, head of legal for RKO. There were three deals that had to be set: Valenti's, Tarloff's and Dick Berg's.

It took from December until February of the new year to put together a three-page development deal for our three clients. It was almost the end of February when we started working on a press release with the help of Warren Cowan and RKO press.

Finally, by late April, we all returned to Jack's apartment at The Peninsula: Dina, Ted, Robert O'Conner, Dick, Erik and Jack. The purpose this time was to discuss the overview of Erik's outline. Both Jack and I felt he was on the right track with the updated story that took the script into the next century, 2004 to 2010. How strange it feels today to look back at that period. Once everyone left, Jack dropped into one of the large chairs in the living room and said, "I feel, Budd, after four long years we are almost there. From Medavoy to Milos, Robby to Laura and Peter. The long journey is now over, thanks to you." I must tell you, coming from Jack at this time really meant a lot to me. That was one of those special moments I looked forward to reminiscing about with Jack and needless to say, will never forget.

As exciting and rewarding as it was to see checks coming into the agency for Valenti, Berg and Tarloff, each signed by Dina Merrill, I started to think about the checks that were coming into the office the previous year signed by Laura Pels. The months that went by, meeting after meeting after meeting and the so-called execs that really did not know "what the left hand was doing with the right hand."

Right before our eyes we could see a slow transition taking place towards Erik and his final draft. The holidays came and went, just like they did with Laura Pels and the script(s) that were written by David Scott Milton. Jack and Dick Berg spent a lot of time together trying to salvage Erik's script.

Towards the end of January Jack asked that I contact Dina, Ted and

Julia Halperin, head of development, to set up a meeting with him and Dick to discuss the second draft of Erik's script. We were also waiting for Julia to get back to us as she was working on her coverage of the script prior to the holidays. Our meeting was for January 29th and was going to be the time to decide on what would happen with Erik and his creative efforts over the past months. Jack had said his script was excellent but was not his book, unfortunately.

It was during this time that Jack sent Milos Forman a memo and asked him to read Erik's second draft: "Budd Moss has dispatched a script of my novel "Protect and Defend" to Robby Lantz. I still remember with affection and delight your early interest in this story. I am hopeful that you might choose to fit it in to your schedule. The script by Erik Tarloff has made many changes to my novel. The essence of the story remains, but your creative instincts are most important which is why I am eager for you to read this script. Thanks Milos. Warmly, Jack"

Robby was coming to LA for one of his very infrequent visits and Jack had asked me one morning at breakfast if Milos had read Erik's screenplay, hoping if he had that I could set up a meeting with Dina, Ted and Berg at RKO before he made his decision. I said to Robby, "The script was long in coming and if you and Milos were interested, she would like to put a supervising 'A' writer on the script to work with Valenti and Milos."

Needless to say, Milos responded to Jack's request by reading Erik's screenplay in quick fashion. It was the following week when Robby sent me a fax per Milos' request to advise Valenti that in reading the script, "he felt this material has deviated too far from the book, from its attitudes, insights and portraits and Milos frankly seems to prefer what Jack did with the entire setup and background."

Robby went on to say "that Milos is always enormously fair and positive where material is concerned that interests him and therefore says that it is probably a legitimate way and, also long as Jack approves it, that will be fine. But it is not, in its present form, at all what he had in mind for a movie based on the book. He is sorry about that because he is so fond of Jack's work but he thinks that, as far as he is concerned, the treatment of the story is wrong."

Robby Lantz, at this point, sent Dick Berg and me a "Saturday afternoon memo" stating that he lamented in writing this memo but Milos Forman's reaction to Erik's script triggered numerous thoughts: "From my very first reading of Erik's first draft, I had both misgivings and anxieties. It was not merely the fact his story diverges almost 180 degrees from the book. It had to do with my instinctive judgment that the story Erik created squirms with what I would describe as 'déjà vu' material, i.e. blowing up the U.S. Capitol building, the chase, the discarding what is the essential element (which Milos found fascinating), that is the political death struggle between the vice president and the president, a story which has not been told on the screen, to my knowledge. What Erik did do right in the final draft was to elevate the love story between the FBI agent and Clem, thereby constructing two parts that first class actors might choose to embrace."

At this point, Valenti said that we needed "a new approach with a new writer." He was not sure that RKO would spring for that or not. Jack kept coming back to Milos' judgment that "the script swerves too violently from the novel and tilts the story away from its original concept," president versus the vice president, with a sub-text of the romance.

Jack finished by saying, "My principal aim is to keep RKO interested, indeed, desirous of going forward. I surmise that RKO is awaiting my summary, which I hesitate to offer. I would like your views on this memo."

Dina, Ted and Julia were anxious to find a new "A" writer and Robby, Dick, Jack and I started to review a short list to see if there was a name that Milos would know and agree to work with. It was an impressive list that included Brian Helgeland, Michael Colleary, Mike Werb, Pat Kelly, Ehren Kruger and Ted Tally, just to mention a few.

At the same time, I sent Robby a note about my speaking with Adam

Davidson about working with Milos and he sounded very interested. Shortly thereafter, Jack sent Adam a very interesting letter, especially since Adam responded with great interest in reading Jack's book.

Jack told Adam that he called Milos to tell him that RKO had optioned his novel. Jack revealed that Ted and Dina would love for Milos to be "supervising producer," to choose the writer and director and generally deploy a monitoring eye over the project. Milos then immediately suggested Adam as the perfect person to direct the film, if he was interested.

Jack told Adam that RKO had contracted with a writer who had turned in two drafts which strayed wildly from the original story. "I was not pleased with either of them." Jack continued, "When Milos read the last draft, he expressed the view that the writer had written a new story that he found unacceptable. Therefore, the RKO strategy is now to find a new writer, but also to see if a talented young director like you finds the story enticing, and then you and Milos would have the most say in choosing a writer. Budd Moss, my agent on this specific project, and RKO have a list of about nine writers they are looking at, none of whom I know.

Given Milos' celebration of your talents, I am keen to get your take on the book. So take the time you need. As soon as you have read it and formed a judgment, would you get back to me? I'm pleased you remembered my congratulatory letter to you. An Academy Award has to be as close to the summit as one can get.

Warmly, Jack (May 12th 1998)."

Robby sent me a note that Adam was coming into New York the next day and Milos was coming back over the weekend and the three of them were planning to get together to discuss this situation. Jack was also planning on going into New York.

The next day Jack sent me a fax informing me that the meeting with Milos, Robby and Adam went splendidly. Jack was very impressed with Adam and said that he had found the book to be fascinating and said that it had captured his interests. Adam was in the final stages of a sound mix for the picture he just completed. Jack concluded, "He will finish the book shortly and then will get back in touch with me and Robby. So everything looks good so far."

Chapter Thirty-Nine

Robby Lantz Invades RKO

Before you knew it, Robby was coming to LA to meet with RKO for our first pitch meeting. For me, it was going to be a treat to watch this "Gentleman Agent" tell Dina and Ted that Milos, who would be attending the meeting, wanted Adam to work with him if there was a deal to be put in place. I had suggested to Robby to bring some of Adam's writing material to show Dina and Ted, but Robby just said that Milos did not have to show anything. He simply wanted to work with him.

The pitch meeting went very well, I thought. We tried at one point to get Valenti on the phone but he was not available. Dick Berg had hoped to speak with him but could wait until the next morning. Even though Dina, Ted and Julia were impressed with Robby and his explaining to them that Adam and Milos have worked together and the chemistry between them will bring a great script, Julia had to show her wisdom by asking Robby to review the list of writers with Milos to see if he would speak to one of them besides Adam.

At this turning point, Dick and I told Jack the next day that he should call Dina and Ted after Julia has reviewed Adams work. Here we were, with RKO interested in two-time Oscar winner Milos Forman, who for the past five years liked Valenti's novel, and having his friend and Oscar winner Adam Davidson write the screenplay under Milos' supervision as an executive producer. And then when the script was finished, subject to Milos' availability, either direct the film himself or have to right to approve another director of his choice.

Once again, as interested as Julia was in Adam's work, she was set on doing her job and getting Valenti and Milos to look at the list again of the top "A" writers in hopes that they would speak to one or two of them. Needless to say, Dick Berg and Robby were "shocked" that here was Milos Forman with a writer, ready to go to work and she was still not happy with the situation. It was Dick's suggestion at this point to either make this deal and make it fast or let Valenti and his book go elsewhere.

On August 6th, 1998, Jack Valenti took it upon himself to send Julia Halperin at RKO the following letter:

"Dear Julia, I'm sorry I was unable to insert myself via the phone into your meeting on August 4th. I have been avalanched by some pesky congressional issues which have held me hostage. Nonetheless, let me offer you some personal comments addressed to moving *Protect and Defend* to a production green light.

First, we have available to us one of the greatest living film directors, Milos Forman. His name and his body of work entices major studios. He is eminently bankable. He is also mightily attracted to actors who want to work with him, and has a kinship with other first class directors in our business. I would judge Milos to be an asset of spacious worth.

Second, early on he was enamored of the novel, and had read it carefully and thoroughly when I first met with him. At that time he was ready to take on the project as co-writer and director. Because I could not offer him the kind of personal time he requested of my collaboration, he moved onto another project. But he knows the material well. He still likes it.

Third, he is ready (1) to be the supervising producer, to help select both writer and director. He believes in the skills of Adam Davidson, who in turn has devoured the novel and has put to paper a script design. And (2) he has declared he is ready to direct the movie himself once he is freed of his current obligation, if it is written by Adam, and if no other director of his choice is available.

By my lights, the above produces a large cinema value not often accessible to a production company. I daresay if RKO wants to partner with a studio or other such entity, the presence of Milos would be the prime connecting tissue.

Therefore, I suggest that RKO ought to embrace Milos and his recommendations as a superior to all other alternatives.

That being said, Julia, may I offer response to the one-page treatment? My belief in the material emerges from what I believe to be the 'characters' in the play, whose development ought to be the centerpiece of the narrative. The Vice President, amoral, with the dash and elan of Clinton and Kennedy; the Russian, Federof, sinister, crafty, sensual; the team of Clem and Toni, idealistic, dutybound to protect the President.

It is the clash of these opposites in the cauldron of presidential election which suffuses the story. I see this story on an epic scale, in Russia where a newly resurgent leader re-assembles power back to Moscow; in Washington; the Oval Office; in the backrooms where the campaign dust-bins are located; in the salons conducted by doyennes of the political society. In short, I see this as a modern day version of ADVISE AND CONSENT, not so much a thriller which is too commonplace in the current cinema.

To repeat: I counsel RKO to go with Milos and his design.

Warmly,

Jack"

A few days later, Julia forwarded a copy of a memo that she had sent to Ted:

"RKO Inter-office Memorandum

Attached please find Valenti's letter (Aug. 6th 1998). I immediately called Budd who conveyed the following:

"Robby Lantz is of the opinion that we could walk into any studio today and make a deal based on Milos' commitment to this project. (We need to clarify that this means that Milos will supervise and co-write [as needed] the script with Adam. We also need to clarify his commitment regarding directing—the biggest draw).

Although we are still waiting to receive Adam Davidson's samples and tape, since Milos is hot to work with him, we should find a way to make this work [for us] or we risk losing Milos.

We are still waiting for Milos feedback to my writer's list, but if Milos does not respond to any names on the list and chooses to work exclusively with Adam, we should be prepared to bring this package (with a thought-out pitch) to the studios.

Ted, the tone of Jack's letter seems to be a warning not to push Milos to work with another writer. Jack, Budd, Dick and Lantz, are ready to go to the studios with Adam and Milos once we have a pitch. If we go to the studios and they want to make a deal, great. I will not fight the team to bring on another writer."

I sent Jack a fax right away sharing with him this memo to Ted and Dina from Julia. I also wrote:

"I spoke to her [Julia] last night and expressed all of our feelings about Milos and Adam. Have spoken to Robby, who informed me that Milos would not want screen credit as a writer.

I suggest that I arrange a dinner at the Hotel Bel-Air on August 21st or 22nd with you, Milos, Dina and Ted and try and move ahead by October 1st, which was the date that Ted set to start the new screenplay.

Marty Shapiro will be back [from his summer holiday in Cannes] on

August 24th and can start preparing the deal memo covering Milos and Adams' deal with RKO.

We are very close to taking that last, big giant step towards that green light, dear Jack.

Warmest personal regards,

Budd"

The next morning I shot off another fax to Robby telling him of the pending dinner with Ted, Dina, Milos and Jack at the Bel-Air. Jack was supposed to have dinner with the Wasserman's and the Kirk Douglas' but would re-arrange his schedule if Milos could be available one of those nights.

On August 11th, I sent Julia Adam Davidson's Oscar winning short film *The Lunch Date* along with his bio asking her to have Dina and Ted look at this as soon as possible.

At the same time, I sent Marty a fax advising him of Robby Lantz, Dick Berg and my meeting with Ted, Dina and Julia to discuss the possibilities of bringing Milos into the project as an executive producer. He would also supervise the writing of the new script by Adam, whom he had worked with in the past. Robby, Jack and Adam had met in New York the month before and Jack felt very good about Adam and his writing.

I also told Marty that RKO had asked Milos to review the list of "A" writers to see if there is someone he would like to work with, but Robby made it clear that Milos wanted Adam. I added, "Besides, Robby said that Adam would save RKO $1 Mil by using him. I told Robby that you would call him when you returned on Aug. 24th."

Even though Milos could not work out the dinner with Ted, Jack and Dina due to his shooting schedule, I was able to arrange for Jack to go to the old Chasen's Restaurant on Beverly Blvd., on the 21st of August. Dick Berg and I had met the other morning and we both agreed that the next few weeks should get us in to a launching position with RKO, Milos and Adam.

Ted, after reading Valenti's letter to Julia responded to Jack:

"As always, you reduce the complexities down to clear issues. As you say, if Milos will agree to executive produce and to supervise and co-write with Adam, maybe we can make this happen.

Naturally, Milos' level of commitment to direct is the most valuable aspect of all. I believe we need to define his interests in doing this. Without Milos' commitment in some documented form, Adam's writing experience alone will not give us or the studios what is needed to advance this promising film.

Meanwhile, we move ahead. I understand we will weave all this together next month when we meet again.

Always with great regard, Ted"

I had arranged with Jack to take him over to Chasen's the next afternoon at 5:30 p.m. to meet with Milos during a production break. Milos managed to spend some time in between shots with Jim Carrey and Danny De Vito for the film "Man On The Moon." Even when Milos introduced Jim to Jack, he would not break character, which Jack and I found very interesting.

I told Robby the next day that Jack told Milos he was pleased that there was this opportunity for Adam to work on the outline and first draft with Milos overseeing the material. Needless to say, Milos made it very clear to Jack that it would have to be at a time that he could devote the proper attention to the material. I was planning on seeing Ted the following week with Marty Shapiro back in town to start putting the first steps together for Milos and Adam on to some RKO stationary.

A couple of days later, Robby sent me a fax:

"I think indeed that we should try and put some foundation under this entire matter, by which I mean that I approve of your remark that some kind of step deal should be prepared.

I know from experience that the ten-page outlines are the hardest things in the world to do and require the most planning and thinking. Are you satisfied that RKO is prepared to put up the necessary front or development money to pay Adam and to pay Milos?

It is not impossible that I will come out again quite soon. If it is absolutely necessary, I will try and find three or four days to make the trip to L.A. It may be essential to do that.

We have had situations in the past where Milos rendered consulting services to the development of a script and in fact we have an established fee for him. He was delighted to see Jack and apparently you all had a good time. Things are going well on the movie. I'm beginning to be alarmed.

Give my best to Dina Merrill and her husband.

Yours ever, Robby"

Two days later, on August 26th, Robby sent me another fax:

"It is not easy to propose any kind of an arrangement to cover the extraordinary position of Milos Forman as a kind of executive producer, supervising the possible RKO movie of Valenti's book.

In all previous instances when Milos worked with the writer or contributed at all to the development of material, usually in the expectation that he would be the director of the work, we established a consultation fee of $250,000, usually applicable against his directorial fees.

I would suggest that RKO be asked for the $250,000 for considerable help already given by Milos, including the suggestion of employing Adam Davidson and his accessibility henceforth whenever possible to Adam.

If the resulting first draft, or whatever will be, shows that the RKO people want to go further and, even more importantly, Milos would like to go forward and be involved in the movie as the supervising executive producer, then he should be paid an additional one million dollars plus one percent of the gross from the first dollar.

I am making this 'proposal' up and if that is an acceptable basis to RKO, then I will have to review it with Milos and with Bruce Ramer and Chuck Scott before it can be made firm. Let me know whether that is enough information. All the best.

Yours ever, Robby"

I got back to Robby the next day and told him:

"Thank you for your very informative letter (fax) regarding the proposal of a deal with RKO for Milos and Adam. I will contact you tomorrow after my breakfast with Ted Hartley, since the main reason for this meeting is to put everything on the table as to the way Jack would like to move ahead with Milos, Adam and Dick Berg.

I had hoped even though I told Marty Shapiro what the basic points were of Milos' deal at Universal, if you could please send me a brief outline [for my eyes only] of the deal, including $5 million, against 7 ½ percent against the gross, etc., this would help Marty so when he meets next week with Ted and his lawyers, we have everything in place.

Marty would like to call you if not on Friday, early next week once our date is arranged at RKO.

Best,

Budd"

When Marty returned, I sent him an overview of what had taken place along with all of Robby's faxes reviewing all of his requests and concerns about Milos and Adam. I had suggested to Marty that we meet the week of September 14th with Ted and Arthur Horan in legal. I had set a tentative time of 4:00 p.m. subject to Marty's schedule.

The next day Robby had exchanged views with Chuck Scott, Bruce Ramer's law partner, who works mainly out of Santa Fe, so that we would have some more reliable proposals regarding Milos. Bruce would be back that coming weekend. Then Robby wrote to me:

"We are in agreement that the upfront compensation should be $250,000 as established and should cover pre-production work including work with the writer and assisting with the casting. After you telling me that Milos really should receive an additional million dollars or a total of $1,250,000 for his services and the use of his name, against 2 percent of the gross, I stick to my proposal of 1 percent of the gross because I don't think Milos wants Jack to think that he is burdening the set up.

I also have your fax of yesterday's date. In the meantime, you will have your breakfast meeting with Ted Hartley.

I think it would be a giant step towards the reality of a movie if RKO would have access to Milos Forman, make a deal with Adam Davidson to start work as soon as he returns from his current acting assignment in "Vojtech," Jansy's movie, and have Dick Berg as a line producer. Incidentally, do you also need a real experienced line producer such as the one who always works with Milos, i.e. Mike Hausman?

There isn't really any need to bring up Milos' directorial terms. Yes, the figures you have are basically correct except that the 7 ½ percent of the gross rises to 10 percent and 12 ½ percent. Also, by the time this picture is written and cast and actually goes into production, Milos may come out of the area of pittance and be paid more than now, so there is nothing to quote without a date.

You talk about Ted and his lawyers. Who are these lawyers? [Here is where Robby's amazing sense of humor always came in to play in our personal conversations.] If it is Ken Starr, we'll have to think things over.

Marty can always call me and never needs a special permission even from my manager, Budd Moss.

I may be a bit forward and ask why on earth you Budd, are not being compensated beyond the agency position? You should have a direct and official association with the picture which you are in fact putting together and even co-producing.

Let the record show that I still like Dina Merrill.

All the best, yours ever,

Robby"

On August 31st I had breakfast with Ted at the Hotel Bel-Air and reviewed the overall deal that was pending. The next day, Ted sent me the following note thanking me for breakfast and said:

"It seems to me the next steps we devised are these:

We have agreed to a briefing and storytelling meeting with Adam Davidson around September 20th.

You are going to ascertain before that date the fees for Adam and for Milos Forman together with availability and writing commitments.

We will thereafter set up a meeting date with Universal and begin discussions about their funding the development of that package.

As you know, I would be delighted and surprised if any studio were willing to make a major commitment to our relatively inexperienced writer and to Milos as a supervising (executive) producer without further obligations by him. However, since you and Jack seem so optimistic, we will give it a full-fledged varsity try. We do want to have a clear concept and agenda before we make this effort.

Let's work on that after the September meeting.

Regards and good wishes,

Ted Hartley"

In the days that followed after Marty and I had our conference call with Ted and Arthur Horan on September 10th and placed all of our deal points on the table, we assured them that our first stop was to go to Universal with our package proposal for "Protect and Defend" with RKO. Needless to say, Robby was also pleased when I called him the next morning, even though knowing Robby there was always a question mark about confirming everything that was still just on paper.

There were many times my dear readers when I felt that what had transpired over the past months with Ted, Dina, Milos, Jack and Adam had happened before. There was a sense of "deja vu," and that what we were doing, we just did before. I could see Jack, Marty, and me at the Cannes Film Festival, walking into the large conference room at the Majestic Hotel with Harvey Weinstein, Mike Medavoy and producer, author Jeffery Konvitz at 8:30 in the morning. There was Warren Cowan and his PR staff already handing out information to the press regarding "Protect and Defend" and the new deal with Laura Pels and Peter Bogdanovich Productions purchasing Jack's book for a high six figure deal. There was Jack Valenti, the "Czar of Hollywood," probably the most powerful man in the motion picture industry, next to Lew Wasserman and Dr. Jules Stein, selling his first novel to be made into a major motion picture, and the deal was put together by his agents, Budd Burton Moss and Martin Shapiro.

I could visualize the breakfast and luncheon meetings, the dinner meetings both in LA at the Hotel Bel-Air with Laura, the Polo Lounge, The Peninsula Hotel, 21 in NYC, the Russian Tea Room with Robby, the

Hay-Adams Hotel in Washington D.C. with Jack. Before I knew it my bedroom started to spin and I could see hundreds of faxes flying through the air. Laura, Gil and her East Coast and West Coast staff yelling at me that "Laura is going to put this deal on hold until further notified." Finally her option on the book was about to expire and Peter Bogdanovich was nowhere to be found. I promised Valenti that the RKO deal was going to happen, and then I woke up in a pool of sweat.

The next day, Marty sent Stacey Snider at Universal Studios one of Adam Davidson's screenplays, "Midnight Climax," and advised her that Milos Forman had attached himself to the project and wanted to develop the Valenti novel, "Protect and Defend," which was under option to Dina Merrill and Ted Hartley at RKO. Marty had also enclosed a copy of Jack's book for her to read. Marty had also sent "Protect and Defend" to David Vogel at The Buena Vista Motion Picture Group at Disney with the same cover letter.

I remember one day at breakfast, Jack said "that this business is a race to wait business." It was now November and I asked Marty to please check with both Universal and Disney to see if there was any kind of an update since Milos was going back to NYC for a week of filming before he wraps up "Man On The Moon."

Robby also thought that if there was no word from RKO at this time, he could arrange a meeting in NYC for Milos and Jack at Universal and Disney if there was someone to speak with. That dark cloud that hung over my office at the Shapiro-Lichtman Building on Beverly Blvd. towards the end of the Pels/Bogdonovich contract started to re-appear as Thanksgiving and Christmas was upon us, like it or not. It was early December and Robby, God bless him, was one of the few who was still at his desk, despite his serious health problems. Jack had called me and told me that he had spoken to Adam about the overall situation with RKO. Robby was going to call Ted in hopes he could find a way to move things ahead in the weeks to come so Jack could then speak with Milos and Adam before he had to go to Canada.

Before you could sing "Dashing thru the Snow," Christmas and New Year's had disappeared and still there remained a dark cloud over my office. It was January 20th 1999, almost the end of a century, when Ted finally checked in with Robby, knowing that Robby had not been well, and sent both his and Dina's best wishes for a speedy recovery. Ted affirmed: "I am prepared to get Adam started on 'Protect and Defend.'"

"I am pleased to hear that we have an agreement that the outline product will be the result of full collaboration between Adam Davidson and Milos Forman and that it will include dialogue sequences of main characters and that it is to be at least 20 pages in length. Adam Davidson /Milos Forman will do the polish to get it to the place at which time we can take it, as a group, to a distributor for commitment and that the first draft will be received with in an agreed upon time frame.

Always with regards,

Ted Hartley"

The next day I sent Ted the following letter [fax]:

"I trust this finds you feeling better and back at your desk. After we spoke last week when I was in Tampa, Florida, I notified Robby Lantz that we had several conversations and that you had agreed to pay Adam Davidson the $10,000 breaking it down with the first payment of $5,000.00. I told Robby that you would call him and work out the back end and that you needed a cap on the time to put the twenty pages together.

Robby will be in his office next week and will be in touch. I also spoke with Jack Valenti yesterday as he was anxious to get an update and wanted to stay close to Milos Forman and Adam Davidson. I understand that you have dropped Robby a note and are prepared to move ahead as soon as possible.

Warmest regards, Budd Burton Moss

c.c. Arthur Horan, RKO Robby Lantz

The next day, Jan. 22nd 1999, Robby was ill as he had been in the past weeks having fallen at home and having serious back problems along with a lot of internal problems, was planning on being in the office the following Tuesday or Wednesday. He wrote me:

"Monday is to be given over to the test at the doctor's office—and then you and I will have a full conversation. This whole discussion with Ted is beginning to be comical. He cannot seriously continue to have these extended conversations about a $10,000 item that will bring the undivided concentration and work of Adam, together with serious input from Milos, and it is all unbecoming to all of us. Milos is determined to do what he can to be of help to Jack and his book. But he cannot be auditioning for Ted and company just so that they have what used to be ten pages and now is twenty pages including dialogue and so on, to be shown to various studios in search of support.

We can do all this with one phone call. Anyone who can have access to any portion of Milos' time would be willing to pay six figures and more just for that. What on earth do they think they're doing at RKO?

Everybody also insists on misspelling Milos' name. It is spelled "Forman" but so far the only thing that he got out of this connection with RKO is an extra "e." He returns it with thanks.

We'll talk. You're a dear man.

Fondly yours,

Robby Lantz"

What continued to amaze me each and every day that we were in touch, as sick as he was, he managed to maintain a remarkable sense of humor over the childish games that were being played out in this crazy business called "Showbiz!" Robby continued to stay at home and at the doctor's office at least once a day.

Several weeks flew by and I sent Robby a note wondering if he had spoken to Ted recently as Ted had sent me a RKO memo card, "will be able to get Adam started on the treatment soon." My note to Robby included:

"I met Jack at The Peninsula for a quick cup of tea. He told me 'that he saw Ted last week and Ted led him to believe that Adam's deal was in place and he was hard at work.' 'NOT TRUE,' I told Jack. Needless to say he was very concerned and said he was going to call you tomorrow. Enjoy your weekend dear Robby. Let us get ready to move on to another studio. (Miramax is my first choice) next week.

Warmly,

Budd"

THE IDES OF MARCH ARE UPON US. I could feel as March approached that the cloud over our office was getting darker and darker. Robby was the first to greet me with a note, concerned about not having heard from Jack recently. As busy as Robby had been, he was very worried about RKO and where we were going at this late date. He was supposed to have dinner with both Milos and Adam but it was cancelled and Adam flew to San Francisco for his sister's wedding. Milos had been locked in trying to finish his editing on "Man On The Moon," morning, noon and night. God love Robby. He said the only lovely thing that had happened to him was a dinner party he had with Baryshnikov and Jessica Lange. What a special night that had to have been.

The next day Jack and I met at his hotel and tried to not only review but to make sense of where we were once again with Ted, Adam and Milos. I kept hearing Laura Pels again telling me that she had put a hold on

"Protect and Defend." I told Robby I would call him the next day. Jack felt as we did; if we couldn't close this up as soon as possible, we should move on to our next bus stop.

The Ides of March was the day before and I sent Robby a Memo to File, telling him that we must find a way to get Ted to sign off on Adam's $10,000. It was hard to believe what we had been going through for this small amount of monies in comparison to the overall deal that would be made if RKO went ahead with "Protect and Defend."

Earlier that month, Ted sent me one of his memo cards asking for an update on the deal. "What were we missing?" I said to Valenti. Since January, Ted had changed the deal that Robby and I had asked for regarding $5,000 to start the treatment, putting a time cap on the 20 pages that were due, and the balance of $5,000 payable when the work was approved by Ted, Milos and Jack.

Ted had left a long voice mail stating that I was spreading rumors that he was holding up the deal and that I was saying that Valenti was disappointed, confused and frustrated RKO would not close the deal.

Robby and I had a 30-minute conversation with Art Huran (RKO business affairs) and told him that Valenti even told Robby over the weekend that he was disappointed that this was dragging out and felt RKO was having second thoughts and "cold feet" about moving forward. Art Horan was going to report all of this to Ted Hartley. To be continued.

MEMO TO FILE; MARCH 16TH 11:19 PM. This message was left on my office voice mail by Ted Hartley. The following day, Robby and I spoke with Art Horan and was able to get Ted to agree to the $10,000.00 as it was originally agreed to when I was in Tampa, Florida approximately o/a January 6/8th 1999:

"This is Ted Hartley. I am concerned about the rumors that are going around about things you are saying about this transaction with the Valenti script. It is not a big enough transaction to us so if this is causing hard feelings we will just take our lien against the project and put it back out and let you guys go do it. My personal relationship with Jack is much more important than any film that is going to be made and seems to me that you and I seem to have trouble agreeing on what each other has said. I don't want to get in the way of our relationship either and if we can't do a good transaction together, we should just avoid it so we can stay pals and be friendly which is what I would rather do. So we have had the same conversation with Robby Lantz that we did directly with the writer in which you and I talked about a number of times except that it is better than you and I have talked about before. I understand that you are complaining that the $5,000 is too insignificant a sum and I should go ahead and write the check regardless of what the agreement is. I just think just because the nature of the way people would like to do business around here, which is basically make an economic analysis and then negotiate it and hang by that unless something comes up to change the transaction. I'm fine if you want to do something else with this transaction. I'll call Jack and tell him that I am turning it back over to him with the agreement of course that we get a lien on any picture that is ever made for the amount that we have already spent. So see if that is a solution for you because if we are not going to go ahead with this in good faith and enthusiasm and have fun doing it, then there no point in doing it. So it would trouble me if what is said is true that Jack Valenti is disturbed because I won't write a check for $5,000 because that clearly is not what has happened and I would be disappointed if that is the kind of things you are telling him so we need to clear this up. So think it over and decide what you want to do and give me a call."

Within hours the machinery at RKO started to go into high gear. Art Horan, executive vice president sent Robby the following letter (fax):

"Re: Adam Davidson/ *Protect and Defend* March 17, 1999 "Dear Robby:

"I have had the opportunity to speak with Ted. RKO will agree to pay Adam the sum of $10,000.00 for twenty (20) page treatment payable $5,000.00 upon execution of a short deal memo and $5,000.00 upon acceptance by RKO of the treatment after notes and consultation. The above is conditional on (1) Milos Forman supervising the writing and (11) Milos attaching himself to direct, subject of course to his availability and approval over the final screenplay, if written.

259

If the foregoing meets with your approval, please call me so we can move this project forward.

Best wishes,

Arthur Horan (RKO Business Affairs)

c.c. Ted Hartley"

From March 17th to April 21st 1999, at least two dozen letters (faxes) between Robby, Arthur Horan, Valenti, Marty and Ted and my office flew back and forth.

Finally, on April 21st RKO sent Robby a detailed two-page short form contract for Adam Davidson to sign off on. It covered two dozen deal points that had not been discussed between Robby, Adam or me. Everything from RKO sole option to credit to work for hire clause to a "sunset" provision, that states "if artist has not delivered a complete screenplay within 18 months of commencement of services, RKO shall have no further obligations to artist here under," etc.

For the rest of the year, deal memos kept going back and forth. Robby's health was failing due to serious back problems which led to several operations. On May 4th 1999, Robby sent me a four-page letter picking apart each of the deal points from RKO's two-page deal memo. As the summer dragged on, RKO had sent Valenti a one-page six-month option extension for the delivery of Adam's treatment which he gladly signed. It wasn't until August 8th, 1999 when Adam finally signed the two-page agreement after Robby had modified it so he and Adam were comfortable with it.

On September 2nd, Robby sent me a note that Adam was going to Washington D.C. to do some research with Jack Valenti and was going to be his house guest on September 12th for a few days and requested that RKO pick up his travel expenses.

On November 18th, Art Horan notified Robby of the extension of Adam's treatment from November 15th 1999. I personally think most people were glad to see 1999 go off into the sunset and greet 2000 with open arms.

Jack started the New Year off with a memo f/y/f to Adam reviewing his draft that was sent to RKO and all parties on January 1st 2000. The months dragged on and on...

Finally in July, Jack, Ted and I met at The Peninsula to review the status of "Protect and Defend" in hopes that we could shop the material to the "majors" and get a deal for Adam to write the screenplay for $250,000. Milos said that once the screenplay was finished he would make the decision whether to direct the film or executive produce it for $1 million.

Each day the clouds got darker and darker. I could see in my dreams Laura Pels off in the distance trying to get to Jack to tell him that she was no longer interested in "Protect and Defend." I then would wake up again in a cold sweat.

On a Friday, Ted and I spoke to Robby. We wanted him to go back to Adam and Milos with one more recommendation, one more deal point, one more... Finally on July 19th, Robby sent Ted a fax that I had hoped he would not send:

"The entire project of 'Protect and Defend' is very dear to our hearts. But I am afraid I have to report to you that, after discussing the proposed 'terms' with Adam who would have the lion's share of work now and with Milos who has already given so generously of his time and imagination, we all feel that we are miles and miles apart, not only financially but in the whole structure of how to set up the mechanics of preparing and developing the movie, that it is best to thank all concerned and most especially you and Dina and allow you all freely to go elsewhere. Milos cannot be available in the manner suggested nor can Adam accept the terms which you have stated.

All of us have done the best we could, out of devotion to the parties, and we hope that very soon we will come together on something that is more easily workable, at least for us.

With warmest regards to you and Dina and thanks to all.

Yours ever,

Robby Lantz

c.c. Milos Forman, Adam Davidson, Budd Moss, Jack Valenti"

On July 25th 2000, Robby sent Ted another four-page follow-up. It seems that Robby had gotten a call from producer Gene Kirkwood whom Ted had brought to RKO as a consultant. Robby wrote:

"I had a very pleasant conversation with Gene Kirkwood and he then reported to you and had reviewed the proposal originally made to Adam Davidson which resulted in a withdrawal of both Adam and Milos from the Valenti project and you are now suggesting to offer Adam a deal of $35,000 for the first draft screenplay to be developed.

I believe the correct offer needs to be $35,441, which is the applicable WGA minimum. I would like to state once more that people like Milos Forman and others are truly excited about the idea of this film. All of us are fond of you and Dina and of course Jack and Budd and normal business procedure and especially Hollywood business procedure is set aside to help all of us get the brilliant idea presented by Milos, and enthusiastically received by Jack, turned into a viable screenplay. The only person who has that talent, ability, time and energy to work on this now is Adam, and Milos, who has worked with Adam before, has no doubt that he will turn out something exciting and workable."

Robby's letter went on to cover everything that had been done to date and what was expected of Adam, Milos, and RKO. Robby talked about Adam beginning full time and would arrange with Jack Valenti's office in Washington appointments with either four key senators or their principal aides to collect as much research as may be needed. This would involve trips to D.C. and elsewhere and it is understood that his round trips by shuttle plane will be reimbursed plus all legitimate expenses such as taxis to and from airports, etc. Robby went on and on as only this master agent knew how.

Robby concluded with the following statement:

"As far as I know, this office represents Adam and Milos Forman, if and when you will call upon their full services. Jack Valenti, the author of the underlying material, is represented by Budd Moss and I do not know who else is involved or who represents those people.

This letter is no attempt to create a formal document but simply avoid any kind of misunderstanding or conflicts at later date. As I have said before, on our side this is very much a labor of love and a pleasure of being involved with you and Dina and RKO and with Jack and this fascinating tale.

With warmest regards, very sincerely yours,

Robby Lantz

c.c. to: Dina Merrill/ RKO, Arthur Horan, Esq., Gene Kirkwood, Milos Forman, Jack Valenti, Budd Moss"

On July 27th 2000, Robby, who was very upset with Gene Kirkwood, sent me the following fax:

"Dear Budd,

I just saw the attached letter from Gene Kirkwood, which is totally unbecoming to all of us. The last help I can give puts me in an awkward position of withholding the information contained in it from Milos, for a couple of days. I suspect it would end everything as it now ends everything from this office unless it is properly rescinded in total.

RKO surely doesn't attempt to insult all concerned. The financial terms as outlined in my letter to Ted had everyone's approval. If the matter is not resolved by the end of the business day in New York tomorrow, I suggest that all concerned forget the entire 'negotiation.' There will be no further discussions, at least not with our office. Please let me hear from you.

Yours ever, (dictated but not read)

Robert Lantz"

Later that day I sent Ted Hartley and Gene Kirkwood the following letter:

"Dear Ted,

I am attaching copies of our letters going back to January 1999 when you and I agreed in principal to have Adam Davidson start on the outline. It took us months to finally clear the air. We are now, a year and a half later, at a major turning point in all the months and years we have been working at this.

The offer that Robby has made to you in accepting the $35,400.00 has been laid out with the greatest of care and Valenti and Milos are behind it and support it. It is crucial to make this work, as you understand that this is the way Milos and Robby need the deal to be structured so Adam can go to work.

I have spent years Ted in keeping this alive. Don't let it fall apart today over the structure of the payments or over travel expenses for research.

Valenti has spoken to the top senators and aides in Washington D.C. who are now waiting for Adam to come down there in August or September. Please re-read Robby's letter with great care, Ted, and allow him to structure this deal as he and Milos feel it should be done. You have Milos in the palm of your hands. I can promise you that once this has been done and approved, you, Robby, and Milos can open dialog on a creative level as the screenplay is being developed. We can find a way to handle the P, H & W—that is minor to what has to be done. Robby's outline for expenses has to be followed. It should not be a problem either.

Ted, as I said to you when we met several weeks ago with Jack Valenti, this is the closest you have ever been to getting this off the ground. You have Milos looking over Adam's shoulders as he writes.

Hopefully, when it is finished, you will have Milos as your director.

Let us go to work!

Warmest Personal Regards,

BUDD BURTON MOSS

cc: Gene Kirkwood/RKO"

A day later, Ted wrote to Robby, and from there Robby soon replied on July 31st with:

"Dear Ted,

Your letter faxed to me on July 28th did much to repair relations between the parties and I thank you for it. But it did not do enough simply because of long-established facts in life and most especially in business life. It was too little too late. And it came after I had told you in my previous letter that the decision has been that, as far as our side is concerned, the matter was dead and closed.

What I said then, I meant and it reflected the difficult and admittedly quiet emotional decision Adam and Milos had to make.

Post mortems don't help. What is to be rescued from a dream set up which also lasted long enough to bring Milos, Jack and Adam into my office many, many, months ago to be a very productive and realistic resolution, which then set apart to the point where we really seem to have nowhere else to go.

There never was a 'business deal' or not one of us could have afforded to give so much time for so little immediate recompense. And even now, on the eve of August 1st, we frivolously lost another month before even the weeks of research could start if the valiant and kind effort you and Budd made on Saturday morning in Los Angeles (at your home) had led to an acceptable alternative.

Milos is by now buried under a mountain of scripts, accompanied by realistic proposals in many seven figures. Adam has finished the last work on the first movie he wrote and directed and we have high hopes for it. Incidentally, in your July 28th letter, you call him 'un-produced.' But, of course, he already won an Oscar, a Palme d'Or, and has completed months of highly paid work on an original screenplay with Milos, which is also again suddenly, total alive.

It was with enormous sadness that Milos had to tell me at the end of Sunday that he simply sees no way in which he can permit this matter to restart and yet still be 'in negotiation.' There are still ifs and buts and reservations to which you are fully entitled but which need not be acceptable to the others.

So I'm instructed to find a way to convey the continued respect and affection that Milos and Adam and, if I may add, myself, have for you and your beautiful wife and your wonderful, electric, stimulating, and wise author, and shall continue to have for ever and ever. The rights to the 'drug' idea Milos proposed and Jack welcomed so warmly and Adam believes could work brilliantly belong to Milos. We make no other claims and have no other reservations. Only regrets.

I would be very wrong if I didn't say a word of thanks from Milos and Adam and myself for the unselfish and untiring efforts Budd Moss made to save the project and to make reality of the hugely promising material contributed by Jack.

Indeed, he sets an example for the huge amount of time and effort, and even cost, that all of us contributed and that very, very, nearly your July

28th letter might have moved forward. It just came too late.

Milos asks that I send his very special admiration and warmest regards to you and Dina, and hopes you understand, just as he does.

May I join in that?

All good wishes, yours ever,

Robby

c.c. to Ms. Dina Merrill, Adam Davidson, Milos Forman, Jack Valenti, Budd Moss"

I found myself spending a better part of the evening with my wife Carolyn, talking about what I thought was the end of this difficult and sometime torturous journey for Jack, Robby and me and wondered just like the Laura Pels relationship, what I could have done or done better to make the RKO deal work? Much to my great surprise when I got to the office on August 1st, Ted's copy of his letter to Robby was waiting for me. It read:

"Dear Robby:

Your letter received yesterday morning gave my heart a tug. We have all labored on this project so long it is hard to accept the finality of your news.

Having not seen your earlier letter until Friday, I missed all the previous discussions and assumed we were moving ahead to define our next steps together. Jack Valenti's letter also received on Friday seemed to indicate that, too. I asked only for some definitions of the upper limits of expenditures that were expected from us. I had not understood that clearly from your gracious letter.

Thus the meeting with Budd Moss on Saturday filled in the blanks and I felt enthusiastic about the proceeding. Your letter yesterday tells me that by the time I received Jack's and your letter on Friday, Milos had already decided he did not want to discuss the project further. So Budd's bringing me up to date on Saturday and my signing off was in vain. I wish it were otherwise.

It is hard to hear about 'damage done' since I felt we were working in the same direction. That is sad as well.

And you are right: the relationships were not about money. But since whatever money was being spent was coming from me, it seems reasonable that I know the extent of my commitment and what plan we would follow together through to a final draft. I am sure Milos understands that.

I do understand that Adam has produced a film that he wrote. I meant no degradation in saying 'un-produced,' simply that from a studio's point of view, Adam has not had a screenplay produced at this level.

You are so good about making things work and such a great example to all of us about how business should be conducted with courtesy and style. No matter what ultimately happens to *Protect and Defend* (which I love and would like to see brought to the screen) it is for me a treat to know you.

With regards also from Dina, who is always an admirer of yours,

Ted Hartley"

On August 3rd Ted left the following voicemail:

"Budd, hi, it's Ted Hartley. I had called earlier this week to talk to Adam to tell him I wished him well and I thought he had done some good work and say we'll find another project. He was kind of in a desperate state. He had just lost some money from a thief and was saying, 'Why can't the project go ahead—I'm ready to work on it now, and I really don't need a particular kind of a deal. Whatever your deal is I'm sure it's fine; I just need to be writing and earning some money.' So, I said, 'Well, gosh, we made an offer, Budd Moss made an offer and Robby Lantz turned it down.' He said, 'I told Robby Lantz that I was talking to you and maybe you should talk to him again.'

I don't know what to do with this thing. I leave it in your good hands but if Adam wants to do it and Milos wants to do it, then I'm still ready to do the transaction you and I talked about.

Great, I'll leave it in your good hands.

Talk to you later."

On August 23rd, 2000 I spoke with Robby to see if there was "one last charge down the hill." Not wanting to give this project up after the time he had put into trying to keep it alive, Robby suggested we give RKO a 48-hour window to make the deal. I then sent Valenti a short note:

"Dear Jack,

I spoke with Robby Lantz this morning, and he feels, as do I, that you and Milos should try to get together in Venice during the festival and review the overall project to the point that if we want to give RKO a 48-hour ultimatum, it should be done right after Labor Day.

I suggested that if you and Milos want to then move ahead, we should meet in New York on September 8th at Robby's apartment, unless he is well enough to go into the office.

Warmest Personal Regards, Budd Burton Moss."

"Dear Jack, and as always, a very special birthday wish to my fellow Virgo!!!"

I then followed up a few weeks later:

"September 6th 2000

Dear Jack,

Welcome home! I trust that between Venice and Deauville, you had a great trip and birthday. Please give me a call when this finds you, as I have spoken to Robby and he advised me of your conversations with Milos. I thought you would want to have this in front of you when we speak.

Warmest Personal Regards,

Budd Burton Moss"

And again about two weeks after that:

"Thursday, September 21, 2000

Dear Jack,

I know this is a trying time for you. My thoughts are with you as you continue to fight those windmills. Good luck!

I had a long talk, as I told you, with Ted Hartley, and told him that there might be a 48-hour window that can be opened soon. He must move swiftly though.

It is important that you call Ted on Friday or early next week at the L.A. office and review your conversations with Milos Forman when you were at the Venice Film Festival. Please call me afterwards, as Milos and Robby are waiting to hear from me.

Warmest Personal Regards,

Budd Burton Moss"

On Monday, September 25, 2000, Ted Hartley called. He recorded our conversation and sent me a transcript:

"Ted: RKO needs further free options from Jack and we need room at other end, two years is not enough.

Budd: Whatever extensions you had before you'd like to keep. Another free option is OK. So three free one-year options consecutively. I need paperwork from RKO to Robby by Wednesday.

Ted: Great. So we need a draft and rewrite from Adam. Let's keep with the understanding that you and I had on that Saturday we worked on this. I need to be able to announce that Adam is writing a screenplay from a Jack Valenti book and that Milos is supervising the script.

Budd: Milos is supervising off the record. I cannot say if he will want an announcement made.

Ted: That would be a deal breaker. He must agree to actively supervise. If he is to do that, then we must be able to announce that. Let's keep with the deal done on that Saturday; $35,400 split in thirds, 1/3 for signing the deal memo, 1/3 for delivery of the first draft, and 1/3 for delivery of the second draft plus not more than $3,000 for submitted project, related travel to Washington D.C. for research.

Budd: I'll get this to Robby in the morning."

On September 26th 2000, I sent Ted the following fax. You could feel the tension on both sides since we all tried to keep the deal alive:

"Dear Ted,

I am in receipt of your fax dated Sept. 26th 2000. I am also enclosing a copy of Robby's letter dated July 25th (which was five days before we met at your home on July 29th. This is the deal that Robby sent you and said that it had to be done this way.).

When we met at Hillcrest Country Club on September 16th, I suggested to you that after numerous conversations with Milos and Jack Valenti that Robby was going to open up the window one more time—in hopes that you would understand clearly that this deal can be made this week under these conditions.

Robby wanted me to tell you that your request to make an announcement can come at a later date. This was not part of the deal that we made on July 29th. Let us get this locked up under these conditions. It has always been $35,400 which half upon signing and the other half upon delivery of the draft, giving you a rewrite or polish and $3000 for related travel to D.C. for research.

I would be more than happy to meet with you tomorrow to close this up. As Jack Valenti told you, this is the only way that Milos will come aboard. Please trust me, Ted. Don't let this self-destruct again!

We all have put too much time into this—we have lost another two months. This is your final opportunity to make this work!

I look forward to hearing from you soon.

Best regards,

Budd Burton Moss"

The next morning at 9:55 a.m. a fax arrived from RKO. Ted could not resist sending in long hand:

"Bud, you forget! My agreement with you was for a draft AND a re-write. (YOU CONFIRMED THIS). If this is changing, then let's forget it. Too tough. Also, I never agreed to a 'secret deal.' If we can't announce it with some indication of Milos' interest, then it won't happen for any offer."

That same day, September 27th 2000, I sent Ted the following fax:

"Dear Ted,

This is not a time to be sending handwritten notes to one another. I would suggest that I meet you and Dina if she is in LA, before Friday, as the window is going to close unless you can respect Robby's, Jack's and Milos' wishes to close this deal for Adam as Robby requested in his letter, and you agreed to on July 29th at your home.(when we met).

There is no secret deal. Your request to announce this was never discussed at that time. I suggest you review that paperwork. If you would like to bring Milos aboard after this deal is put together (with Adam) from Robby, I believe that Milos is ready to perform as executive producer for 1 Mil, and points. Read paragraph # 3 carefully. You have a draft and a re-write.

Ted, please understand this; it took a lot of effort between Milos, Jack and Robby for me to advise you that you have a very brief time to put this together as Robby has requested.

Please, just one time, honor Robby's letter with no added problems. I spoke to Valenti yesterday and we will work out his options.

Regards,

BUDD BURTON MOSS c.c. ROBBY LANTZ"

Ted followed up that evening with the following borderline "rude" voicemail:

"I assume the paragraph you're referring to in your notes this morning is on page 2 of the Lantz office's July 25th letter. If it is not that, you don't either cite the letter or the page number, so I have to guess at this, but I believe it's that paragraph which begins "Adam will be paid ½ of the $35,000 at the start and a quarter into 75 pages and a quarter when the first draft is going to be delivered." There is nothing in it about a second draft, there's nothing in it about paying, not paying until a second draft is going to be delivered. Clearly, you as an agent would not endorse that kind of project for things of two drafts. The payment is made when the second draft is completed, this is what you and I discussed at the house.

Budd, you don't want to spend any more time on this. I'm not going to re-negotiate this transaction. Let's just quit friends, if we 'can' do what you and I agreed to at the house which is two drafts, payment along the way for those drafts not both pay the money for the first draft and hope we can get a second draft. It's got to be a standard one and two draft kind of transaction. This deal can't be a secret. In that letter he talks about, Milos Forman is going to put in his full services as supervisor. If that's a secret and nobody is supposed to know it, then I don't think Milos Forman knows about it. So I don't want to be tricked, I don't want to be screwed around anymore. I have a lot of movies to make, and this one doesn't sound like it's going to be one of them.

If we can't do what we talked about and we can't talk to people about what we're doing, including reporters when we talk about projects we're doing, and we have to tiptoe and not mention Jack's name and not mention Milos' name or not tell people what we are doing, then I don't want to do it either. You normally wouldn't have to put that in a contract, and I'm surprised this is coming up now and you're saying it's a contract breaker. Just call me, tell me you can't do it the way we agreed, and let's forget about it. Thanks Budd. Goodbye" Hang up!

It seems that after every voicemail message that Ted left, some with threats, some with a sense of him not knowing or remembering what was previously said or what was in the contracts he had agreed to, another fax would come the next morning from him in the form of an agreement.

On September 28th 2000 that was the case again:

"Dear Bud,

RKO is prepared to engage Adam Davidson at the $35,000 (SAG minimum) for writing services for *Protect and Defend*, half to paid upon commencement of writing, the next ¼ upon delivery of the first draft of the screenplay and the final ¼ paid on delivery of second draft based upon revision notes. This is applicable against a writing bonus (up to $250,000) of 1% of the hard budget for sole writing credit.

It is RKO's custom and expectation that we receive pages periodically during the drafting process. We need to establish start and delivery dates.

I have agreed to a reimbursement of not more than $3000 in applicable, substantiated travel/ research expenses.

Other germane issues are: 1) the transparency of our agreement that Milos oversee and participate in Adam's writing and his taking an active role in notes, conferences, and 2) the multiple extensions of the underlying rights. "Have we missed anything else?

Sincerely,

Ted Hartley"

The next day, September 29th 2000, I received the following fax from Robby:

"Dear Budd:

Happy New Year or whatever!

I am rapidly fading but have just received the fax that you forwarded to me from Ted Hartley. I will of course send it to Adam at his parent's home in Los Angeles and tomorrow to Milos when he returns to Connecticut. And we will discuss it.

So what you get from me here is my gut reaction and you are fully aware that my gut has been out of order for several months.

I think you have done a heroic job of holding this together for all concerned. But this letter, again, has more holes than an imported Emmentheler.

The payment he agrees to is still slightly less than minimum but basically that is what he means. This is not for a first draft screenplay according to him but includes a second draft 'upon revision notes.' I telephoned Thomas Jefferson and even he would not offer such an open-ended deal to a slave.

This is applicable 'against the writing bonus' which it never was; it is Adam's fee for a screenplay. Nor is it 'up to $250,000.' It is $250,000 and not even RKO could tell us today what is meant by 'one percent of the hard budget for sole writing credit.'

A reference to RKO's 'custom and expectation' about receiving pages while the writer is creating not only the screenplay but the whole story line is (a) a custom that went out of existence with RKO; (b) would be totally absolutely and completely unacceptable to Milos if he is to be involved.

From people who have wasted months and months of irretrievable time to say now 'we need to establish start and delivery dates' is worthy of Jack Benny.

It was my understanding that he would make available a pool of $3,500 from which to draw applicable, substantiated travel/research expenses. By the terms of this agreement, the Writer, after possibly paying taxes and, God forbid, agents would have to advance expenses, too, until he gets 'reimbursed.' But I am certain Ted didn't mean it that way. Also, over the weekend I am asking Rick Lazio and Hillary Rodham Clinton to negotiate with the shuttle airlines for a better deal for Adam should he have to work for RKO.

Now we come to the Wagnernian last paragraph. Thrown into this whole overly generous and quickly determined deal to make a young writer older but richer, is an 'agreement that Milos oversee and participate in Adam's writing and is taking an active role in notes conferences.' In other words, he is to throw in his talent and time in active work, which he takes very seriously, as if he were an employee of RKO. Can you picture his agent agreeing to that?

In the last line of his well-intentioned letter, he asks, "Have you missed anything else?" The answer, even in Hollywood, where everybody has a car, is "Yes, the bus."

Forgive the tongue in cheek tone but I cannot bring myself in a direct communication to you to dissemble. My clients are totally free to decide whatever they wish and may have reasons of their own. But you are of course totally free to show this note to Jack and he and Milos may want to talk over the weekend because Milos' devotion to Jack and to Adam is so genuine that he may offer to pay me to go back to Berlin, the sooner the better.

Love to you and your wife.

Yours ever,

Robert Lantz (dictated but not read)"

The next day, October 6th 2000, Robby faxed Valenti:

"Dear Jack:

I propose to send the attached letter I drafted today to Ted Hartley, provided you have no objection and there is no objection from Adam.

The unspeakable waste of time that was involved in endless discussions over next to nothing, i.e., the paltry sum of money and which has by no means ended with Ted's latest effort to reassure everybody, have served as a serious warning to Milos not to continue on this path.

He loves the potential of your book and of his additional idea. Above all, he loves you and Adam, but he also has had enough experience in the movie business to realize that this is no way to start a picture.

Budd is the absolute hero of the occasion and will not take No for an answer. But for the sake of your project, let us reassemble when your basic work is free of encumbrances. We all like Ted and especially Dina but the making of a movie from scratch is based on a professional conduct or pattern, which has not been followed here.

As this decision affects all the parties, we do not want to send off the letter to Ted until we have your and Adam's consent.

Milos is back in Connecticut and will be happy to talk to you.

Anybody will be happy to talk to you.

Yours ever,

Robert Lantz

cc: Adam Davidson

Budd Moss

Milos Forman"

The attachment Robby refers to above follows:

"Dear Ted:

I am afraid all of your kind efforts and Budd Moss' wonderfully inventive deal-making capacity has come to naught. Too much time has gone by and Milos feels that kind of delay and argument over initial steps does not bode well for the long and troublesome and often harrowing journey that is the making of a movie, as you well know.

In the circumstances, as Milos is inundated with proposals and must make a decision momentarily and as Adam has to go to work at long last on a new project—the screenings of his film Way Past Cool, in New York have been very successful—let us call an end to this and remain friends and hope for an easier next chance.

Milos asked that I convey his warm regards to you and Dina, also.

Yours ever,

Robert Lantz

cc: Jack Valenti

Adam Davidson

Budd Moss

Dina Merrill"

For all of us it was a great disappointment, especially for Jack as he really believed that Ted and Dina could have made this film work.

We were all so close.

I had never known a more creative and driven agent than Robby Lantz. Even when he was ill, he managed with what strength he had to come to the office and send one of his memorable faxes maintaining his great sense of humor all through the years. What were we going to do next?

It took me over a month to re-group. After several meetings with Mark and Marty, I put a list together of some of the most important executives I could think of at that time and started making calls again and sending out copies of Jack's novel to producers like Marty Katz at Disney, who had expressed interest in reading the book and meeting Jack. Producer and friend of Valenti, Thom Mount. Producer Johnny Veitch at Columbia. Close friends and producers, David and Mark Wolper. Oscar winner, writer Stirling Silliphant. Producer Mark Carliner. Producer Dick Berg, whom I knew when he was at Universal Studios. I remember sending Jack a note about my meeting with Dick and giving him a copy of the book which he read from cover to cover and found it very exciting and was "looking forward to meeting you when you next come to LA."

Prior to all of the happenings with Laura Pels and RKO, I had several meetings in 1995 with Dick Berg and was able to have Jack and Dick speak on the phone about his interests regarding "Protect and Defend." With Valenti's summer schedule, I could not set up a meeting with the two of them until early August.

Marty was on holiday at his villa in the south of France, overlooking the romantic village of Cannes. Mark Lichtman and I had several conversations with Dick and thought it advisable to get a letter of intent, which Dick faxed over the next day covering the Shapiro-Lichtman representation and commission arrangements.

There were several scheduling problems in the weeks that followed and finally Jack had to reschedule our appointment with Dick and Marty at The Peninsula Hotel.

The meeting went very well and I knew that Jack and Dick would get along. Shortly thereafter, a press release went out thru Warren Cowan's office of the new merger with Jack, Dick and his partner, Allan Marcil, to produce "Protect and Defend" as a major motion picture for TV /miniseries.

"What are some of your thoughts Budd about casting?" Jack asked the next morning at our 7:30 a.m., breakfast at our regular table at The Peninsula. "Jack, there are so many ways of playing the VP as you know. It just so happens that Carolyn and I went to a private screening of a film that I had spent over two years working on with producer Walter Shenson, 'Ruby Jean and Joe' by James Lee Barrett. Walter had given up and someone came along and picked it up and put Tom Selleck in the lead role."

I had known Tom and his beautiful model wife, Jaqueline Ray, when they were in a terrific actors workshop headed by a New York/ Pacino/ De Niro/ Cassevetes, actor-director by the name of Sal Dano. He and his wife Linda lived in an old Beverly Hills apartment complex off Burton Way near Robertson Blvd.

Along with Tom in this actors workshop, there were several other aspiring young actors including Roy Thinnes, Leslie Moonves and Sal's wife, Linda, who went on years later to become one of the most successful daytime Emmy Award winning TV stars— something I had a lot to do with. At the beginning I was able to find a great but short lived TV series called, "The Montefusco's" to get Linda started. Les tried and tried but with little success and one day found himself years later running CBS and becoming one of the most powerful and highly respected icons in our industry.

I told Tom about "Protect and Defend" and that I was representing both Jack and Dick Berg, who he knew very well. I thought Tom would make a great VP and told him that I would like to speak to Jack about this and set up a meeting the next time Jack was in town.

I called both Dick Berg and Jack and arranged several meetings with Tom, which went very well and Dick thought Tom was a serious choice as did Jack. At the same time, I had been in touch with Alan Alda's agents in New York, who Jack knew over the years and we all agreed that there was not another actor around that could be more perfect for Kells, the president of the United States. I had arranged for Alan and Jack to meet in Los Angeles in mid-January to talk about "Protect and Defend."

Jack personally sent Alan a copy of his book over Christmas with a handwritten note: "Dear Alan, I hope you might find this story of some modest fascination. Maybe you'd like to see it on the screen Starring Alan Alda! Wow! Love to Arlene. Warmly, Jack."

I also had called Toni Howard, one of Hollywood's major motion picture powerhouse agents at ICM, regarding a possible meeting to bring her up to date with the progress of "Protect and Defend" with Dick Berg who is the father of Jeff Berg, the president of ICM at that time. One of Toni's special clients was Jimmy Wood's, who Jack wanted for one of several key roles.

After several calls to Toni, who just was too busy to meet right now, she suggested we speak on the phone and that I send her the script or outline of "Protect and Defend," which I did and reminded her that Jack had sent Jimmy the book right after it was published. I also reminded her of her early days at MGM as a secretary and the few times we went to the famous Daisy Disco for a few drinks and a dance or two and then home early. I remember she was a very good dancer.

Sometimes it amazes me how things get done in Hollywood, especially when you are a very important agent at ICM and we find ourselves waiting for the paint to dry. I had spoken to Toni toward the end of January having sent her the treatment. All of a sudden it was late March. To the best of my knowledge, Toni had yet to send Jimmy the outline. Finally the next month, I received Jimmy Woods' address and Jack sent him the novel.

Then in May, Jack asked me to contact Toni to arrange a meeting at The Peninsula for either drinks when he got in from D.C. or breakfast the next morning with both Toni and Jimmy. At the same time and at the same agency, ICM, I had told Valenti that I had spoken to Jack Gilardi whom I go back with to the very first day that he and I became motion picture and TV agents at General Artist Corporation in early 1960. Was that a long time ago!

One of Gilardi's clients was Charlton Heston, who could be the frontrunner to play Kells, our beloved president. Valenti and Dick were very anxious to have that meeting when Dick returned from Europe in the middle of June. I sent Gilardi the novel right away by messenger.

Jack moved very quickly being the talent agent he was. He contacted one of his favorite producers, Robert Halmi, Sr., at Hallmark Entertainment in New York. He sent him the Valenti treatment along with the book advising Halmi that Chuck Heston was very interested in playing the president of the United States and Jimmy Woods was very interested in playing the VP. Dick Berg would produce, William Kelly, who wrote "Witness," would write the new screenplay, and Joe Sargent would direct the political thriller. All of a sudden we had ourselves an exciting package, as they say.

And then everything came to an abrupt stop. It was December 1995…and the project had slowly worked its way into the closet for no reason at all.

Chapter Forty

The Collapse at RKO, Addis and Berger to the Rescue

After the collapse of the Laura Pels deal, and the RKO deal with Ted Hartley and Dina Merrill, I needed a long breather. Actually, I was just about ready to throw in the towel. I headed for Maui with my wife, Carolyn, and son Geoffrey, taking some time to cleanse the mind and the soul. As I swam with the turtles in Napili Bay, I made a mental note of ten independent production companies that I wanted to take one last shot at before I called Valenti and told him that I had failed.

Emmy Award winner and producer ("Holocaust") Buzz Berger and I had been friends going back to MGM days when he was in casting and I had just become an agent at GAC and was covering the Metro lot, with several other new hot agents including Robin French, Bobby Littman (just over from England), Barry Diller (never thought he would amount to anything), Abby Greshler, Phil Gersh and Fred Specktor to mention a few of the agents at that time.

When I returned from Hawaii feeling refreshed, I called Buzz and said, "Let's meet at Starbucks in Westwood Village and go over the list I put together, starting with Tom Cruise Productions." I'd been his agent for about 30 minutes when Dolores Sancetta, a great NYC agent, brought him and John James to me for West Coast representation.

John Davis at Marvin Davis Co., Brillstein-Grey, Keith Addis at

Industry Entertainment—Buzz and I met with all of them. Keith was #10 on the list and if that list fell apart, it was all over for me and "Protect and Defend."

Buzz and I first sat down with Keith Addis in March 2004 and after several meetings and phone conversations, Keith having a great respect for Jack and for his novel which he read from cover to cover, and being a diehard Democrat, said he wanted to meet with Jack and take an option on "Protect and Defend" on April 21st 2004. From that time on, Buzz, Keith and Nana Greenwald, head of development for Keith, spent days, weeks, months and yes, a year trying to find a top "A" writer to bring to the table. We called every agent and every agency and the list grew longer and longer.

Finally, we came to the end of the list and I said to Valenti, "If we still want to get Milos, we have to get Robby to go to Keith and tell him that Milos wants to work with Adam Davidson." Against Keith's better judgment, Adam came aboard and spent weeks going over the outlines in his mind as to where he wanted to take the book.

After months of frustration, as if a script was being written just for Valenti, Jack's longtime close personal friend, Lorenzo di Bonaventura, left Warner Brothers as president and headed to Paramount with the help of Sherry Lansing to head up a new production company. I told Keith that this is what we had been waiting for. Timing is everything!

Within a week Keith called Lorenzo and told him that he was working with me and Valenti. Lorenzo suggested we meet at Paramount as soon as possible. What followed was meeting after meeting with Valenti, whenever he was in town. He would come right from LAX to Paramount and then over the hill to Universal to report to Wasserman, and then to The Peninsula Hotel for most of his other meetings. Within weeks, Lorenzo and Keith cut a deal and Lorenzo was going to take an option on Jack's book and out of his discretionary funds, pay Adam Davidson to start writing the screenplay.

Adam and Erik Howsam—Lorenzo's number one assistant along with

Nana and Keith—started working on the first draft. Weeks once again turned into months just like our deals with Laura Pels and RKO. Adam had to take several TV jobs to direct which sadly slowed down the process. Despite Lorenzo speaking with Robby Lantz, Valenti, and Milos Forman, Adam kept dragging his feet as far as finishing the first draft. Finally in June of 2005, over a year later from our first meeting with Keith Addis, Adam turned in his script. It took weeks for everyone to read it and then we tried for weeks to get everyone to the table for Lorenzo's notes. Call after call from Valenti to Lorenzo, Lorenzo to Keith to Buzz and Erik Howsam, and the script all of a sudden went into the closet.

At this point, had it not been for Buzz Berger's help and guidance, we would never have gotten this far. Finally, Erik Howsam called Keith and me and said, to everyone's great disappointment, the "Brown" team at Paramount did not feel that "Protect and Defend" was right for Paramount but there seemed to be some interest in the script with Paramount Classics. From that point on I could never get a direct answer from Erik.

It seemed like we were in a bad movie because we could never get a report from Lorenzo and what his comments were. He now was in production with four other new films. He was going between Scotland and England, Vancouver and Hollywood. It was now my feeling, after speaking with Keith and Buzz, that Lorenzo to this date had yet to read the script. Valenti was let down and very disappointed in Lorenzo. Jack tried many times to set a personal meeting with Lorenzo in July, August and September of 2006 but could not get him to the phone let alone to the table. The next time I had breakfast with Jack at The Peninsula, I suggested that since Paramount had passed on Adam's first draft, that Jack, Keith and Lorenzo meet with Jack's long-time friend, Brad Grey then president of Paramount Studios. We tried for weeks to set this up but Lorenzo's office kept pushing back. Every time we had a date from Valenti, Lorenzo could not be found. Finally, when Jack was in Sun Valley with his annual business convention headed up by the Allen organization, Jack ran into Brad and told him that he had been trying to set up this meeting, since he had a development deal with Lorenzo for his book "Protect and Defend. " Brad said he knew nothing about this deal (which I knew was going to happen) but to tell Lorenzo to set it up when he was back in town.

Chapter Forty-One

Lorenzo Would Not Return Valenti's Calls

Jack wrote to Lorenzo and also requested an additional $35,000 for Adam to do a major re-write, come up with some dollars for Milos Forman to supervise Adam's re-write, and then re-submit it to Paramount along with a meeting with Brad. I said to myself that Lorenzo must have had his head in a hole somewhere in the Mojave Desert, as there was never a response from him.

Finally, it was December 2006. Jack sent three final faxes telling Lorenzo that if he would not respond personally to his calls or letters, to have someone from Lorenzo's office, like Erik Howsam, head of production, call him, Keith Addis, or me and tell us that Lorenzo was officially not going ahead with the project. Paramount had picked up Valenti's option on the novel two times and now was going to drop it.

On December 13th 2006, I sent Jack a note that on the front page of Variety, was an announcement that Lorenzo was going to do a CIA feature with Jason Blum and David Wise. It seems that Lorenzo did speak briefly to Jack but he never gave me an update as to what was said.

Jack's response the next day was just, "Budd, I called Lorenzo twice. No response. Jack."

On December 15th, I said to Jack, "I think a stronger fax is probably the last resort. Will try and call you after lunch."

The next day Jack said, "You are probably right. I called twice on Thursday and once on Friday. The irony is he was there, his secretary said he had just gone into a meeting and would call me back. Not!"

The holidays shot by us so fast. Maui has always been a haven for rest and for clearing my mind and shooing the cobwebs away from a very difficult and frustrating time. This trip especially I found myself on the phone and at my computer, even though it was hard to find anyone until early January, when Jack said to me that "Lorenzo will have my last letter to him Monday. If I don't hear from him in a few days I intend to write him and tell him I am ashamed by his callous treatment of someone who has been his friend and defended him against some folks who are relentlessly opposed to him."

Jack was in the process of sending Lorenzo what was to be one of two final letters to him. The following is a copy of Valenti's December 18th 2006 letter to Lorenzo:

"Dear Lorenzo,

You are a longtime friend and so very close to my family {Jack's daughter, (Courtenay, had worked for Lorenzo for years at Warner Brothers Studios} which makes me feel a bit intrusive in my bombardment of you with phone calls over this and last month. Therefore, let me declare a "CEASE FIRE." What I most devoutly wish is some message from you to me delivered by someone on your staff responding to my query. If you are no longer interested in pursuing "Protect and Defend" or if you have no inclination to offer some funding to Adam Davidson to bevel and polish his last draft of the script as well as funding to Milos Forman to work with and supervise Adam's creative re-draft (Milos would be able to perform these labors in March or April of 2007), then my colleagues and I would love to move this script to others to see if they are interested. I have several folks in mind for this kind of scrutiny. I think I know the heavy burden of work that grapples you at this moment. I don't want to interfere with those tasks. What I am asking for is a decision on your part that can be conveyed to me by one of your colleagues, and not intrude any further on your time. Is this possible?

With affection,

Jack"

I was devastated at how humbling it was to Jack, a giant in the industry, to have to say to his longtime close friend, "Have one of your associates give me a call." Jack was simply despondent over this treatment.

There was no response. On January 5th 2007 Jack sent another letter:

"Dear Lorenzo,

On December 18th, I sent you a letter (attached). I again say to you I know how overwhelmed you are and I don't want to add any burdens to you. But I do need to get an answer from you. I need to know if you intend to pursue the "Protect and Defend" script which is in your hands now. If you do, there has to be some funding for Milos Forman to work directly with Adam (Davidson) on a final script.

If that is something you do not choose to do, I really do need to know that. If the latter is the case, then I would like your permission to take the script in its current form to others in the community to see if they find it attractive. You don't have to spend any more time on this except to come to a decision and let one of your associates give me a call to tell me what you have decided.

Many thanks,

Jack"

I told Jack that I thought his letter(s) to Lorenzo were long overdue and that I was still in shock that he had not responded, especially since the two had spoken briefly in D.C. I told Jack that I was going to bring Keith Addis up to date; when I did, Keith told me that he too had not heard from Lorenzo in two months as close as Keith was to him also.

Over the following days, Jack, Keith, Robby and I spoke about trying to bring in another writer if Lorenzo would not accept a rewrite with Adam and Milos supervising. Jack said on January 12th that he had made his LAST call—with emphasis on LAST—at 11:00 a.m. Of course, Lorenzo was not available.

We had come to the end of a long road with Lorenzo, which saddened all of us.

Most importantly, Valenti had stood by Lorenzo's side at Warner Bros. when Bob Daley was out to get Lorenzo's head, according to Jack. This is why Jack could not figure out why Lorenzo put up a brick wall and refused to speak to him. Was it because Lorenzo did not have the balls to say "no" to Valenti?

I met with Jack in his suite at The Peninsula and he wanted to move on. He said point blank: "I don't care if I never see or speak to Lorenzo again."

Chapter Forty-Two

I Don't Care If I Ever Speak to Lorenzo Again

Everything came to a standstill for the next week. I suggested to Jack that since I was no longer associated with Shapiro-Lichtman since they closed their doors, that we could go elsewhere with "Protect and Defend." I wanted to go and see Jim Wiatt at the Morris office to bring him up to date on this long and agonizing journey that all of us had been going through, especially Jack.

Rather than calling Jim, Jack sent him the following fax on January 22nd 2007:

"Dear Jim, (by hand)

I miss seeing you, old friend. I aim to remedy that lacuna soon. (I have been trying for weeks to use that word 'lacuna' and now I did it.)

A longtime friend of mine, Budd Burton Moss, is also a veteran agent. I wrote a novel "Protect and Defend" that Milos Forman liked and wanted to adapt for the screen but wanted me to take off four months to co-author the screenplay. I told Milos I had a day job. The project lapsed but Budd came to me and took it on. He performed miracles to the extent that it is now at Paramount, with Lorenzo di Bonaventura's production office. It was quite an agent feat.

I recount all this because Budd is also working with Larry King and his production company on an enticing project for me to host. Would it be possible for Budd to visit with you briefly? He has one trait which I find both beguiling and indispensable: he never gives up. He is always moving forward. This is, to my untutored agent's eye, the key to success.

Oh yes, in the next month you will be getting galleys of my book, 'This Time, This Place: My Life in War, the White House and Hollywood.'

To Elizabeth, my loving embrace, always given lovingly, Jack"

On February 2, 2007 I met with Jim Wiatt, then president of the William Morris agency, and related the whole tragic story to him. I told him that since I was no longer with Shapiro-Lichtman since they closed their doors in October 2006, and there were no strings tied to "Protect and Defend," that I wanted to bring Jack, Buzz and the script to the Morris office and let them represent the project.

I also told Jim Wiatt the sad story about Lorenzo not returning Valenti's calls. Jim was furious. He called Lorenzo the next day and told him off. How dare he treat his longtime friend this way after he saved his ass so many times at Warner Bros. It was soon after that that Lorenzo found Jack at The Peninsula and shot over there in person, and asked Jack to forgive him, which Jack related to me.

It was just a few weeks later over the 79th Oscar weekend, on February 24th when Jack and I had lunch with Larry King at The Peninsula to discuss Director's Choice. A one-hour TV talk show that Jack would host along with some of the greatest directors in Hollywood and why they "chose that actor or actress" to star in their blockbuster feature. Jack had expressed to Larry that this was "just what he was looking for." As I sat there I found myself thinking of the first time that Carolyn and I went to the 41st Oscars with Jack, his beautiful wife, Mary Margaret and family at the Dorothy Chandler Pavilion. It was the year of "The Godfather," produced by Al Ruddy. Along with the Oscar for

Best Picture, Marlon Brando won for Best Actor but he declined his Oscar. My high school pal and client when I was an agent at the time at General Artist Corp., won Best Supporting Actor, Joel Grey along with Liza Minnelli for their stunning performances in "Cabaret."

Little did anyone think after almost 40 years of attending the Academy Awards that this year was going to be the last one Jack and Mary Margaret would attend. Jack told Larry that he was going into New York after the awards with Kirk and Anne Douglas for Kirk's new book and then they were going home as Jack had been having some eye problems. Once that was all taken care of, he was going to come back to get started on "Director's Choice" and promised me that he was going to set up a small office in Beverly Hills and "we're going to finally get 'Protect and Defend' finished." He also promised Larry that he would do his first new book interview with him. His new book "This Time, This Place, My Life in War, the White House, and Hollywood," was a remarkable account of Jack's journey as a decorated pilot in WWII, his years in the White House with LBJ after the tragic assassination of President John Kennedy in Dallas, which he was witness to, and the memorable years as President and CEO of the Motion Picture Association of America.

After all the years that passed from 1992, when "Protect and Defend" was published, the long journey that took place with Milos, Robby and Jack, I eagerly looked forward to his return in June as we had so many marvelous plans ahead of us. Sadly, we were not going to be granted our wish.

As I described earlier, within weeks after Jack and Mary Margaret got home, Jack had gone to Johns Hopkins University Medical Center in Baltimore, Md. on March 27th, where he was having tests for his eye problems. It was at this time that Jack suffered a fatal stroke.

The funeral was held on May 1st 2007 at the Cathedral of Saint Matthew the Apostle, one of the most beautiful cathedrals in the country, where JFK's funeral service had also been held. The cathedral was located just a few blocks from the White House where Jack had served for over three years as special assistant to President Lyndon Johnson and later in D.C. as chief of the Motion Picture Association of America. Eight days later, he would be buried with full military honors at Arlington National Cemetery under a veteran's gravestone, which listed both his war decorations and his years as president of the Motion Picture Association of America.

Valenti had been a passionate film industry lobbyist, deflecting criticism of Hollywood and fiercely combating threats to the industry such as film piracy. The service at the cathedral was standing room only for Jack. Friends and family members from DC to LA gathered to honor a man at home in the power structures of both cities. Kirk Douglas recalled for his fellow mourners a time he spent with Valenti after a long, frustrating wait for a Washington meeting. Valenti told him to abandon his post and come over to the White House.

"If you were Jack's friend, your troubles became his troubles," Douglas said. "When the time comes for me to be upstairs waiting for St. Peter to see me, I expect Jack to find me and bring me to the big man." Among the other attendees were Michael Douglas, his wife Catherine Zeta Jones, Mike Medavoy and Steven Spielberg, to mention just a few. The political side of the spectrum was represented by House Speaker Nancy Pelosi, House Majority Leader Steny Hoyer and Senators Patrick Leahy, Dianne Feinstein, John Kerry and Ted Kennedy, among others.

The list of honorary pallbearers, among them big names from all aspects of Valenti's life, included California Governor Arnold Schwarzenegger and his wife Maria Shriver, TV producer Steven Bochco, TV host and former LBJ staffer Bill Moyers, Warren Buffet, Clint Eastwood and me. I was honored that Mary Margaret called me and said, "Jack loved you and I know he would want you here to say goodbye to him."

I find myself now, eight years later reflecting on how Jack and I first meet in 1966 when he came to Hollywood as president of the Motion Picture Association of America. Jack took our industry, which needed his intelligence and guidance, and over the 39 years as the newly appointed "Czar of Hollywood" he covered the world and gave Hollywood a new respect for the kind of great film making that it has today.

My journey with Jack and his novel, "Protect and Defend" is not over yet as I have a new screenplay in development and hopefully with the creative talents of Constance Towers Gavin, Edward James Olmos and a young and talented writer, Nic Izzi, we hope to have our film produced next year by a major motion picture company.

Chapter Forty-Three

Tom Bosley Meets "Happy Days" 1973

At the time when I received a call from casting lady Milly Gusse at Paramount somewhere in 1973, who said, "I have a great pilot script for Tom Bosley," and suggested he join the cast of "Happy Days" with Ron Howard, Marion Ross, and Anson Williams, and soon to join the show, Henry Winkler, "The Fonz," I would say that Tom was the most successful working actor I represented since the Burton Moss Agency opened in 1967.

The series, produced by Garry Marshall and directed by some of the best directors of the time, including Jerry Paris, was an overnight success and lasted for eleven years on ABC.

The cast was remarkable to say the least. Marion and Tom became America's "Number One" TV parents. Ron Howard could have stayed another ten years on the show if he had wanted to. He enriched everyone's lives during the short time he remained with the series. To this day Ron has an open door for me at Image Entertainment. Donny Most added creative talent too as did Erin Moran and Scott Baio and many others.

And then there was this unbelievable young actor who learned what acting was all about from the Yale Drama School and on the streets of New York in his early film days. Over the eleven years of the series,

Henry never knew the word "NO." Whatever was asked of him, he was the first person to do what was needed. He was always the first one on the set and usually the last one to leave even if he was not in the first set up of the day or the last one.

When Henry Winkler was cast for the role of "Arthur Herbert Fonzarelli," nicknamed "The Fonz" or "Fonzie," he had first been seen in 1974. Garry Marshall, the director/producer, originally had a completely opposite physical look in mind. Garry wanted a hulky, blonde Italian model type. When Henry, an MFA student from Yale, created his character for his auditions, Garry was amazed at what Henry did. Henry said, "The Fonz was everybody I wasn't. He was everybody I wanted to be."

His mother and dad were always there for the tapings, and they being from the old world, had to have instilled in Henry the word "integrity." He was thankful for those on "Happy Days" who helped make him such a major star on the series. One day the network came to Garry Marshall as the show was coming to the end of the tenth season and it looked like it would be cancelled because they could not afford the increase they would have to pay the cast members, especially the big jump in Henry's salary as he was one of the highest paid actors on TV at the time. He was getting $100,000 dollars a show. Even though all the cast had become wealthy from the series, they had hoped for one more year since Henry said he was leaving. He asked to meet with Garry and the "suits" and finally said, "If I am willing to stay one more season, will you keep us on the air? I will ask the cast not to ask for their increase and stay on another season at their current salary." Without Henry there would not be an eleventh year. He then went to Tom and Marion and told them what he had done for his love of his fellow actors and what they and the cast and crew did for him to make him one of the most important and successful actors in Hollywood for all those years.

Over the years that my son Geoff played AYSO soccer and I was his coach, I had made a deal with Mike Eisner, who was then the president of Paramount and his son Eric was on my son's team, that once a month, if we won one or two games, I would take the kids from the team to lunch at Paramount and then to the pre-taping of "Happy Days." Henry would always come over and sit with the kids and soon he remembered their names and a month later when they would come on the set, he would say, "Hi Eric. Or "Hello John, did you get a goal last week?" Or "Hi Geoff, is your dad really a great coach?" And yes, even today when I call or email Henry about "something," when he is out, within hours his assistant would call asking "what message can I give to Mr. Winkler for you as he is in New York?" God bless Henry Winkler and may he have another one hundred years in Showbiz. His new TV series "The Winklers" is in development at ABC and hopefully is on the air in the near future.

Chapter Forty-Four

"Murder She Wrote" Meets "Father Dowling"

A year later, after "Happy Days" finally came to an end, I received a call from Tom who said he had just gotten a call from Angela Lansbury, a longtime friend, who he had worked with in the past. She told Tom that she and her husband, Peter Shaw, were going to produce a new series for CBS called "Murder She Wrote" and she wanted Tom to play the town Sheriff, "Amos Topper." The setting was a small New England village, somewhere on the coast of Maine.

Most of the series was shot on the back lot of Universal at the New England village set, but a lot of the other outdoor locations, especially "Jessica Fletcher's" scenes, our mystery writer, were filmed in Mendocino, California. From time to time, during the three years that Tom was filming, and especially when I had a client like Ruth Roman or June Allyson guest starring on the show, I would fly up to San Francisco on an early morning flight, rent a car and drive up to Mendocino which was a four-hour drive and get there around 1:00 pm for a late lunch, spend the day on the set and have dinner with Tom and then drive back to San Francisco in the morning.

One afternoon a few years later, I was on holiday with Carolyn and Geoff and we were staying at the Cipriani Hotel on the Grand Canal in Venice. We had just gotten off the speedboat from St. Mark's Square when I spotted Fred Silverman walking across the garden to the bar. I told Carolyn that I would meet her and Geoff back in the room but I wanted to say hello to Fred, who from "Happy Days" was one of Tom's biggest fans.

Over the years that I knew Fred, he was president of NBC, CBS and ABC TV and whenever I was in New York, I would always have an open door to his office. "Hey Fred, what brings you to Venice? Looking for a new location for a series? What a nice surprise seeing you here. Are you with your family?"

As we walked into the bar, Fred said, "Grab a stool and let me buy you a drink."

"What are you having?" I asked.

"I am having a 'Bellini.' Next to Harry's Bar across the canal, they make the best here. They are made with fresh white peach puree and a fine champagne. How is Tom doing? Is he still on "Murder She Wrote?""

"Almost three years now," I said.

"It is interesting that we should meet here in Venice of all places. I have been thinking of Tom recently, since for the last couple of years I have been trying to get the rights to a very important series of mystery books written by G.K. Chesterton called, 'Father Brown Mysteries.' They're based on Father John O' Conner going back to the 1800's. I have been having difficulties with the Chesterton estate for some time now...if I can't make a deal soon, I am going to take Father Brown out of London and put him in Chicago or Cleveland and call him Father Kennedy or Father Dowling. He is a priest who solves his crimes with a strict reasoning process. I think this would be a great idea for a series for Tom. Have another Bellini, Budd."

"I think Tom would enjoy doing a series like this. Maybe he and Angela Lansbury could solve some of these mysteries together?"

"Why don't you give me a call when you get home Budd and we can set up a meeting with Tom, and if he is interested, we can meet with Viacom."

We just finished our third Bellini as Fred grabbed the check.

"Off to dinner!" he said.

I thought it was worth a call to the States that night when we got in from dinner. Tom was always an early riser so my call to him, nine hours later at 7:00 a.m., did not bother him, especially when it is from his agent from Venice, and it was regarding work. Needless to say he loved the idea of Father Dowling and wanted to know when he should tell Angela.

"Hold on Tom, let's have our meeting first."

The meeting with Fred was two weeks later. It was a quick lunch at the Polo Lounge and three weeks later, Fred had a draft and sent it to Tom and the next day we met with one of my old friends, former agent, Tommy Tannebaum, who was in charge of packaging at Viacom. Everything started to spin. I met with Tom's lawyers and Viacom's lawyers. The deal was in place and Tom called Angela and told her that he was going to make a pilot in Denver and needed ten days off. I then followed it up with production at "Murder She Wrote." I told them that if the pilot sold we would be leaving the series at the end of the year. Tom had a recurring contract with the series and it was "always when available" so there was no problem and Angela was very excited for Tom.

The pilot was made and sold and the series went on NBC January 20th 1989 for one season and then the network was going to drop the series when ABC decided they wanted to pick it up, and the series lasted two additional seasons. It co-starred Mary Wikes as Father Dowling's housekeeper and Tracy Nelson as "Sister Stephanie," who did most of Father Dowling's legwork.

Sadly, ABC could not keep it any longer and at the end of 1991 the series was cancelled. From Bellini's in Venice with Fred Silverman in 1988, Tom and I had a very enjoyable couple of years.

Chapter Forty-Five

Hollywood Royalty / Constance Towers and John Gavin 1967

When it comes to representing "Hollywood Royalty" I would have to put John Gavin and Constance Towers on top of the list. When you have clients over the years that have worked with John Wayne, John Ford, Hitchcock, Lana Turner, Susan Hayward, Kirk Douglas and Yul Brynner, you have to give them special attention and care. When they are seen at the "A" parties with heads of studios and networks, the Sherry Lansings, the Poitier's, the Lear's, the Daley's, the Schlatter's and the various Presidents of countries, especially Nancy and Ronnie Reagan, the Bush's, and Mexico's former president Vicente Fox, they deserve and expect "special services"—with the exception of Connie and John.

When I first met Connie, she was starring in a production of "The Sound of Music" at the famous Jones Beach Amphitheater in N.Y. in 1967. Never having seen this production before, I could not see where Mary Martin could have done a better job. As beautiful as Julie Andrews was in the Academy Award winning film with Christopher Plummer, Connie gave Maria a feeling of great understanding, warmth and a devotion to God that I did not see in other performances over the following years.

I attended this production with Irma and Burt Bacharach, Sr. They became friends of mine over the years having first met them with Carolyn Jones. I would usually find myself stopping by to see them at 200 E. 57th Street when I first got off the plane on many of my trips to New York over the years. Irma and Burt were New York's most famous "First Nighters" to every play that opened on and off Broadway. Burt was a well-known freelance writer whose humorous articles would appear in the New York Times, the Post and numerous papers around the country.

From time to time, Carolyn and I would run into their talented son, Burt Jr. and his beautiful wife, Angie Dickinson and they would tell me how much his mom and dad looked forward to my frequent visits to their apartment. Once in a while, we would find time to meet at The Russian Tea Room where I always knew we would have the "Number One" table as we walked into this famous restaurant right next door to Carnegie Hall. On any given day there was Leonard Bernstein, and his legendary agent, Robby Lantz, Walter Cronkite, Barbara Walters, De Niro, the mayor, The governor, Brando, Mia, Frank, George C. Scott, Pacino, Larry King and all the "hot" actors that were currently starring on Broadway and whomever was conducting or playing next door, including agents and directors—the Neiderlander's were there and of course so was Mr. Broadway, Gerald Schoenfeld and the Coat Check girl who came back one day as Madonna.

Connie's career in Hollywood was a very busy one. Here was this tall, elegant and classic blonde actress who you would have thought was born into royalty and educated in the finest boarding schools in Paris or Switzerland, and then you would find out that this cattle raising cowgirl was born and raised in Whitefish, Montana. Go figure!

I remember being a John Wayne fan when I used to go to the Hitching Post movie theatre in Hollywood with my brother, Herbie, my mom and dad and watched "Stagecoach" when I was probably ten years old.

From the time she came on the screen with John Wayne in "The Horse Soldiers" (1959) with William Holden, Hoot Gibson and all of John

Ford's favorite cowboys, you knew she was on her way into "Hollywood Royalty." She continued to star in films like "Sergeant Rutledge" with Jeffery Hunter and working with director Sam Fuller in "Shock Corridor" to mention a few.

In 1969 Connie made her Broadway debut in "Anya" and then in productions including "Carousel," "The Sound of Music," "Kiss Me Kate," "Oklahoma," "Camelot," "Mame," and then she met Yul Brynner and joined him in "The King and I" where she and Yul thrilled audiences for over 800 performances. I remember going to see Connie and Yul when "The King and I" opened in Los Angeles in 1976, which was the start of their national tour, working their way to New York.

It was in 1954 when I was in New York and saw my first Broadway musical. It was a brand new production of "King" starring Constance Carpenter and a very young Yul Brynner. Sadly, the legendary Gertrude Lawrence had just passed away. I had been in New York and staying with Margo Jones, the famous director and producer of the Margo Jones Theatre in Dallas. It was my first time in New York as a young and aspiring actor, and Margo had promised when we first met in San Francisco that "when you come to New York, 'Darlin,' you stay with your Auntie Margo and you will see the theatre through my eyes and you will never forget it as long as you live!" "Life with Father," "Wish You Were Here," "Picnic," "Oklahoma" and one of the most exciting productions of "Porgy and Bess." Add to that hotspots like "Sardis," "21," "The Stork Club," "The Copa," and "The Russian Tea Room." As the years have gone by, the production of "King and I" even today remains the most beautiful and memorable production in my life, and I told this to Connie when I saw her in their magical production.

Chapter Forty-Six

John Gavin Joins Burton Moss Agency

I remember in the late 60's when I had just opened the Burton Moss Agency, meeting John Gavin at one of the early talk shows that I went to with Carolyn Jones. John and I started talking backstage about the "business" and telling him how much I enjoyed seeing Connie Towers in "The Sound of Music" at Jones Beach.

Connie and Jack had been dating at that time and were planning on getting married. I told John that I would like very much to meet with him in the near future, we exchanged phone numbers and promised to get together soon.

John had a very successful career over the years. Universal Studios had been grooming him to be the next Rock Hudson. He made his debut in "Behind the High Wall" with Sylvia Sidney and Tom Tully. Over the years, the film became a classic film noir. Three years later, he made another classic film, a remake of "Imitation of Life" with Lana Turner, and "A Time To Live and a Time To Die" directed by Douglas Sirk.

In 1960 John achieved cinematic immortality by appearing as Janet Leigh's lover in Alfred Hitchcock's "Psycho" and by playing "Julius Caesar" in Stanley Kubrick's film, "Spartacus," with an all-star cast including Kirk Douglas, Charles Laughton, Laurence Olivier, Jean Simmons and Peter Ustinov. Over the years, John had said, "I had no idea that these two films would become classics. Had I realized that, perhaps I would have paid more attention to my career."

John and Connie were actively involved with Hollywood politics and Gavin became president of the Screen Actors Guild from 1971 to 1973, having followed his close friend, Ronald Reagan, who was the president of SAG from 1947-1952 and again in 1959-1960.

John decided to go to Broadway and appeared in the musical version of "Two for the Seesaw" called "Seesaw." John and Lucie Arnaz replacing Ken Howard and Michele Lee and then took the production on its national tour.

When I went to see the production, I found myself reminiscing with John about my travels back in 1958 with my wife Ruth Roman who starred in the national company of "Two for the Seesaw" with Jeffrey Lynn. It was a small world, I called it.

In 1978, I had gone over to 20th Century Fox to visit my favorite producer, David Gerber who I had worked with at General Artist Corp. and had spent several years with when I placed Hope Lange in his series "The Ghost and Mrs. Muir." He was in the process of getting ready to produce a new "doctors" series, called, "Doctors' Private Lives," a weekly series dealing with the personal and professional lives of two California heart surgeons. The pilot had all the makings of a successful TV series. Gerber had been testing various name actors and actresses for the four leads.

Gerber and I had been speaking about several of my clients, including John. He was hoping that he would test for the pilot, but like Hope Lange, he had read the script and found it interesting but really did not think he would like to do a weekly series. He did not feel at that point he wanted to test.

"Let Gerber make an offer and then I will let you know if I want to do the pilot."

The tests went on for several weeks and finally they had their choices for all four roles.

It was September and the Emmy's were taking place at the Pasadena Civic Auditorium and I was there with my wife, Carolyn as was Gerber, with his wife, Larraine Stevens, who I was representing at the time. It was crunch time and the network was forcing Gerber to set his actors for the pilot which was scheduled to shoot in a week.

Carolyn and I were in the lobby when Gerber came up to me.

"Budd, I know that this is last minute but I have to speak with you alone."

I gave Carolyn our tickets and asked her to head for our seats. Gerber grabbed me by the arm and we walked into the men's room. I did not think this was the best place to be alone. "Gerber, you are not Howard Hughes, why do we have to go into the bathroom."

"What is it going to take to get Gavin to do this fuckin' pilot? The network needs a name for the lead and they really want John Gavin in the series."

There we were, standing in front of the urinals throwing figures back and forth as many of our mutual friends were coming in and out, wanting to shake our hands as we kept talking. Finally Gerber came up with some realistic figures. I was writing them down on the paper towels, leaning against one of the urinals. John knew that we were close to getting an offer but I was playing it very cool. I told Gerber that I was going to call him and started looking for a pay phone as the Emmy's started (God what I would've given for a cell phone in those days). I had given John some figures that seemed to work. He wanted to think about the offer but I told him there was no time. He asked me what I thought about the offer and told him I wanted a little more for the pilot and was not that worried about his weekly series if the pilot sold.

Gerber had gone back into the theatre and I sent an usher down to get him.

We were now back in the men's room, back in front of the urinals as I was jotting down the various deal points and Gerber agreed to give John an additional $5,000.00 for the pilot but I think I had to give him a few extra days of shooting if needed.

"Go call Gavin and get this fucking deal put together or I am going on to my next choice!" The pilot was made and sold with John, Ed Nelson (from "Peyton Place") Donna Mills, who was the hottest actress at the time, Barbara Anderson and Larraine Stevenson (Gerber's wife). It was made as a two-hour mini-series and ran from March of 1978 to April 1979, and as excellent as John was in the series, even with his movie star looks and his superb acting ability, much to everyone's disappointment, the show was cancelled.

Chapter Forty-Seven

Constance Towers Joins "Capitol" TV Series

It was in 1980 that CBS asked John Conboy, who was the producer of "The Young and the Restless" to produce an equivalent in day-time during the summer of 1981. "Capitol" became the first soap opera to be produced in Hollywood since "Y and R" began in 1973. The show's title sequence during its early years showed aerial scenes of Washington D.C. during the winter of 1981. Years later, a computerized sequence was instituted, showing the glamour and sex along with the Washington Monument and the Jefferson Memorial.

Connie called me one day and said she was going over to meet her longtime friend, John Conboy, for lunch at CBS. "He has an idea for me to be in a new daytime series he has in development."

I wished her good luck. Within days, Connie was going to be set to play the lead in "Capitol." The phone calls and faxes started going back and forth between my office and CBS legal. I was able to read one of the first scripts that Connie gave me as I was anxious to see if I could help cast the series.

Conboy wanted to try and get the best "Name" actors if possible for some of the other great roles. I submitted many of our "Name" actors at that time but the only actress John sparked to was Beverly Garland. For years, Beverly was one of the most sought after actresses. From "My Three Sons" with Fred McMurray and the "Bing Crosby Series" to all the episodic TV from the 60's into the 70's.

John was excited about Beverly playing the role of Myrna Clegg opposite Connie's character Clarissa Tyler McCandless, the down-to-earth matriarch opposite vituperative and vindictive Myrna. The two women were best friends in their youth and had been rivals over the love of Baxter McCandless.

Beverly loved this role and tested for the part, and for weeks I tried to put the deal together but it seemed that CBS was not that sure about Beverly. They just wanted to think about it. Finally I was told by CBS legal that the producers had decided to go in another direction which was a great disappointment to everyone, including Connie, who was her biggest fan. On several occasions I tried to find out who got the role but I was told that the deal was not closed and I said to myself, I am sure Connie will tell me.

The casting was almost through and the company was getting ready to go to Washington D.C. for the first week of filming. For a daytime series in the 80's John had put together a great cast including Rory Calhoun, Richard Egan, Ed Nelson, Julie Adams, Teri Hatcher, Debrah Farentino, David Mason Daniels and Nicholas Walker to mention just a few of the great actors that joined the series in the years to come. "Capitol" was on the air from March 29th 1982 to March 20th 1987. CBS produced 1,270 episodes.

I made plans to go into D.C. for a week to be there for Connie and spend some time with Jack Valenti at the Motion Picture Association of America, World Headquarters. It was February 1982 and as I arrived at the Watergate Hotel, much to my great surprise, standing there in the lobby waiting for the limo to take her to the set was Carolyn Jones. There stood "Myrna!" I should have known. I think we both were lost for words. We both wanted to say, "What are you doing here?" "You look great Ms. Jones," I said.

"So do you Mr. Hollywood Agent! I heard you have a beautiful wife, named Carolyn and have a son, which I knew you wanted so very much. I am so glad for you Budd, I really mean that! I hope you think of me once in a while when you speak my name?"

"Ms. Jones, your car is here!" said the bell captain, breaking that moment of our lives together. I could see a tear in her eye, as she said, "I am so happy to be working with Connie. She talks about you and how very special you are to her! I hope to see you on the set when you get back to town!" And she was gone.

"You look good, too," there was an echo in my head. We both, I am sure, had a flashback of our saying goodbye to one another in anger, disappointment, and having betrayed one another on the door steps of her home on Beverly Drive where we lived together for almost six years.

Here we were just coming out of a "twilight zone." Almost thirteen years came and went. Almost two years after we broke up, I married Carolyn Gerry in 1970 and two years later, we had a son together, Geoffrey Michael Moss. Carolyn Jones didn't wait to let the body get cold. She and Herbie Greene had been having an affair almost from the time she went back to New York to do the Pinter play, "Homecoming," or longer. I had heard that she had to sell her home on Beverly Drive as she had very little monies left having bought a house in Palm Springs where they lived for almost seven years in a self-imposed exile. They wrote several books which did not make the New York Times best sellers list. I had heard that her first book she wrote with Herbie, "Twice Upon a Time" was a poorly told version of a famous movie actress and her life going from the top of her career, and slowly into the famous toilet. All of Carolyn's friends, husband's lovers and enemies were in there including, Aaron, Budd, Herbie and a lot of her enemies. Only their names and faces had been changed to protect the "guilty." The book was called "Dirty" and was not a big seller. Most of Carolyn's friends did not read the book.

Chapter Forty-Eight

A Sad Farewell to Carolyn Jones

Long before Carolyn ever thought of starring in "Capitol" she had kept a very closely guarded secret and that was that she had been ill for some time since 1981 and only Alisha, her husband Red Buttons, and June Allyson were aware she had been diagnosed with cancer of the colon. In February 1981, Carolyn had been vomiting blood and when the doctors did their tests, and discovered that the cancer had ravaged her colon and spread to her liver, they removed two thirds of her colon and Carolyn continued on, the best she could.

She told all her friends she was having treatments for ulcers. Towards the later part of year, the cancer seemed to have gone into remission, but later in 1982, while filming "Capitol," it returned and spread like wildfire. The doctors fought back with massive injections of drugs but nothing could help at that point. Seeing that the end was near, in October of 1982, she decided to marry a young actor, Peter Bailey-Britton, who she had been living with for almost five years after she and Herbie had broken up.

Carolyn wore a lace and ribbon cap to hide the fact that she had lost her hair.

The wedding was attended by Alisha and Red Buttons, John Astin, June Allyson, Richard Egan, Jim and Henny Backus and a few close friends.

In the meantime, Carolyn quietly went through the treatment. She would go to work on "Capitol" during the day and went to the hospital down the street from CBS, Cedars Sinai, where she underwent her chemo. No one knew. She kept her illness a complete secret for most of the time she was filming the series, with only a few exceptions: Connie, the producer John Conboy, Junie, and the Button's. I had no knowledge at the beginning until several months later, when one morning I had gone to the set to see Connie and I saw Carolyn in her dressing room and I asked if I could come in. She stared at me for what seemed to be a lifetime. She looked pale. Her beautiful blue eyes were empty sockets and they looked hollow. Her dresser was there with her and Carolyn asked her to come back in fifteen minutes.

"Close the door, baby," she said softly. I leaned over and kissed her on the cheek.

"I am not doing well as you can probably imagine by my looks." She paused and then said, "I have cancer of the colon, Budd…I have been fighting it for months and tried desperately to keep it quiet but it has taken over my body and the chemo is having a hard time trying to beat it. I have to go over to Cedars after the next set up, I am dying slowly." Tears were running down her face and I tried to hold her for a moment.

"John Conboy has tried to have a closed set so I can do my scene in a wheelchair which has been written into the script."

"My God!" I said to myself. That was why there was the quick wedding she and Peter had over the weekend. I was lost for words.

Almost at the same time, John Gavin was going through a major transition in his life. After "Doctors' Private Lives" he became very moody and found himself getting very active in the world of politics. In 1981, John's closest friend, President Ronald Reagan, asked him to be the next U.S. Ambassador to Mexico.

It was the perfect job at the most perfect time in his career. His mother,

Delia Pablos Golenor and her family, were very prominent ranchers in Sonora. John had a degree in the economic history of Latin America from Stanford. He had business interests, developing property in Central America and Mexico and he spoke fluent Spanish.

It didn't take long for Jack and Connie to agree that this new post in Mexico was of major importance to both of them. When "Capitol" finally got started in 1982 they knew that it would be difficult to be apart even for a few weeks or months at a time, but soon they were able to work out the schedule between Connie, her life as Clarissa McCandless, and her life as Mrs. Ambassador Gavin.

I remembered how Connie would spend twelve hours on the set of "Capitol" and then head to LAX to catch a 7:00 p.m. Mexicana flight to Mexico City. Connie found herself on numerous occasions changing outfits in the small bathroom on the flight in case there was an event she had to get to once she had landed.

There at the airport would be the ambassador's bulletproof Lincoln with a bodyguard waiting for her as she cleared customs. Jack would be waiting up for her to have a late supper together and then to bed as he would head to the embassy by 9:00 am and Connie would start with her new household problems and getting ready to prepare a menu for a reception for 350 guests that afternoon. Later that day she found herself dealing with major problems in re-doing their new home in Mexico—a twenty-room ambassador's residence that was an eye sore. The furniture in this villa did not match. Each ambassador would end up leaving pieces of furniture here and there. The first thing she noticed was the roof needed repairing and the walls were dirty. Connie rounded up some of the finest Mexican artisans and a well-known decorator, Tom Morrison, as she launched her restoration. The job was far from finished, but she already borrowed artwork worth $2 million dollars, including an Andrew Wyeth and a Georgia O' Keefe painting that were soon hanging on the freshly painted walls.

In the beginning, the new ambassador to many was a joke, especially when his TV commercials pitching Bacardi rum was seen all over

Mexico, and two of his horror films, "Jennifer" with French actress, Lisa Pelikan, Nina Foch and Bert Convy (1978) and "La Casa de Las Sombas" with Yvonne de Carlo, and Leonor Mansco (1976) were still at the theatres, which didn't help the new image that he was trying to create.

Nevertheless, according to many insiders that have known the previous five or ten U.S. ambassadors over the years, they said that John was the best by far and was better prepared than many. Within two years, the Gavin's had become Mexico's glamour couple at all the embassy parties and the elite social circles in the city. (Courtesy of "People Magazine/ Doris Klein Bacon 1983).

Once Connie and "Capitol" were up and running at their new home at CBS TV City, I would find myself just minutes away at my office off San Vicente Blvd., and Wilshire Blvd. At the beginning I would try and drop by at least twice a week, if only to tell Connie how great she and the show looked and what a terrific job she was doing. It also would give me the opportunity to see if Carolyn was working that day, just to give her a thumbs up and a quick, "How nice it is to see you in front of the camera again Ms. Jones. You look great!"

As the show settled down and the great ratings kept coming in, on occasion when Carolyn was working, she would say, "Come by tomorrow, I have a short day and we can go down the hall to the executive dining room or drive over to the farmer's market to get a great seafood salad or a tostada."

Every once in a while, some old fan would spot her and either ask for an autograph or comment on how they missed Morticia and were glad to see her on "Capitol. "

From time to time Carolyn would talk about our lost relationship and the mistake she made running off to do the Pinter play on tour for a year and not wanting to address our personal relationship and wondering if she should or should not get married at that time. Assuming that I was not aware of her relationship with Herbie at the time and their secret affair, she tried to tell me that she did not want to start but she was overwhelmed by Herbie and his convincing her that she should end our relationship and marry him.

No sooner had they gotten married, they moved to Palm Springs to their new adobe home and he told her that her acting days were over and to start her new career as an author. Their first of two books, "Twice Upon a Time" were poor attempts at hiding behind a thin story about an actress being married to a powerful producer and her various affairs and her relationship for over five years with me.

She would tell me of her love for Herbie and about the hard times they were having and even his mental and physical abuse she would take over the years when they were in Palm Springs.

We found time to talk about my Carolyn and son Geoff, I even brought photos from time to time to show her and she would smile a sad smile knowing how proud I was of my son, and my beautiful wife, Carolyn. By then, Geoff was almost eight or nine.

One day, early on in the first month or so of the series, she confided in me how much she needed this job as she was really broke but at the beginning of trying to get this job, she was told that Beverly Garland was close to being cast. Carolyn was upset that she was taking this job away from her, knowing that I had the deal on the table for Beverly and she was such a close and personal friend during the years that she was married to Aaron.

As the series started to take hold and during most of its run the show had steady ratings and held on in the middle of the pack of soaps. Both the down-to-earth Clarissa and the scheming matriarch of Clegg Clan, Myrna, were hard at work setting their course on "Capitol."

It was probably early June when I came by to see Connie that I would ask her how Ms. Jones was doing. I had not seen her on my last couple of visits. I think she said something like her shooting schedule had changed and she had some time off.

When I finally got caught up with Carolyn, she just said she was getting some tests and thought she had some ulcer problems and left it at that. Knowing her as well as I did, I said to myself, something doesn't sound right.

By August I managed to see Carolyn again and said, "Let's see if we can't have lunch next week?" She looked very tired and despondent. Obviously she knew that the end was in sight. By October she decided to marry Peter and was determined to finish the season.

It was not too much longer after that, Carolyn took ill and had checked into Cedar Sinai Hospital near CBS. I had called her husband Peter on several occasions to see how she was doing and asked if it was okay to visit her. Peter said it would be fine but she was very weak. I managed to see her twice before she went home. The first time she was sleeping and I sat with her for a little while holding her cold hand, until the nurse came in with some medication she had to take.

A couple of days later, Peter called me and suggested that if I wanted to see her again, now was the time. He was planning on taking her home the next day because the doctor said she had very little time left. I thanked him for the call and went right over to the hospital.

Carolyn was weak but alert. "Don't I look fancy in my new hat?" she said in a very weak voice, referring to the plastic shower cap she had on to cover her bald head, as I pulled a chair over to be next to her. "I get to go home tomorrow the doctor said." "I know. I am sure you will be happy. I know Red and Alisha will be there to keep you company. Give them my love," trying to find something to say to her. "I love you so, Budd," she whispered ever so softly. I leaned over and kissed her on her forehead and then on her lips.

"I love you too, Ms. Jones." There was a smile on her face as she slowly drifted off into a sleep that the medication for her pain brought on. I found myself sitting there for another five or ten minutes, knowing that I would not see her again. Funny, what thoughts go through your mind at a time like that? We did have for a better part of our six years together a great time, but Carolyn was so motivated and could not handle her career slowing down. Aaron Spelling was always there for support and encouragement. "The Addams Family" was a gift from the gods that gave her that great shot in the arm once again to be working, and on a hit TV series. It was at that time we decided to get married in the near future and threw a star-studded Hollywood engagement party to end all parties. For the next year or so we were at every "A" party and every premiere. On many occasion we would pull up to the theatre in a limo, hit the Red Carpet, say a few words and then move into the theatre waiting for the lights to go down; and then find the rear exit with some of the other actors who had the same idea, and then into the parking lot where our limo was waiting and then off to Chasen's or La Scala for a late supper.

It was late in July when I said my goodbyes to Carolyn Jones. As I left Cedars and walked to the corner to get my car, a soft summer breeze came down Beverly Blvd. from the beach. It was one of those breezes that I would feel at times that made me feel I had done my best over the years, and even though I knew that there was a definite ending, a finality to a brief moment in my life, for me there was a future out there, my beautiful wife for the past thirteen years, a son who was almost ten years old and a career as a successful Hollywood agent.

I stayed in touch with Connie in the weeks to come and then I received a call from June Allyson, who I shared many years of friendship going back to MGM days and then as a client and Carolyn's closest friend and confidante. "She's gone, Buddy," was all a teary Junie could get out.

It was August 3rd and the end came very quietly for her, Junie told me later that day. Carolyn was going to be cremated the next day and the service was going to be on August 5th at the Glasband-Willen Mortuary on Santa Monica Blvd. It was a small group of Carolyn's loved ones. Along with Peter, both Red and Alisha were there to support Peter; John Astin, her leading man from "The Addams Family," gave a lovely eulogy; June Allyson, Connie Towers and some of the cast members from "Capitol" and a few of her fans came to say goodbye. I think all of us kept looking for Aaron to show up for one last farewell but according to the trades, Candy told him that she did not want him to go and that was final.

The following week, Carolyn was laid to rest with her mother at Rose Hill Cemetery in Santa Ana, California. It was her request that her urn be placed on her mother's heart in the coffin.

R.I.P. Ms. Jones.

Chapter Forty-Nine

Hunter Tylo Meets "The Maharaja's Daughter" 1993

Over the years I would work with a number of great NYC agents on a split commission basis when I made frequent trips to the East Coast on business. I remember how excited I was in the late 80s when I first met Hunter Tylo, who was represented by two terrific lady agents, Sames and Rollnick. Hunter was absolutely stunning; the closest thing I ever saw to Ava Gardner. I was sure I could do a great job for her.

Jackie Smith, an NBC casting woman was crazy about Hunter and told me about a new role coming up on "Days of Our Lives." The role was one of those classic staples of daytime soaps: twin sisters— one good, one evil. What a great opportunity for Hunter. I negotiated a three-year contract for her with NBC, but by the time Hunter had appeared on a dozen shows it was obvious that her characters were not working out as everyone had hoped. Since the NBC contract contained their standard option period, they did not exercise her pickup. As disappointed as Hunter, Sames and Rollnick were, I told them all not to worry. There was a lot of work out there for her.

Within a month, "The Bold and the Beautiful" was looking for a new leading lady.

Hunter tested along with four or five other leading ladies. Christie Dooley, one of the best daytime casting ladies in the business and a personal fan of Hunter's work, called me over the weekend to tell me she got the role. We were all thrilled about this great break. Hunter began playing Dr. Taylor Hayes on "B and B" in 1990 and quickly became a tremendously popular daytime star with a devoted following.

"The Maharaja's Daughter" was a three-part miniseries to be filmed in India at some of the most beautiful and far-flung locations in the world. The producers were two Italian gentlemen, Guido Lombardo and Anselmo Parrinello, who were major players in the Italian film industry. Renowned director Burt Brinckerhoff, my partner Marty Shapiro's client, was signed to direct, and Burt's old friend, Bruce Boxleitner, was close to committing to the male lead.

The female lead character was a fun and modern role for any actress. She would play the favored daughter of a very wealthy Indian maharaja, a former ruling princess in India, who had been given permission by her father to go to Montreal, Canada, to study medicine and become a doctor. She in turn promised to return to India after completing medical school. While living and studying as an independent woman, she falls in love with a Montreal police officer and when she returns to her father and country, her focus is to persuade her father to permit a marriage not to a prince of her own class, but to the very attractive "prince" of Montreal's police force.

Hunter Tylo became obsessed with landing this role. She was absolutely certain it was her destiny, and that this miniseries would catapult her into worldwide superstardom.

So one night I sat in a suite at the Beverly Wilshire Hotel with famed casting director, Lou DiGiaimo and the two producers from Rome, waiting for Hunter to show up for her audition. She was nearly two hours late for her appointment; one of her assistants had called my office to tell me that she was working later than she thought on "The Bold and the Beautiful" that evening.

Earlier that day I had told her to put a little dark make-up on, along with maybe a scarf over her head to give her a regal look. Needless to say, we were all in shock when she came through the door in a white sari and full Indian makeup, complete with the red dot on her forehead, apologizing for running so late. The producers were utterly charmed by Hunter. She had done her homework and was fully prepared for her reading. I excused myself and told Lou to call me downstairs in the bar, when she was through with the reading. I was on my third glass of Pinot Grigio nearly an hour later when Lou came to get me. "Come on back up, Budd, we have to go over this very difficult schedule to see if it can work. They love Hunter and want her for the lead in the film."

In the world of "soap opera" (daytime TV) your run-of-the-mill soap star is usually given two weeks off each year for vacation time. If the actor wants to do a movie or TV guest shot, the producers will make best efforts to make it work, but add the time taken off to the actor's contract.

Now comes the hard work, I said to myself as I gave the bartender my credit card. Lou reached over and grabbed my card. "Put this on room 799," he ordered, giving the bartender a $5.00 bill.

"Thanks," I said and up we went to see Hunter and the producers.

She was having a Coke as I came through the door. She walked over to me and gave me a warm hug, whispering in my ear, "Don't fuck this up…I want this movie to work. It will make me a star around the world."

We sat with the producers and went over their 12-week schedule. It wasn't going to be easy. The producers wanted Hunter to get off for 12 weeks to do this film.

"Three months," I said to Hunter, looking right at her.

"I know the Bells will work this out, Budd. Go and see them next week," she said airily, smiling at the producers. "I know they will do everything to re-arrange my shooting schedule on 'Bold.'"

I broke out into a cold sweat, knowing very well that in all my travels among soap actors, this was almost never done. I was not looking forward to calling the Bells to make an appointment to discuss this. But there was no time to waste; production started in four weeks.

The next morning I waited for my partners Mark and Marty to come into the office. Mark usually showed up around 10:00 or so and Marty quite often got in a good game of tennis and arrived either before or after lunch. The Shapiro-Lichtman offices were on Beverly Blvd., near Robertson in Beverly Hills. We were a block from the world famous Ivy restaurant and a few doors from Madeo's Italian restaurant, in the Pierre Cossette "show business" building where ICM had their offices for many years, along with my dear friend, Warren Cowan, one of the truly great PR men, along with a host of indie production companies.

When Marty and Mark arrived we got together to strategize. Hunter had gotten the role, and that was the good news. The bad news was I knew I had an uphill battle ahead of me. I laid out the production schedule. We all knew that there was no way it would work. Still, it was my job not to fuck it up, in the words of Hunter Tylo. My secretary came down to Marty's office and said that Michael Tylo had called several times and needed to speak with me ASAP. I told the boys that I would come back later.

Michael Tylo was a soft-spoken, chain-smoking actor who had first met Hunter in New York when they were working on "All My Children" in 1970. It wasn't until 1987 that Hunter and Michael finally got married, the year their son Michael—Mickey was his nickname—was born. (Hunter had been previously married to Tom Morehart in 1980 and they had one child together, Christopher.) It was a difficult marriage due to the fact that Michael's career had slowed down and he found himself playing both mom and dad to their two young boys.

Michael showed up in our offices about an hour later. He looked terrible and worn out.

"What's the matter?" I asked.

"Budd, you have got to make this work for Hunter. She needs a role like this to get her into primetime. The soap world I know better than anyone… you can get stuck there forever… the money is good but not like what you can make in primetime."

"Trust me Michael, I will do the best I can." It was obvious, to me at least, that they were having marital problems and Hunter was anxious to get out of town. I called and made an appointment with the Bells, creators of "B and B." I had known this wasn't going to be easy, and I was right. From the first moment that I spoke to Bradley Bell, he was cut and dried. He said there was no way to get Hunter off for more than two, maybe three weeks, at the most.

"I can tell you Budd, that in the world of soaps, your request is unprecedented here too at 'Bold and Beautiful,'" he said pointedly.

Once the offer was on the table from Lou, and I told Hunter that the Bells did not see that there was any way this was going to work, Hunter told me in no uncertain terms that the Bells had to make this work, and demanded a meeting with Bill Bell and his wife, Lee Phillips.

I called Bradley the next day and told him that Hunter wanted to come over the next day after lunch to speak personally with the Bells.

"Budd," Bradley said, "I don't know that there will be a meeting about this."

When I told Hunter, she said, "I want that meeting. Tomorrow. I am coming down with the flu bug and might not be able to come into the studio."

Hunter then called the assistant A.D. and said she was running a temperature and they needed to re-schedule her work day. Production knew very well what she was doing when Hunter did not show up for work the next morning. After lunch, Bradley called and said that the Bells could meet with her the next day after lunch. I have to hand it to her, Hunter came in with her game day face on. I had asked Marty to come with me to make sure that this meeting was a meeting to remember.

The Bells were as cordial as possible at first… but as the meeting went on and I explained to the Bells that we were prepared to rework Hunter's contract with them and CBS, and were willing to add on another year to her contract with no additional raises, they held firm. I had gotten a small preview at her reading, but I suddenly saw another side of my gorgeous client.

"I am going to do this fucking movie whether you like it or not. I know you have the ability to work out a schedule with my character, it is not that difficult. If you want to fire me, you can do that, but I told the producers in Rome that I will be in India in four weeks and I don't give a shit what happens to me or my role on 'Bold and Beautiful.' This is a star making role and I am leaving the show if you don't let me off so sue me if you want." Marty and I sat frozen in our chairs.

Bill Bell said to Marty, "Let us talk to production tomorrow and see what they have on the boards, and Marty, speak to Burt Brinckerhoff and have him go over their schedule in India and find out how many days she works and how many days she has off over the 12-week period and get back to us."

Without another word Hunter got up and walked out the door. Marty and I were right behind her as we said our awkward goodbyes to the Bells. To make a long story short, Hunter won. I spent the next couple of weeks finalizing Hunter's contract with the Italian production company attorneys, going back and forth endlessly with the Bells, CBS legal, and Marty Shapiro. Finally, it was done. I had worked it out so that on three separate occasions, Hunter would leave the location in India and either fly to LA to shoot a week of "The Bold and the Beautiful" and possibly continue on to Toronto to shoot there and do some second unit filming. Needless to say, at our agency, Mark Lichtman and Marty were so pleased that I had been able to pull this almost "impossible" deal off. For those that live and die in the soap world, this was a major coup and unprecedented as far as "The Bold and the Beautiful" was concerned.

I admired Hunter, despite all the headaches, for taking on this Herculean challenge, knowing full well what lay ahead of her. This miniseries was going to be a major event for her and her career; and it was all of our hopes that she would be able to pull this one off. What a major opportunity for our "rising star" and for all of us.

Between Burt Brinkerhoff and Lou DiGiaimo, the casting on the film turned out very well. Some terrific actors were brought over from Hollywood. Bruce Boxleitner, the male lead, was looking forward to working with Burt and Hunter. Tony Lo Bianco and Burt Young (of

"Rocky" fame) were cast to play key roles. One of India's most prominent actors, Kabir Bedi, played the role of Chandragupta, the maharaja. At Hunter's request, I arranged for her drama coach, Ivan Chubbuck, to travel with her and work with her once she got to India, for a couple of weeks.

All seemed well as production commenced. But almost immediately I started to receive calls at three or four in the morning from producer Anselmo Parnello. From the start, as Burt would say, Hunter would not listen to or absorb from any of the people who had been hired specifically to help her develop this fairy tale princess or independent woman character, and even dismissed the help of an Indian woman who had written a book about the difficult break from patriarchy in Indian society.

The first few calls were polite. "Budd, could you do me a favor, as I am beginning to see a pattern developing here. Hunter is running very late to the set every day, and she needs to work harder on her lines with her acting coach that we brought over at great expense."

Chapter Fifty

Hunter and Her Snake Charmer

Then stories started filtering back to me from Anselmo and other members of the production staff about how Hunter had become enamored of one of the animal trainers. I knew Hunter was a true animal lover; having been born and brought up in Fort Worth, Texas, she had started riding horses at a very early age and was an excellent horsewoman. She also had a great passion for reptiles, especially snakes. She adored her pet boa constrictor named "BJ" (never did find out what the initials meant) and kept a large collection of exotic and unusual pets at home. It didn't take long to surround herself with another menagerie of animals, children and more exotic pets on location.

The exotic Indian animal trainer was of the Buddhist faith and explained to Hunter how the practice of Buddhism would change her life. Soon the two of them were spending long days together on her spiritual purification. I was told from numerous reliable sources that she would spend hours with the snake charmer, sitting in the lotus position with tiny tambourines on her fingers and humming for hours at a time. The next thing I heard through the grapevine was that Hunter was claiming that she was suffering from a "demon attack," resulting in confusion about her troubled marriage to Michael Tylo and her entire life.

I must have received two dozen increasingly frantic calls from Anselmo and other members of the production, begging me, for one reason or another, to speak to Hunter about her lack of professional behavior, to say the least.

I came to dread the sound of the phone ringing at three in the morning as I knew that the latest report from the set would make me feel like crawling into the bathroom and vomiting. What had I done to deserve this? I'd had a fairy princess, and suddenly I felt like Doctor Frankenstein wanting to destroy the monster that he had created.

Needless to say, it was almost impossible to reach Hunter directly. And on the rare occasions when I was able to get her on the phone in India, she would say, "Not to worry Budd, I have it all under control." And off she would go.

When she returned to the States for some pre-taping of "B and B" I tried to spend some time with her and talk to her seriously face to face, but it was almost impossible due to this problem and that problem or "Let's meet later," etc. Try as I might, I could not get any answers from her.

As production was getting ready to wrap up and head for Canada for the last stop, it was apparent once again from word of mouth that Hunter and "her guru" were having problems. Rumor also had it that either she wanted to bring her Buddha advisor/elephant trainer/snake charmer with her or he was pushing to stay with her and come to the States. It took three full days to get Hunter ready to leave India without her constant companion. One story that made the rounds was that when her luggage was finally put into the limo, three members of the production crew were there too, solely to make sure her luggage got to the airport and on the plane. Unfortunately, she and her "guru" had such a long, drawn-out tearful farewell that the limo gave up and left. Much to her dismay, Hunter was forced into a cab.

Anselmo was there to tell the driver to get her to the airport as quickly as possible and probably handed the driver an extra $100.00 in cash.

The cab driver was crazed from the very beginning, knowing that he must get to the airport as fast as possible. Reports came back that Hunter pestered him the whole way, repeatedly directing him to go this way or that way through the crowded Bombay streets. "Hurry, hurry, hurry." As they finally started down what seemed to be an open road, all of a sudden a truck that was coming towards her car swerved and the cab driver turned his wheel to avoid hitting him. The car started to spin and went into a ditch and rolled over, the car started to smoke as Hunter lay there unconscious, from what witnesses told Anselo days later.

A few bystanders started to rush over to the cab and a young man bravely pulled open the door. With the help of a few other people he managed to pull her out of the car before it caught fire and exploded, the driver, unfortunately, was dead.

They never found out if the cab driver had been killed in the crash or burned to death when the car went up in flames, the details from that point on were fuzzy. One report was that Hunter was taken by a passing car that had stopped back into town to a nearby emergency hospital and given as much care as possible. By the time that the limo carrying her luggage got to the airport and people kept waiting for Hunter's cab to arrive, everyone started to worry. The A.D. started to backtrack and by the time the plane was ready to leave for the States, word came back that there had been a serious accident just outside of town, but no one knew who was in the cab or what had happened to the passengers. The flight finally took off without Hunter.

Anselmo and the production company went on high alert. Every hospital in Bombay (and there were a lot of them) was called with very little success. Finally late that night, a hospital on the far end of the city reported that an American woman had been brought to the hospital, almost unconscious, with serious wounds. Anselmo (or whoever had taken charge) ordered an ambulance and a team of doctors to go to this hospital and bring Hunter to one of the major hospitals in the city. The reports were told that she had suffered a broken shoulder and fractured arm, a few facial cuts and a very bruised body, but it was a miracle she

337

hadn't burned up in the car explosion.

I am certain that Hunter had to believe that her new-found faith in Buddha had protected her.

I was told that her "friend" found her at the hospital and refused to leave her side. The next day, against the advice of the top doctor there not to travel for at least a week, the producers took her out of the hospital and back to the hotel for the night. She had a shoulder and arm cast and quite a few bandages. They made sure that Hunter was up to traveling and managed to get her on the next flight back to the States.

To this day I am still amazed and stunned by what took place after Hunter returned to Los Angeles. Not wanting word of this near tragedy to get out to the press in India—let alone in the States and in Europe—within a 48-hour period, a large blanket of secrecy was apparently thrown over the entire city of Bombay. The police were contacted, both hospitals were dealt with, and those that were there at the scene of the accident were located and told the accident officially never happened. Hunter had not been seen in either hospital, and no cab driver had been involved much less killed.

Several short reports did crop up in the press that Hunter's limo in Bombay had been involved in an accident and she broke her shoulder, or better yet, rumors flew among her fans that the day before she was to return to the States she wanted to take one last ride with her lover and fell off her horse. But apart from these flurries, the story was over, never to be mentioned again.

After all that, the miniseries was never shown in the U.S. But much to everyone's great surprise—except Burt, Mr. Lombardo and those Italian money people that had made deals with Germany, Italy and France—the film was a wildly successful six-hour miniseries in Europe, winning Hunter even more fans in Italy, where she was already beloved for her work on "B and B."

Hunter's friends, admirers, detractors and fellow workers told so many conflicting stories about the shoot in India that there's no telling what really happened.

Though I had the opportunity to see her a few times, Hunter never had time to tell me what happened, either being embarrassed or just not wanting to go into the whole epic story of her finally finishing up the film. I hope one day that she will come forward with the real story. All I know is that the princess was kissed while sleeping and when she woke up could never remember what had happened in her dream.

Chapter Fifty-One

Tom Bosley Meets "Beauty and the Beast" 1993

Almost all of the talent agents around the country subscribe to what is known as the "Breakdown Service," which we get off our computers. Each day, morning, noon, and night it tells you what is being cast on TV, features, and the theatre. It is a great service and you then submit your clients' materials through this program, which forwards those materials to the casting director directly.

One morning, there was "Beauty and the Beast" to be produced as a joint venture between Disney, their first Broadway musical, and a major Broadway production company, "The Dodgers," headed up by Michael David, Broadway's hot producer. "Tommy" was their biggest hit the year before. I noticed that Jay Binder was casting the production, who I called right away and started pitching various clients for the different roles. I suggested Tom Bosley for "Maurice" the father of "Belle" ("Beauty"). Jay being a very well-known and respected casting director was a fan of Tom's and said he was in the audience when Tom won his Tony for "Fiorello," based on the famous mayor of New York, Fiorello La Guardia.

What with Tom's great track record going from "Happy Days" to "Murder She Wrote" to "Father Dowling" he was considered a major TV star and should demand top dollar even in the theatre.

"Disney does not have a lot of money, these days, Budd!"

"I would think there should be room to pay Tom at least $10,000 a week!"

"Budd, it is not one of the major roles. You might be able to get between $5,000 and $7,500.00 a week if you are lucky. Let's see if he even likes the role and wants to audition for the producers. Where should I send the script and the music?"

After "Father Dowling" went off the air, Tom and I sadly parted ways due to the fact that Tom's wife, Patty, wanted him to be a movie star and had not been pleased with what I had done for his career, making him one of TV's greatest "Fathers" through "Happy Days," let alone what Tom was able to put in the bank over these many years. Not having spoken with Tom for a long time, I decided that this would be an appropriate time to break the ice. Tom was surprised and excited by my call at the beginning when I told him of the interest by Disney and The Dodgers, but he wanted to know what kind of monies they wanted to pay.

"I am not too sure at this time in my life and career if I want to leave Patty and move back to New York for a year," said Tom.

I told Tom that they were going to send him the script and the music next week. Tom had expressed great interest again and was eager to audition in Los Angeles first. The date was April 28th at the Debbie Reynolds Studio on Lankershim in the valley.

Tom's audition for the Disney brass and the Dodger organization went very well. I think that both Mike Eisner, Jeff Katzenberg and Tim Rice, of Weber and Rice fame, and Alan Menken, who wrote the music, and the director Robert Jess Roth, Michael David and Disney producer Bob McTyre, all were impressed with Tom's audition.

I had decided to drive out to the audition, wanting to see Tom after all these years and to give him some moral support. I thought Tom was in there for a long time as I walked back and forth from one side of the

342

parking lot to the other. Soon Jay Binder and Mark Simons came out with a non-expressive look on their faces and then lit up and said, "Tom was fantastic and we want to bring him back to New York on May 13th." I was lost for words.

"We are now halfway there, Tommy!" I said to him as I shook his hand.

The following day, I received a call from Robert Strickstein, head of business affairs for The Dodgers, who I had been in touch with about Tom's overall deal. I told Strickstein that Tom needed the following: weekly expense monies, a hotel, a driver to take him back and forth to rehearsals, etc. I was not happy with the $2,500 per week salary that they had offered. I was looking for other ways to make up for the low salary. Tom was concerned about what it would cost him each week, running his home in Beverly Hills and what it would cost him in New York.

It was up to me to be more than just an agent at this time, I had to find additional monies "in the air" to help Tom with his expenses. What could I do? Day after day I would either speak to Bob Strickstein or go over his head and send communiques to Michael David, Bob McTyre, or one of the major producers of the show. And I had no problem sending the head of Disney, Mike Eisner, a c.c. of my faxes.

It was now time to go back to New York for Tom's final audition. I decided to go back with him. Disney had picked up his flight, hotel and per-diem for the three days. It was now May 12th and we were on our way to what I had hoped would be Tom's return to Broadway.

The audition was going to be at the famous Michael Bennett Studio, where a few years before, "Chorus Line" had been created. When we got there, we were greeted by Jay Binder. He told Tom that basically the same people that were at the Los Angeles audition were there and a few others from the production company. Once Tom went in, I found myself walking the halls of the famous 890 Broadway that belonged to Michael Bennett. Tragically, Michael did not have the opportunity to enjoy his great success. He had passed away shortly after from AIDS.

It seemed that when Tom was still in LA, Michael David had sent Tom a new song that was written by Tim Rice and Howard Ashman just before Tom was to leave for New York. He liked the song but did not have time to rehearse with Seth Riggs, his singing coach and said that as much as he loved the song, he would not work on it until he knew he had the role, which was fine with the producers.

Tom was the first actor to go into the audition. It was now "hold your breath time" for the next 48 hours. When Tom came back out, some 15 minutes later, he felt that he did the best he could and wanted to go back home to be with Patty in Los Angeles. Tom was so excited about his audition and felt so confident that we walked forty blocks back to the hotel afterwards.

The next day I got a very early phone call from Jay Binder. "They loved Tom," Jay said. "Tom has the part of Maurice." Both Michael David and Jeff Katzenberg are planning to call Tom also. Tears had come to my eyes, not only for Tom but for me, too. It was months of pushing and pulling, trying to be low-keyed about the play and Tom doing it. The hard part now was ahead of me. It was only May and the play was going into rehearsal October 4th for six weeks in New York and then move to Houston, Texas for two additional weeks and then open October 30th through January 2nd 1994. Then there was a break and then they were renewing rehearsals in New York February 14th 1994 with their first public performance on Broadway March 3rd 1994. (Authors note: due to productions delays, the play finally opened on April 18th 1994.)

Shortly after the announcement, Robert Strickstein sent me a three-page deal memo stating that this is what the overall contract would look like. There is very little "wiggle room" as far as changing the deal. Since Tom was asked to be a presenter at the Tony Awards on June 6th, I told Michael David and Robert Strickstein that I did not want to start negotiations until we could meet in person to review the basic deal for Tom.

My appointment with Michael David at the famous 1501 Broadway Building was at 1:00 p.m. I had suggested several weeks before I came in, to take Michael to lunch at the Oyster Bar but as luck would have it, he had a bad case of food poisoning and was having soup for lunch. Little did he know that I too had gone downstairs to a Chinese noodle bar and had some matzo ball soup.

I was looking forward to meeting Michael for some time now. I thought I was going to meet a tall, 6' 3" Yale theatre graduate in his dark blue pinstripe Brooks Brothers suit. That his offices were going to look like Lew Wasserman's office across town at the MCA building on Park Avenue and 57th Street—all dark wooden panels, a library filled with brown and green leather first edition books and 18th century desks and furniture that Jules Stein, founder of MCA, personally picked out for Lew and the other agents. Did I have another guess coming? I was sitting in the waiting room reading the weekly Variety newspaper when out of an office came this bearded, 40-year-old producer in Levis, dirty Reeboks, and a real Brooklyn Dodger sweatshirt. "Hi, you must be Budd Moss," he said, reaching out to shake my hand and pulled me into his office.

"Good God," I said to myself. The room, which was very large, had several pinball machines with either "The Green Hornet" or one of those 40's radio heroes, an antique pool table, football helmets and bats hanging from the rafters and baseball uniforms, soccer balls, hockey helmets and sticks! It looked like the sports bar at Yankee Stadium and God knows what else.

"Have a seat!" the couch looked like it was 200 years old and had never been cleaned. He pulled over an overstuffed leather chair and said, "Tell me about you and Tom Bosley and how can we put this deal together?"

Between May 14th and June 4th, when I was going to New York to meet with Michael David and The Dodgers about Tom's overall deal, Tom and I met several times to discuss things, knowing that it was not going to be an easy deal to put together.

My meeting with Michael David was very pleasant. We spoke about Tom's long and successful career from "Happy Days" to "Murder She Wrote" to how "Father Dowling" came to be. And we talked about my years with Marty Baum, who he knew of and his great success over the years as a Broadway agent, and my leaving General Artist to open the Burton Moss Agency. We spoke briefly about representing Rita Hayworth and Cyd Charisse, Carolyn Jones and Ruth Roman and her tour of "Two for the Seesaw." I could see that he wanted to get to a pending deal for Tom and said, "Thanks for coming to see me. It is not too often that a Hollywood agent would come all the way back to meet with me."

The one important point that I wanted to share with Michael was an apartment for Tom at Disney's expense. This alone would probably be the difference in making or breaking the deal. The apartment with $1,000 a week expenses could close the deal. What I was talking about was another $2,500 in addition to the apartment for six months. This could be done as a signing bonus or a "holding fee" if there was a problem to show a weekly expense. Michael sat there for a few moments not knowing what to say. I told him that we really wanted to find a formula that could make this work.

"Let me think about it," was about all he could say at that time. "We all hope that it will work out. We would be thrilled to have Tom join us. Let me take you down the hall to meet Robert Strickstein, who is head of business affairs. He will help put the deal together with you."

My brief meeting with Robert Strickstein was an indication that there was little time to put this deal together and that Disney had very little monies for the actors.

I thanked him and headed for the street, feeling that my trip to New York was worthwhile. However, I had a lump in my stomach as I got into my cab and headed back to the Lombardy Hotel to get my thoughts together before I called Tom to tell him of my great meeting with Michael David and Robert Strickstein. Tom wanted to know right away what the deal was. I told him that Strickstein was going to layout the whole deal for us in the next week or so. I did not want to put the $2,500 a week on the table just yet!

Over the following weeks, Strickstein went over various points about Houston— Tom wanting to bring Patty there, loan out information, and numerous points that we needed to put into the deal memo. I wanted to make sure that Tom had his billing in a very special place separate from the other supporting actors. The cast was almost in place and a very talented and almost unknown actress by the name of Susan Egan was going to play "Belle" and a superb actor by the name of Terrance Mann was going to play "The Beast." Their credits where going to be above the title of Disney's "Beauty and The Beast." Then there were eight co-starring roles that would be in the same size as Susan and Terrance, and then a lot of supporting actors.

I wanted Tom's name to be after the supporting actors so it would stand out. I arranged:

And

TOM BOSLEY

As

"Maurice"

I received a call from Strickstein advising me that Tom's deal memo was being faxed to me the next day.

Tom and I had met several times while we were waiting for THE FIRM OFFER in writing. We would have lunch down the street from my office off Beverly Blvd., at "The Ivy." I had prepared Tom over the past weeks that the weekly salary was going to be low for all the actors and Tom seemed to be prepared to accept the $2,500 when I first told him, much to my great surprise, but was anxious to see what I was going to arrange as far as expenses, per diem and whatever perks I could come up with. I did have a game plan.

When the contract, dated June 30th 1993 arrived by fax, I called Tom and told him I was going to fax it to him and his lawyer and business manager. I suggested to Tom that he look at it, call his lawyer and then Tom and I would go over the two-page agreement, step by step.

The overall deal was what I called a "step deal" as the contract would be for six months and would cover the New York rehearsals, then the Houston "Theatre Under the Stars" rehearsals and opening for five to eight weeks, then back to New York for an additional two weeks of rehearsal and the New York first public performance.

Chapter Fifty-Two

And I Thought Being a Brain Surgeon Was Difficult?

The contract was for a six-month run of the play commencing with the first public performance. It covered a first class air fare ticket from New York to Houston or two coach tickets if Mr. Bosley wanted Mrs. Bosley to join him and he would be responsible for the difference in price; a dressing room with a phone that Mr. Bosley would also be responsible for his calls; and his private dresser.

In Houston, they would provide a car rental. In New York I had arranged a car and driver that would be provided by the company once the play opened. Tom wanted to have a driver that he had used before, so the company would pay Tom $250.00 per week toward his car and driver, and vocal coaching; at the request and expense of the producer, Mr. Bosley would take vocal coaching in Los Angeles under the supervision of the musical director. The contract addressed house seats, hair dresser, and it went on and on.

One clause that I insisted on was a favored nation clause which made Tom very happy to know that no actor in the show was going to get more than Tom. This was a major point that I had hoped Tom would feel that the salary he was receiving was the top salary and no other actor was going to receive more monies.

At this point, I thought we would have a chance to make our deal, but

Tom, his lawyer and most importantly his business manager could not see how Tom was going to be able to run his home in Beverly Hills and at the same time live in New York without losing monies.

Tom was ready to walk away from the deal, even after I had spoken to Bob McTyre and Michael Eisner about how excited Tom was about being in Disney's first Broadway musical. Tom wanted to meet with Jeff Katzenberg but I told him at this point, I think Jeff would pass on it, leaving it up to Strickstein to keep trying to make the deal work.

Finally, after talks with Patty, the lawyer and the business manager, Tom called me and said, "I have to pass Budd. I have not worked in almost two years after "Father Dowling" and my leaving you, which was a big mistake, but I would be losing monies, I would not even be breaking even."

It was over the 4th of July holiday that I sent a fax to Strickstein, Bob McTyre and Mike Eisner. I told Robert that I was writing this letter with regret that my client, after weeks of negotiations, felt that we had come to an impasse. We were deadlocked based on the fact that if Mr. Bosley did the play, he would be losing money as the deal was now structured. Tom also regretted giving up the opportunity to appear on Broadway in Disney's first musical. It also meant a lot to Tom being able to return to the theatre where he first began.

I had spoken to Eisner, Laura Fox and Strickstein regarding Disney finding another $2500.00 a week for expenses, which was not an unreasonable request based on a hotel costing between $2,500 and $5,000 a month for a one-bedroom apartment. His meals at $100.00 a day was a low figure. If his wife Patty came back to stay with him for a while, this would come close to $6,000.00 per month, not including transportation, along with his normal living expenses.

I had come up with what I was hoping would be a very creative idea, without telling Tom at the time. Disney World, from the time it first opened in Orlando, would bring stars from Hollywood for a week of P.R. and fun and games for four or five of his/her closest friends. They would pick up the tab for all of this and give the star a check at the end of the week for $15,000 dollars. How could anyone say no? I had arranged this for Tom, Cyd Charisse, Gary Coleman from "Different Strokes" and the most popular "Miss America" of them all, Mary Ann Mobley.

Why not give Tom a guarantee of another personal appearance during a time when he was not in the play? Disney could find a way to increase the revenue for Mr. Bosley not only in Florida, but in Anaheim, Japan and France where there were other Disney Worlds. Also, Disney could guarantee employment appearances on their eight or nine TV shows and features. Tom could also bring projects to Disney on a "First Look Basis." Why not let Tom Bosley be Disney's Roving Ambassador?

At the beginning, Strickstein must have thought I was crazy. But knowing that they could lose Bosley, he took my suggestions to Disney.

What transpired in the following weeks was very interesting. After Bob Strickstein received my first fax thanking Disney for their interest in Tom appearing in "Beauty and the Beast" and that regretfully we were going to pass, he told me that he was going to send us a "thank you note" and they were now going to move on to their next choice.

When he received my second fax dealing with a "Service Contract," it seemed to spark some additional interest. It was a way to create other avenues for Disney to find that extra bit of monies to help keep our deal alive. Even Bob McTyre, who was the final word for Disney along with Eisner on keeping the budget together, thought it was a very creative and interesting idea. Having had my "off the record, we never had this conversation" with Eisner that day, his personal secretary, Lucille, said to me, "Michael does not want to get involved at this point and wants you to have Bob McTyre in New York work it out with you and Strickstein."

When I last spoke to Strickstein towards the end of the month, he said, "That strange as it seemed, Disney was trying to work things out and it really was up to Mr. Eisner at this point."

I knew that Strickstein, Michael David, and Bob McTyre were not happy with my calls to Eisner and the c.c.'s to him at key points of our deal, but Michael and I go back to early Aaron Spelling days when he was the head of ABC daytime and then head of programming and then moved on to the head of Paramount Studios while Tom was starring in "Happy Days." And "the piece de resistance," which nobody knew about, was that Michael's son, Eric, was on my son's soccer team and I was the coach!

Michael would come every Saturday with his wife and bring cases of Gatorade, pizza, and sliced oranges for the kids after the games. I tried to get him to come to some of the soccer practices, but he would always say, "Budd, I am the head of Paramount and as much as I would love to come, I have a studio to run. But bring your soccer team to lunch when they win a game, and I will introduce them to "The Fonz" and when possible I will arrange for them to see some of our new movies in our private screening room from time to time."

I then sent Michael David a final fax with a c.c. to everyone making sure that he knew that Tom did not want to walk away from this and we were trying every way possible after almost four months of trying to put a respectable deal together for Tom and for Disney. We were closer than ever. The only thing we were still trying to do was to finalize an apartment or a hotel for Tom for the first six months of his contract. We still needed another $1,500 per week to cover his living expenses.

At that time, since everyone had taken their 4th of July holiday the previous month, I was going to take my wife Carolyn and son Geoffrey to our very private beach and bay at Napili Point, on the island of Maui for her birthday. God, was I looking forward to a rest and to go swimming with the turtles in the bay. I really thought that I had done the best I could to make this deal work for Tom.

Before I left on August 23rd, I sent Michael Eisner one more letter hoping that Disney was going close up the deal by working out the

"Service Contract" and send Tom and his family to Orlando as Disney's Star of the Week for $15,000 and apply that to his monthly per diem. Tom also was going to submit several projects to Disney in hopes that they could be optioned.

I wanted to make sure that everyone knew since our early meetings in LA and NY that Tom was ready to go to work and start tomorrow with his singing lessons. From August 27th and all through September, Bob Strickstein, Jim Schriber, and I banged out Tom's new contract with a sense of urgency and eagerness knowing that the first rehearsal date of October 4th was not too far off.

Strickstein sent copies to everyone. The opening of the new contract read:

"As we reviewed on Wednesday afternoon, the following is our best and final offer for Tom Bosley's services in *Beauty and the Beast*. If these terms are acceptable to you, we will proceed with trying to secure an additional $10,000 for ancillary services from the Disney organization as detailed in your memo of August 23rd to Michael Eisner." Finally, my job as Tom's new agent again was almost complete. I had one more stop to make when I was back in New York prior to the start of rehearsals and that was to go to The Regency Hotel on Park Avenue to see Jonathan Tisch, the president of the Regency. I had known him over the years since I first met him at his apartment, along with my very special friends, Michele and Larry Herbert, the president and CEO of "Pantone Colors," who lived on the floor above him.

The Regency Hotel was the premier hotel on Park Avenue and I wanted to see that Tom was there for as long as he was in the play. Rooms started at $500.00 a day and up. Jonathan Tisch said to me one day, "I enjoy making deals for stars in show business. As long as my hotel guests see Tom Bosley walking through the lobby twice a day, I will give you a one-bedroom suite on our second floor where our offices are. There are about ten one bedroom suites available and I will give one of them to Tom for $100.00 dollars a day."

On September 2nd, Strickstein had sent me a fax with various deal points that were still "open" stating "I will begin "preliminary scouting" of accommodations in New York during rehearsal which meet his requirements, but I look forward to your research as well. All transportation etc. will be dealt with after contracting is completed."

It was with great pleasure to notify Strickstein that "my scouting" had paid off and Tom was going to The Regency and that I had worked out a deal with Jonathan Tisch. Needless to say, he was more than surprised.

On September 14th, I sent Michael Eisner a personal letter thanking him for his belief in Tom. I wanted him to know we were off to New York for the start of rehearsals and then off to Houston for our out of town opening, which I planned to attend.

On September 17th I sent Tom a fax congratulating him that the deal was finalized and thanked him for hanging in there because there were so many times that the deal could have exploded, but with care and patience and my believing that I knew how to make this work for all of us, we succeeded.

Finally the day had arrived when all parties concerned went back to the Michael Bennett Studio: The Dodgers, Mike Eisner and Jeff Katzenberg, the director, Robert Jess Roth, and our stars were now going to meet for the first time. Alan Menken, who wrote the music, Howard Ashman and Tim Rice, who wrote the lyrics, and Linda Woolverton, who wrote the book. There was Tom, Susan Egan and Terrence Mann, Gary Beach, Beth Fowler, Eleanor Glockner, Heather Lamberts, Stacy Logan, Burke Moses, Brian Press and Kenny Raskin. Most of the production staff met during the day along with Matt West, who was going to do the choreography. I even got to say hello to Jay Binder and his partner Mark Simon, and most importantly, Robert Strickstein and I got to shake hands and said to one another, like Snoopy and the Red Baron after WWI was over and the two fighter pilots expressed, "Job well done," as they were drinking their root beer.

For Tom Bosley and me it was the end of a long ride, going back many years. I had told Tom that one day he would be back on Broadway and I had kept my promise. Before we knew it, it was opening night in Houston at the "Theatre Under the Stars." Patty Bosley and I sat in the fourth row center and then for the next hour and a half, with the assistance of "The Disney Magic," we were transported to the amazing world of "Beauty and the Beast." When the play ended, there were standing ovations that went on and on.

Tom could see where we were sitting and he threw Patty a kiss and one of his marvelous smiles.

That night was the beginning of almost a two-year love affair for Tom Bosley, "Belle," and of course "The Beast" and for me too. No sooner then we said farewell to Houston, it was time to head for the most famous of all theatres on Broadway, THE PALACE.

"Playing the Palace" has always been the dream of every Broadway performer since the theatre opened in 1913. For many years the Palace was the preeminent vaudeville theatre in the country and an engagement in this theatre meant that a performer had "MADE IT." The who's who of entertainment royalty that has performed on this stage includes Will Rogers, Ethel Merman, Judy Garland, the great magician Harry Houdini, Bette Middler, Shirley MacLaine and Ethel Barrymore, to mention just a few.

In 1965, the Nederlander's turned it into a legitimate theatre with the opening of "Sweet Charity" starring Gwen Verdon. Since then, it has housed star-studded hits including Lauren Bacall in "Applause" and "Woman of the Year," Richard Kiley in "Man of La Mancha" and George Hearn in "La Cage aux Folles" that my longtime friend Alan Carr produced. And on April 18th 1994 the theatre was transformed into the magical world of Disney with "Beauty and the Beast" which proved to be one of Broadway's greatest successes playing for a total of thirteen years at the Palace for 5,461 performances.

Broadway critic David Richards wrote, "*Beauty and the Beast.* Disney does Broadway, dancing spoons and all. As Broadway musicals go, *Beauty and the Beast* belongs right up there with the Empire State Building, F.A.O. Schwartz and the Circle Line Boat Tours. It is hardly a triumph of art, but it'll probably be a whale of a tourist attraction. It's Las Vegas without the sex, Mardi Gras without the booze and Madam Tussaud's without the waxy stares. You don't watch it, you gape at it. That nothing in Dubuque comes close."

Susan Egan ("Belle") went on to be a big star over the years as did Terrance Mann ("Beast") whose Broadway credits go on and on. Burke Moses ("Gaston") was so handsome, he almost took "Belle" away from the "Beast." Gary Beach ("Lumiere"), Kenny Raskin ("Lefou") and the lovely Beth Fowler ("Mrs. Potts") all added their talents to this great cast. Tom who played "Maurice," "Belle's" father, had been TV's favorite father for years and the audiences loved him from the minute he walked on stage. What a historic night. A night I will always remember. Tom Bosley and Budd Moss at the Palace Theatre. "WE MADE IT!"

There I was as the curtain was coming down on "Opening Night" standing with a packed audience cheering this brilliant cast on for what seemed to be a ten-minute standing ovation. I looked around in the first three or four rows. I could see Mike Eisner and Jeff Katzenberg shaking hands with Bob McTyre, their number one man from Disney. Michael David and Bob Strickstein from The Dodgers who I fought with over the many months, trying to make the best deal I could for Tommy. Michael David looked over my way and gave me "a thumbs up"!

For the next two years, Broadway and the Palace Theatre was his home. As Tom's agent and longtime friend, I made a promise that I would bring him back to Broadway, and I kept that promise.

Chapter Fifty-Three

Tom Bosley Meets "Show Boat" and "Cabaret" and a Final Curtain Call

Tom joined The Burton Moss Agency in 1968 and the first film I put him in was "The Secret War of Harry Frigg" with Paul Newman. But Tom decided after seventeen years of back to back work through three TV series and over 100 TV productions and numerous commercials, he followed his wife's, Patricia's, view that they could not understand why he was not a giant movie star and would be better off with another agent.

Sadly, we went our separate ways for over three years and then one day, I saw that "Beauty and the Beast" was being done by Disney and I said to myself, there has to be a role for Mr. Bosley. I had told Tom at that time that one day he would be back on Broadway and I kept my promise through thick and thin over some twenty-five years later.

Time was going so fast and Tom and Patty had moved to Palm Springs. Tom had been running into some bad weather with his health. We all knew that Tom was a big smoker and tried for years to quit.

In 1998, just five years after Tom left "Beauty and The Beast," Garth Drabinsky, one of Canada's most infamous producers, called me and ask if Tom would be interested in going out with a new production of "Showboat" for a year with Karen Morrow. From the beginning of putting this deal together, it was a joy to work with the casting people because everything that Tom wanted, they gave him and were thrilled to do it and on top of that, they said, "We would like to pay Mr. Bosley $10,000.00 a week."

I had a hard time trying to play it cool after the months I spent putting the deal together for "Beast" and Tom would only get a favored nations salary of $2,500.00 a week along with all the other stars of the show.

As difficult as it was at that time, with health problems popping up along the way, Tom enjoyed the tour and Patty found herself coming into the various towns along the way and spending time with him. Even I had a great time visiting "Captain Andy" along the Mississippi during the run of the play. Little did we know in Hollywood at that time that Garth Drabinsky, Livent and his partner were going to be convicted and sentenced to prison for fraud and forgery the following year.

From "Showboat" Tom returned to Palm Springs with his family, where more tests and less work followed. Tom on occasion would do some episodic work from time to time. And then I got a call from the famous Roundabout Theatre that was going to do "Cabaret" at the infamous Studio 54 in 2003. Tom was thrilled to go back to work and on Broadway one more time. His leading lady was going to be Mariette Hartley. Tom enjoyed playing the rather small but very important "Jewish store keeper." Once again, his fans flocked to Studio 54 to see him and wait at the stage door for him to come out and sign their photos and autograph books.

When Tom came home he finally said to me, "Budd, I think it is time to let me slow down and come to a stop. I have more tests to do and need time to get better." We never spoke about his having lung cancer. It was just one test after another.

I had not seen Tom for a long time, even though we would speak regularly once or twice a week about the business and we both spoke about getting together for our long overdue lunch one day.

Finally, in October of 2010, Tom called me and said that his daughter's, Amy's, son Ethan was going to have a Bar Mitzvah and they were coming in for the week and would stay at their favorite little hotel just around the corner from where I live in Westwood—The Beverly Hills Plaza Hotel on Wilshire Blvd., a charming three leveled Mediterranean type hotel.

I so wanted to see Tommy because it had been several years and yet I had mixed feeling knowing what Tom had been going through with his chemo and radiation treatments.

This had been a forty-two-year relationship with a lot of bumps along the road, but there was a warm and loving friendship that went along with our working together.

As demanding as Tom was over the years, he was a die-hard professional and was right most of the time when he wanted something done. From day one, when we would have our weekly lunch, we laid out our "Grand Plan." Tom knew that I was considered an excellent agent and fought hard for my clients over the years. I admired Tom as a multi-talented actor as he did with me and my work as an agent. I remember saying to Tom at the beginning of our relationship, "Let's make a deal...I will never tell you how to act if you promise you will not tell me how to be an agent!"

We shook hands on that and there were very few times when we hit a wall about some problem that got worked out in the end anyway.

As I walked across the patio and around the beautiful swimming pool and fountains, I started to feel a deep pain in my stomach and my heart. I stood by the door marked 201 and took a deep breath as I knocked. As the door slowly opened, there was this frame of what used to be Tom Bosley, his famous voice saying "Come on in Budd" with as much warmth that he could reach for, but the ravages of cancer had taken its toll. Not only was Tom totally bald but he must have lost so much weight that you could only recognize him by his voice that was still filled with energy. Patty was there at the door too, as we embraced one another after all those years.

This was not the first or second time that I had seen what damage can be done to our bodies by cancer. I almost went into a shell for the time being, trying to see what was there at the beginning of our time together.

"Come and sit. What would you like to drink, Budd?" Patty said. "We are going to have a vanilla shake. Would you like one?" Tom quickly said as I sat on the couch. "Great!"

You could almost feel a sense urgency from both of them. They knew as I sat there, that I was having a difficult time focusing on the moment after a year or two of not having seen Tommy.

"How are Carolyn and Geoffrey doing?" Patty said with the house phone in her hand, "Oh this is Mrs. Bosley, would you please connect me to room service... Yes, this is Mrs. Bosley in 201. Would you please fix us three of your vanilla shakes and some cookies that go with it. Yes, three shakes, and make them thick!"

I quickly said, "How exciting it is Tommy for your grandson to have a Bar Mitzvah!" Amy must be thrilled, especially having both of you here. Where did the time go? It seemed like only yesterday that Amy was thirteen, going on twenty-one. I remembered when we were all in London at the same time and I took you both on your first 'Double Decker' bus ride to Buckingham Palace to see the changing of the guards."

We tried to find something else to speak about and soon there was a knock on the door. "Room Service. Vanilla Shakes!" What a treat at 11:00 in the morning. We found ourselves talking about Ron Howard and his great success. About Marion Ross and Henry Winkler who had just called Tom in Palm Springs a few weeks earlier, just to say hello. Henry was one of a kind. You can meet him once or twice and a year or two would go by and you would bump into him at a party and it was, "Hi Budd, how are you doing?"

We chatted about the great success that Tom had back on Broadway and opening night of "Beauty and the Beast" at the famous Palace

Theatre. The vanilla shakes were great and then the phone rang; "Hi Amy, guess who is sitting here with us? Yes, it's Budd Moss. Yes, we will come by in about an hour… Amy said to say hello!"

As we finished our shakes, I looked at my watch and finally said, "Well, you have a busy couple of days ahead of you. I better let you get ready to see Amy and especially 'the Bar Mitzvah Boy,' Ethan. Please give Amy my love and wish them a blessed day." We put our arms around one another and hugged each other very tightly, each of us knowing deep down in our heart of hearts, that I would probably never see Tom again, after this sacred moment in our lives.

As the door closed behind me and the number on the door got smaller and smaller as I walked away around the beautiful swimming pool and fountains, I almost wanted to run back and just tell Tommy one more time how much I loved him as a friend and client over the years, but I found myself getting too teary to go back.

The next day as everyone was getting ready to put their best synagogue outfits on, Tommy started to have chills and shivers. He did not look well and had to go back to bed. Patty was not too sure what to do other than to call Amy. With all that she had on her mind at that time, she told Patty to call their doctor, Joel Hirschberg. Patty had to leave word that it was urgent. Maybe fifteen minutes went by before he called back.

As Patty was describing the symptoms, Dr. Hirschberg said, "How far are you from UCLA?"

"Maybe ten minutes, if we hurry."

"Call 911 and get over there right away and I will call over to admittance and meet you there."

Patty called Amy back, who said, "I will meet you there!"

Once the paramedic's got to room 201 and prepared him for his quick ride to UCLA, not fifteen minutes had passed before he was at UCLA and checked in.

As the Baer family started to prepare themselves for this joyous and most sacred event in every Jewish boy and girl's young life, Tom and Patty's day started to darken and get worse. The doctor had Tom in ICU as soon as they got there. For some time, Patty had told me years later, it was touch and go.

As all the relatives and friends that came from near and far to be witness to this day "That is a commandment and a law that when a Jewish boy becomes thirteen years old, he becomes accountable for his actions and becomes 'Bar Mitzvah.' He then becomes able to participate in all areas of Jewish community life." Soon, the relatives and friends, continued to make their way, later that day to the synagogue for the Bar Mitzvah, many not being aware of what was happening to Tommy.

Amy managed to stay in constant contact with Patty, getting reports on how he was coming along. It was later on that evening that the doctors and nurses began to take hold of Tom's situation and had him under their watchful eye.

Patty was able to tell Tommy how beautiful the Bar Mitzvah was and how proud Amy and her family were watching this moment in Ethan's young life take place. Patty could tell that Tom understood everything, if only by his squeezing Patty's hand as she sat by him for as long as the nurses would allow her to be there in ICU.

Soon it was time to take Patty back to the hotel for the night but Amy assured her that she had every moment of the Bar Mitzvah filmed. And once the doctors told Amy they were going to move him to his hospital room, she was going to bring the video over to show Tom and Patty the whole service, which I am sure brought tears to their eyes.

Tom's brother Richard and his wife Barbara came over later that day to see him, as did many of the other loving friends and relatives, knowing how ill he was. They wanted to share whatever few minutes they could knowing that this might be the last time they could tell him how much they loved him.

The next day Tom had made a lot of improvement and after all the doctors checked him out, Dr. Hirshberg told him and Patty that he felt Tom was ready to go back to their home in Palm Springs the following day, which was just about an hour and a half drive without too much traffic.

Patty put a call into their driver and the following day, Amy, her husband and three children came over to UCLA to send Tommy off with a smile on his face, thinking all was going to be okay for the next couple of hours.

Little did anyone have any idea that less than an hour away from their home, Tom told Patty that he started to feel ill again and thought it best to call Dr. Hirshberg again and see what he suggested since he was having those chills and shakes all over his body. Thank God for cell phones at a time like that. Patty was on hold for almost ten minutes as she told the doctor's exchange that it was urgent. Once she had him back on the phone, she told him that Tom was reacting the same way as he did at the hotel but twice as bad. Tom was stretched out on the back seat of their car, shaking severely.

Dr. Hirshberg said, "I will call to Eisenhower right away and notify them that you will be there within the hour and send the doctors his records from UCLA!"

Patty told their driver to go as fast as he could. Tom seemed to have passed out but his body was still shaking violently. Finally, with the "Emergency" sign in view, Patty kept telling Tommy that they were there and it would only be minutes before the doctors would treat him. She was hoping he could hear her. As they pulled into the driveway, there was the ER team waiting with the gurney and all the equipment that was needed to save Tom's life. Patty was a nervous wreck and once they got him into the ER she told the nurse that she lived ten minutes away and had to get home for a few minutes and then would return. She could barely speak to the driver who knew what was happening. Patty was in tears racing to their home. She changed her soiled clothes quickly, picked up their dog, and with their grandson, Jason, went racing back to the emergency parking lot. As she went in to the waiting area, the two doctor saw her and walked over to her. "Mrs. Bosley, we have done the best we could. Tom had passed away and we were able to resuscitate him for a while but he is now in ICU and connected to all the machines. You can go in a see him but he will not know you are there."

Patty was beside herself and sat there with Jason for a longtime. She then managed to call Amy to tell her. Amy said that she was on her way there. Patty and Jason waited for over two hours and once she was there, they all sat with Tom, saying their prayers and giving thanks to this remarkable human for giving them such a beautiful life that they all shared together.

On October 19th 2010 at the Old North Church at Forest Lawn Cemetery, Hollywood Hills, Tom was laid to rest. The celebration of Tom's life was so beautifully expressed by so many of his loved ones. Garry Marshall, Henry Winkler and Ron Howard all spoke about their years with Tommy as a loving friend and a fellow actor as did some of those that were so close to him. Marion Ross, Anson Williams, Donny Most, Erin Moran, Scott Baio and all the cast of "Happy Days" were there to say their final farewell.

I was close to Patty after the services and put my arms around her and told her how fortunate I was to have spent all these years with her and my special friend Tommy, and what great joy we shared working together for over forty years.

Chapter Fifty-Four

UCLA's Carolyn Shea Meets Aaron Spelling 2003

Over the years as an agent, I have taken great pride in finding new talent to bring into the industry. During my years at General Artists Corporation, I negotiated both Larry Hagman and Barbara Eden's deal for the series, "I Dream of Jeannie," Elizabeth Montgomery in "Bewitched," and Mia Farrow in "Peyton Place." When I opened the Burton Moss Agency, I placed John James in the "Dynasty" series, Tom Bosley in "Happy Days," "Murder She Wrote" and "Father Dowling," Hope Lange in "The Ghost and Mrs Muir," John Gavin in "Doctors' Private Lives," Constance Towers in "Capitol," Robert Pine and Randi Oakes in "CHIPs" and Ted Bessell in "That Girl." I also discovered Carrie Snodgress who became an Oscar nominee for "Diary of a Mad Housewife."

I also placed Dyan Cannon in "Bob Carol, Ted and Alice," for which she received an Oscar nomination, and Sally Kellerman in "M.A.S.H." and she also received an Oscar nomination.

In 1992 I found myself merging my agency with two longtime friends, Martin Shapiro and Mark Lichtman and headed up their Motion Picture/TV Department for Talent and brought in Motion Picture Association of American president Jack Valenti as a new client along with other important actors.

Having been an avid jogger over the years, I found myself at the UCLA track five to six times a week in the early mornings, and I got to know the women's track and cross-country coach, Eric Peterson.

It is there, according to Hollywood folklore, that Budd Burton Moss plucked Carolyn Shea, a top Jr. All-American athlete from Waterville, Maine off the track and got her budding acting career started. On several occasions, I mentioned to Eric that she reminded me of an actress by the name of Hope Lange who I represented years ago. I gave Eric my card to give to Carolyn, and asked her to contact me if she was interested in knowing about the wonderful world of show business.

It was early 2003 when I saw a casting breakdown for a short film by a director who I knew from Chapman College, Michael Mohan. I called him at Fox Searchlight and told him that I wanted him to meet a newcomer, Carolyn Shea for his film. Needless to say, Carolyn was extremely nervous to read for her first film. The reading went well, though she was "not right" for the role. However, Michael asked Carolyn to coffee to discuss a different project that he had in mind that eventually became "Run, Attack, Fly," a ten-minute short film that I ended up packaging with three other clients, and co-executive produced.

It was her first time in front of the camera, and with the help of Michael, Matt Twining, who played her brother, and Robert Ginty, who played her father, off she went. The film depicts a star high school runner who struggles under the pressure of an overbearing father and coach. The main connection between fiction and reality was running.

For her first time in front of the camera, she did a marvelous job. She was a natural. The film turned out very well and its world premiere was in Carolyn's hometown of Waterville, Maine at the annual film festival hosted by Peter Fonda, whom I had known over the years along with the Fonda family. Needless to say he was surprised to see me in Waterville, Maine.

Anxious to get Carolyn's career started, but having to work around her busy school schedule, I had contacted the Spellings' casting director, Pamela Shae, and with my long history with the Spellings, Pamela agreed to meet Carolyn and look at her film.

Pamela normally does not take time out to look at young actors' demo reels, especially with the actor sitting with her, but we were an exception. Not only did she enjoy the short film, but Pamela was more than impressed at how natural Carolyn was. Pamela assured Carolyn that she would look for a small part in the near future on one of Aaron's TV shows.

I had also called E. Duke Vincent, head of Aaron's production company, and longtime friend, to ask if he had a moment or two to say hello to Carolyn. When we went over to visit with Duke, he could not have been more charming. Duke promised Carolyn that he would look at the video as soon as he could and we said our goodbyes.

It was then time to go over to Aaron's office. I introduced Carolyn to Aaron's longtime assistant, and major influence from the early Dick Powell days, Renate Kamer. No one ever passes her desk to see Aaron without her permission. She was the keeper of the keys and knew Aaron's every move and made all of his appointments over the years. I had known her since my early Carolyn Jones days.

I told Renate that we had been over to see Pamela and Duke, and that we just wanted her to tell Aaron that we came by.

"Aaron is so busy, Budd. He is in two meetings back to back, as usual."

I asked her to just tell Aaron that I missed him and hope to see him soon knowing that he had been very ill over the years. She agreed, and we went into the elevator and down into the bowels of the Wilshire Court parking lot, heading for my car. A few minutes later, as we walked down the long walkway, I could vaguely hear someone calling. We kept walking until Carolyn said, "Someone is calling your name."

When I turned around, there was dear lady Renate walking as fast as she could, yelling, "Budd, come back! Aaron wants to see you and

Carolyn. He wants to watch her film!"

I was somewhat taken aback that after all these years, that Aaron would send dear Renate down into the garage to find me. Carolyn was very excited, trying to catch her breath, as we walked back to the elevator with Renate. Suddenly Carolyn fiercely whispered, "The film, the film!"

We had left our only copy in Duke's office. I told her not to worry. Into the chambers of Aaron Spelling's office we went as five or six executives and writers were heading out, getting a good look at this darling young co-ed from UCLA.

When Aaron finally came to the door, we hugged for a moment, and I asked how his wife Candy was. I introduced him to Carolyn and we exchanged a knowing grin, remembering how we had shared another Carolyn (Jones) years ago, and that I had also married a different Carolyn.

"Aaron only has a few minutes, as he has another meeting" said Renate, looking at her watch.

"I was hoping Aaron, that you could take a look at Carolyn's acting debut."

Aaron smiled, and told Renate that he wanted to take ten minutes to look at the film, and to call the network to say he would be a bit late.

"The film, the film!" Carolyn said. It was in Duke's office.

"Wait here and I'll be right back!" I said.

Aaron and Carolyn started talking as I ran down the hall. Duke was just sitting down to watch the film. You should have seen the look on his face when I told him that Aaron wanted to watch it! I pulled it out of the TV set and raced back.

The lights dimmed and Aaron took Carolyn by the hand as we sat watching the film. He watched with great interest in her performance both as an athlete, and as a promising young actress. When it was over, he kissed her on the check and said, "Yes, Budd is right. You do look a lot like Hope Lange, and should do very well in this business. Just listen to Budd. He is the best agent in town and knows great talent when he sees it."

With that we hugged again and kissed on the cheek, not knowing if I would ever see Aaron again due to his illness. He wished Carolyn a great future in the business. With that, Renate whisked him off the elevator and into his limo for his network meetings.

As we left, I told young Carolyn of our years together as friends and our years as friendly enemies when I was engaged to his ex-wife, Carolyn Jones.

It was little moments like this that you always remember as you travel through this business. Aaron was one of the giants of TV. At one time, he had so many shows on ABC, that the network was nicknamed "Aaron's Broadcasting Company."

He also holds the Guinness World Record for being the most prolific television producer, and yet he would still take the time to watch this first short of a young actress he had never met before because of our long relationship. That was what made Aaron so very special.

I look back at this brief moment with Aaron and Carolyn as one of my favorite moments as an agent. After that, Carolyn met a lot of people, from David E. Kelly (from her hometown of Waterville, Maine) to Larry King and Sidney Poitier. But to this date, she will always remember this very special moment having her first audience with Aaron Spelling.

It was not too long before I got Carolyn her first job on "Passions" for NBC making this her daytime debut. After that, Carolyn made two additional short festival films along with a Nike demo short for a student film at USC and a pilot called "Foxxy News" playing a kooky weather anchorwoman.

Carolyn Shea had a touch of Grace Kelly and a touch of Sharon Stone. It will be interesting to see what road she will take as she moves up the ladder of success as a talented young actress.

Chapter Fifty-Five

Bob Barker "America's Favorite TV Host/ And All I Got Was 10%— not" 2007

I DIDN'T EVEN GET MY TEN PERCENT!

I've known Bob Barker since his early Miss Universe pageant hosting days going all the way back to the late sixties. I used to bring "stars" in from Hollywood to serve as judges. It was a great way for our clients to get a free trip to countries all over the world. After I merged with Shapiro-Lichtman, he was a signed client of the agency. I approached Bob with various offers for television appearances, commercials, etc.— offers totaling probably a million dollars or more. He turned them all down. He was looking to do another movie after the success of Adam Sandler's "Happy Gilmore."

One morning in May 2007 I got a call from Mel Berger, a 35-year veteran of the William Morris office who had handled a number of celebrity memoirs. He explained that he had found me through Celebrity Service, a company that locates representatives for stars and industry executives, and wanted to talk to me about a possible book for Bob Barker. He followed up with an e-mail the next day, saying Random House was interested in doing something "Short, sweet, memoir-ish, that plays to his fan base. In a way, similar to Don Rickles' book which is not long and has some great, great stories." I told him that I was now a personal manager and freelanced with a lot of celebrities, including Bob, and that I'd very much like to work with him and the Morris office to bring Bob an offer. I asked Mel how we would work together in terms of fees, since my commission as a manager is 15%. Mel said that the Morris office did not split fee commissions on book deals, something that I knew from being an agent for many years could not be true.

Mel concluded, "Look, I have no problem in letting you handle the deal with Bob Barker, since I have some writers that would like to work with Bob. You can go ahead. I'll put you in touch with Susan Mercandetti at Random House."

Needless to say, I thought that Mel was more than a gentleman in letting me take over the book deal. Little did I know that this would come back to haunt me in the months that followed.

As always when dealing with Bob Barker, I immediately called Henri Bollinger, Bob's longtime friend and PR person, and told him about the call without going into too many details. Henri said that over the years, various people in publishing had come to Bob about doing a book and then for one reason or another, never followed through. As Bob was finishing off his last few shows of "The Price Is Right," Henri suggested I hold off for a little while, and then he would set up a meeting for me at CBS with Bob. I sent Mel Berger a note to update him, asking meanwhile if Mel had any creative input as to what kind of deal he could put on the table that I could take to my meeting with Bob.

I had visited the set numerous times over the years since I represented numerous models working on the show, including Dian Parkinson who currently had a sexual harassment lawsuit against Bob. I called him and a meeting was set for Studio 33, the Bob Barker stage, at CBS on the next-to-last show taping (ever) of "The Price Is Right." The very last day would be a zoo. Being with Bob and Henri on the next to last day of Bob Barker's career at CBS was very nostalgic and sentimental, to say the least. Backstage personnel were sad, happy, and thrilled to be there at this time. Even one of the makeup ladies I knew had tears in her eyes and was going around blowing her nose, knowing I guess that the next day she was going to have to start looking for another job.

Henri was there to meet me and we walked into Bob's star dressing room. Bob was still dressed in his Levi's and sport shirt, which is the way he always went to the studio and then, with various dressers, makeup artists and hairdressers they would get him into his Bob Barker costume. We shook hands and greeted each other warmly.

"What news do you have, Budd? Henri thinks you might have an interesting book deal pending?"

I told him that Mel Berger at the Morris office had been contacted by Random House to see if there was a Bob Barker book deal out there. I explained that he reached out to me through Celebrity Services, told him about the Morris Agency's no-split policy, and how Mel and I had agreed that I could handle this project myself. I gave Bob a copy of Don Rickles' book. Bob seemed a bit preoccupied; no doubt he was caught up in doing his last couple of shows.

"Let me get past tomorrow's show. I'll give this some thought," Bob said.

I told him that Mel Berger had put me in touch with senior editor Susan Mercandetti at Random House and that she would like to speak with him whenever he was available. "I will give you and Henri a call to follow up real soon."

I walked over to my favorite corner backstage where I could see the screaming audience and Bob coming out on stage to announce that this was going to be his next to last show of "The Price Is Right."

Over the next few weeks I spoke with Susan several times, and finally, after checking with both Bob and Henri, a meeting was set up for the three of us at Bob's home in one of the early Hollywood neighborhoods off Outpost Drive, just walking distance from the world famous Grauman's Chinese Theatre where stars had left their hand and footprints, and sometimes a few kisses too, in the cement for all the world to see years later. I alerted Susan to our meeting, and suggested she put down some thoughts about the book's direction, and told her we would have a call with her from our meeting.

She sent a long letter, saying, "I think Mr. Barker could give his public, in book form, an intimate, candid backstage pass to his shows, his life and his passions. That, basically, is what I'd like to read. I would like to find him a writer and though I have nobody in mind at this moment, I would work with him to find someone suitable. Perhaps, as a way to begin, I could have a writer spend a week with him to determine what shape such a book could take. I know you would like a dollar figure but I can't give you that until I know what we're talking about. Perhaps you could tell me what it would take to get him interested in pursuing such a project. I'd like to do this quickly as to not let too much time pass since he has been off the air." I printed this out and took it with me to my meeting.

When I arrived at Bob's home, Henri Bollinger was already there waiting for me. As hot as it was on this July 3rd, Bob wanted to sit out in the garden since he had some painters working inside. I gave Bob Susan's letter and he studied it for a good five minutes and then handed it to Henri, with a nice smile.

Chapter Fifty-Six

Bob Barker Meets Random House

"Looks interesting," Bob said to Henri. Bob's home phone rang almost exactly at 2:30 p.m. He walked through the doorway, and picked up the phone and said hello to Susan. He held her letter in his hand as he spoke to her for almost a half an hour. Bob told her he was very interested and wanted to take the next couple of steps as far as finding a writer he could work with. Susan said she would speak to her boss and get back to us after the 4th of July weekend.

At that time, and with great care, I explained to Bob and Henri how Mel Berger had contacted me and that as a literary/book agent, the Morris office would get 15%, which was standard in the book world. As a personal manager, I was also able to get 15% commissions from my clients. Bob was emphatic about only paying 10%. I told him that Mel Berger was willing to step aside if there were commission problems but I wanted to see if Mel would split a 15% commission with me.

The next day, July 4th, I sent Susan a note, thanking her for the great phone meeting and telling her that Bob felt that this was now the right time to do his long-overdue book. I also had another conversation with Mel Berger at the Morris office. He said, unfortunately, that the Morris office couldn't do the split I proposed and once again reiterated that he would let me put the deal together and take the 10% commission. If I needed any help, he would be more than happy to assist. I was amazed by his integrity and thanked him for bringing this pending deal to me. It was time to do a big book deal!

On July 10th, I spoke with Bob and told him that both Mel and Susan highly recommended writer Pablo Fenjves, and that I was going to fax over his credits. There was a long, dramatic pause and then Bob said, "I think we should have an American writer, not a Spanish writer."

I told him that Pablo had been born in Venezuela in 1956 and was raised in the States, and to please take a look at his credits as they were very impressive.

"I want a writer that knows the Midwest. What it's like to be in a snowstorm in Missouri in January, someone that is as 'American pie' as I am. Can we find a young writer (male or female) that knows me, the show, and can get out there with the fans on any given day to help make this a truly Bob Barker American Success Story?" He also pressured me to get some sort of offer in writing.

Susan soon responded.

"Dear Budd,

As discussed in our phone conversation, I would like to offer Mr. Bob Barker an advance of $100,000 for a mutually agreed upon book. The writer I mentioned, a very enthusiastic fan, is still available and eager to spend some time with Mr. Barker to determine what shape such a book might take. Please advise as to the next step.

Susan"

It was at this point the Mexican stand-off began. Bob insisted that he has to have a full contract in front of him before he went any further; Susan reasonably explained that until she knew what kind of book we had, Random House could not get the lawyers to send out a contract, other than the advance she had mentioned and standard royalties. I asked if there was a bigger advance available and she said it would depend on the book. Meanwhile, Bob kept insisting on meeting other writers than the "foreign" one Mel Berger and Susan heartily endorsed. I appealed to Susan for help, and she wrote a lovely letter directly to Bob reiterating her enthusiasm for the project.

At that point Henri Bollinger jumped in, pushing to get the word "deal memo" on Susan's correspondence. I could feel that she was getting a bit hot under the collar when she sent me the following email:

"The words 'deal memo' are irrelevant and unnecessary, particularly as I've laid out our intentions clearly. I did not see any reason to do this. I have truly gone as far as I can go without having any idea whatsoever where we are headed."

Things were going rapidly downhill. I called Henri and told him that I thought we all needed to meet again face to face. On July 23rd I drove down Sunset Blvd. and stopped at In-N-Out for a strawberry shake, contemplating my pending meeting. I had a feeling that it was going to end with my crashing into a brick wall. I was right. Once again the meeting was at Bob's home. Once again we sat in the garden. But Bob was not the cordial, genial host this time.

"Tell me again about this deal and how it came to you?" were the first words out of his mouth. I could see that he was very upset. I ran through the story (again) about Mel contacting me through Celebrity Services.

Then Bob really started yelling. "Your name is listed in the Celebrity Service papers as a personal manager to Bob Barker!" he yelled. "You are not my manager!"

At one point Bob had indeed been a signed client of mine, back in the Shapiro-Lichtman days. I told him that I did not know that I was still listed that way, and pointed out that I was no longer an agent. I was a manager—what else could I be called?

Bob continued to berate me. He said that I had lied to him. He said that he had done some checking around and called Norman Brokow, former head of William Morris Agency, who told him that if he was handling the deal, he would have asked for a $500,000 to $1 million advance. I had known Norman for more than 40 years, what else could he say? Henri, whom I considered a friend, kept looking at me; I knew that he felt embarrassed for me.

Bob looked at me and said, "I should forget this whole deal! What would you do in my position, Budd?" he asked me several times.

All I could do was keep telling him again that I had not lied or deceived him. From the very beginning I had asked Mel Berger if we could split a 15% commission, and Berger kept saying they did not split deals at the Morris office and was happy to turn the deal over to me. I had kept Henri informed of every development every step of the way.

Finally, Bob looked at me and said to Henri, "I am going to let him represent me on the book deal. But the deal is going to be for 10 percent! If you want 15 percent there is no deal. Ten percent—is that clear?"

With a sigh of relief, I said that ten percent was confirmed. All I wanted to do was get out of there, but we still had the writer problem. When I mentioned Pablo's name again, Bob said angrily, "I keep telling you. I want an American writer. I don't want people to think that I'm a bigot." Then, under his breath, "even though you probably think I must be." I looked over and saw Henri wince. I could not wait to get away.

The ride back out Sunset Blvd. to my home seemed like it would never end. All I could see in my rearview mirror was Bob Barker's red face yelling at me and saying to Henri, "What should I do with Budd? Do I forget about the deal?"

Once I got home I had a couple of drinks, took a deep breath, and sent an email to Susan requesting a $500,000 advance and a list of other possible writers. She was taken aback. "Whatever fee we end up paying will be our best offer but before we do anything, Bob has to be willing to take the next step and meet with some writers."

I spoke to Bob and told him this. He was back to being quite pleasant and said, "Fine. Tell her I look forward to seeing the list of writers and I'm willing to meet with them in the weeks to come."

The next day I received a brief note from Susan saying, "Just to make clear: I did not offer, nor is there an offer of $500,000 on the table. It may be what Mr. Barker would ultimately like to see but that is not an amount I am comfortable with, particularly given the lack of a proposal."

I was trying desperately to keep everything moving. At this point, I started to reach out to various literary agents to get some names of writers that might be a good fit. I tried to reach Susan several times; clearly she was losing interest. As the days turned into weeks, and the weeks turned into August, I sent Susan some names of various writers that were recommended to me by several of the big agencies, hoping to nail down some writer meetings with Bob. Her response was not encouraging.

"I have a number of projects in full swing and I'm leaving for a few weeks at the end of this month. I strongly suggest you put a proposal together, quite honestly, it is the best way to proceed. Once you and Mr. Barker have identified a writer with whom he is comfortable and can determine what he would like to say in a book, then, at that point, I would be most interested. Good luck."

The doors were closing at Random House for my Bob Barker deal. I immediately sent Susan an email saying, "Don't let this fall apart," and redoubled my efforts. I went back and forth with a prominent Dallas agent, Jan Miller, who represented a number of important writers, including Digby Diehl, who lived in Los Angeles and appeared to be an ideal match as Henri Bollinger had known him for years and liked him. Weeks of wrangling ensued between Susan, Jan and myself concerning who would pay the writer, how much the fees would be, and setting up a personal meeting between Digby, the most likely candidate, with Bob.

On the morning of August 10th I woke up to two emails that gave me one of the few migraine headaches I've had in twenty years. The first was from Jan Miller, reminding me to call Susan to find out what Random House would pay the writer. I knew the answer to that one.

The second read: "Budd, I have decided to withdraw my original offer for a book from Mr. Barker. Please do not refer agents or writers to me.

We have respectfully decided to move on. Good luck with this project. Susan."

I broke out in a cold sweat and felt the beginnings of a migraine headache settling in to my grey matter. There was no kindest regards, sincerely, or thanks for all your hard work these past few months. The journey had come to an abrupt end. I was not going to get my 10 percent for what could have been one of my most successful deals in the last 30 years.

To add insult to injury, Bob went to Norman Brokaw at the William Morris Agency and asked them to make a new deal with another book company. He recommended Digby Diehl as his first choice to write the book. Their book, "Priceless Memories" from Hachette Publishing, was released in August 2009.

ADDENDUM

The following was published on July 14th, 2015, in the National Inquirer:

"Game show legend BOB BARKER, forlorn and forgotten at 91, is determined the animals he loves will split his $70 million fortune!

"The Price Is Right" host is "painfully alone at a time when his spirits could use a lift," said a friend. "He had an amazing career, and has done so much good work as an animal rights activist, but his retirement hasn't been as fulfilling as he'd hoped.

"He's invited to events hosted by animal rights groups, but hardly anyone checks in with him regularly.

"Bob has complained: 'I'm alone, and I feel like that every day.'"

After hosting game show "Truth or Consequences," Bob served a record-breaking 35-year run on "Price Is Right." He was ousted in 2007 and replaced by Drew Carey in a reported move to attract a younger audience.

A sexual harassment controversy, initiated by "Price Is Right" model Dian Parkinson filing a lawsuit following a three-year affair, also damaged his reputation.

"Bob feels like he was put out to pasture by Hollywood," said the source. "He says people in Hollywood have long memories, and the sexual harassment charges unfairly clung to him."

He's long battled back problems, suffered two strokes and grappled with skin cancer and failing eyesight. His wife of 36 years, Dorothy Jo, died in 1981, and the couple had no children."

Bob's now dead-set on dying broke, said sources, by giving away his vast fortune to animal groups."

Chapter Fifty-Seven

"The Wizard of Show Business Is Gone"

When showbiz giant and super-agent Martin Baum passed away, a lavish memorial service was held at CAA in Century City, Marty's employer for the last thirty-some years. It was a beautiful and fitting tribute to a legend; however, I was surprised that his various obituaries made so much of his association with CAA and barely touched on his pioneering days as an agent in New York as a younger man. As the co-head of Baum-Newborn, a New York agency, Marty merged their agency with General Artists Corp., an active talent booking agency with a small motion picture division throughout the 1940s. There are so many tales to tell of those days that were overlooked when he passed. Marty changed my life when he hired me as a Hollywood agent in 1960, and it is Marty I have to thank for more business adventures and personal friendships than I could ever have imagined.

It was late October as I drove home over Laurel Canyon after a meeting with actor Bill Shatner and my book agent David Vigliano. The book we met about, later became "Shatner Rules: Your Guide to Understanding the Shatnerverse," which I was responsible for making the deal for Bill. I was able to get him a very large advance of $500.000, which he recently thanked me for not remembering back four years ago that I brought 'Vigliano and the deal to him. "How soon we forget?" someone famous once said.

I was listening to KNX news radio for traffic alerts. The news at the top of the hour began with, "Noted Hollywood agent to the stars Martin Baum passed away today of heart failure after a long illness." The agent's health had been failing in recent years, but Marty Baum was Marty Baum, meaning that despite his illnesses, he still managed to make it into his office at CAA two, three and sometimes even four days a week. He was truly one of the most driven men I have ever known in 50 years of being an agent and in this business, that's really saying something.

My first thought was for my dear friend Sidney Poitier, who had been Marty's client from day one of his storied career. The two men had remained very close throughout the years. I decided to wait to call Sidney until the next morning, knowing that he would be immediately bombarded with a hundred calls—if he even felt up to answering the phone that night. When I reached him the next day, Sidney sounded sad but resigned to the fact that Marty was gone. Sidney had been aware for the past month or so that it was just a matter of time and that time had come at last. "He's finally gone, Budd, and I know that it is to a better place."

As the week passed, we spoke several times and Sidney suggested that I accompany him and Joanna to the memorial service. I also received emails and calls from Marty's daughter Fern and son Richard, wanting to make sure I would attend. They knew that I was one of the very few who went back with Marty all the way to the Baum-Newborn agency days in New York in the fifties.

On the appointed day, November 16th, 2010, Sidney, Joanna and I exited our car and joined 250 invited guests filing into the beautiful auditorium/screening room at CAA's new offices on Avenue of the Stars in Century City, across from the Century Plaza Hotel. Family members, stars, studio heads, and a host of agents were all there to pay their respects.

Fifty-some years of showbiz agency history flashed in front of me. There were the five former Morris agents—Mike Rosenfeld, Michael

Ovitz, Ron Meyer, William Haber and Roland Perkin— who had opened CAA for business in 1975 with a $35,000 line of credit and a $21,000 bank loan in an office furnished with card tables and folding chairs. A year later these young men convinced Marty Baum to join them. By doing so, Marty brought in real motion picture stars, directors and producers: Oscar winners Sidney Poitier, Walter Mirisch, Gig Young, Julie Andrews, Sterling Silliphant, Richard Attenbourgh and Blake Edwards—just to name a few. Marty and his client list turned the tide of the new agency's fortunes.

Many of the star agents present had, like me, known Marty for decades: Bill Haber, Fred Specktor, Jack Gilardi, Mike Medavoy, Jerry Goldstein, Ted Witzer, Herman Rush, Alan Riche, Meritt Blake, Sandy Bresler, and on and on. I did stop for a fleeting second to see if Marty's two very special secretaries from Baum-Newborn days, Sandy Newman and Sue Mengers, made it to the services. However, it was the new giants of CAA who took over the memorial. Richard Lovett, Brian Siberell, and Jon Levin who told the famous Ed Brophy and Stanley Kramer story about the time Marty made a great deal for Ed—long after he had passed away. Then Rich Baum brought everyone to tears speaking on behalf of the family.

Then our beloved Sidney stood up very slowly, made his way from the second row up to podium. Very softly at first, his famous voice hushed, he began to speak:

"In my eighty-three years of life, I never met another man as amazing as Martin Baum has been in the unfolding of his life. He was a wizard—pure and simple. His smile was always quick—and his laughter genuine.

His instincts, on the mark—nearly always—at the minimal, there was something remarkable about the man. Stories—you have heard—but even they have only scratched the surface—a glimpse at the list of artists represented by Martin Baum will speak loudly of his accomplishments.

But the totality of his life will leave its imprint on those who have been privileged to have known him as the remarkable human being that he was—as the quintessential agent he had become in the professional lives of so many of his clients.

Wizard, I say—because I've watched him at work. I was among others whose careers were enhanced by the craftsmanship of Martin Baum's professional skills. In a period in which it was not considered possible, Martin Baum challenged the status quo—and began fashioning a career for the young African-American actor that I was.

He remained my agent across my entire career—except the time when ABC briefly seduced him to take over their motion picture division— which was short-lived. He then returned to his first love—the agency business. Though times passed—and memories dimmed, Martin Baum's commitment to his clients will be remembered by each of us. So rest in peace Mr. Wizard, until we meet again—as surely we will."

When my friend had finished speaking and when all the farewell speeches were over, a professional-quality 10-minute video was shown documenting Marty's life with his wife Bernice and their children, as well as many of those he worked with. And then the impeccably produced memorial was over.

Sidney and Joanna were so busy greeting so many friends and associates he had not seen in years that it took almost half an hour to work our way out of the building and make it over to Spago's, where Richard and Fern, Marty's son and daughter, had invited more than a hundred of Marty's personal friends for cocktails and snacks. I grabbed a table in the private room before the crowd moved in. Sidney was so generous with his time. As sad as he must have been, he kept a big smile on his face and greeted all those who came over to the table to extend their sympathies warmly. Producer George Schlatter, actor Hugh O' Brian, who worked with Sidney in one of his earlier films, and Walter Mirisch, sat with us for a long time, as did Marty's secretary from GAC days, Carol Dudley Katzka. An hour and a half had passed when Sidney looked at me and said, "Buddy B, time to take it home." In just a few minutes we were back at his lovely Spanish villa, behind the Beverly Hills Hotel.

The two of us went into the living room where we sat for almost another hour talking about early days. Meeting for the first time when we were practically kids on the set of "Blackboard Jungle." Rehearsing day and night in Chicago just before his stardom in "Raisin in the Sun." And the many film achievements he and Marty shared: an Oscar-winning performance in "Lilies of the Fields" making him the first African American to win an Academy Award for Best Actor. "To Sir With Love." "The Defiant Ones." Sidney standing up for me as my best man when I married a non-pro, Carolyn Gerry, for my second, lifelong marriage. The many, many lessons Marty had taught us both. Sidney's unforgettable roles in "The Heat of the Night" and "Guess Who's Coming to Dinner." The wonderful night in 1992 when the American Film Institute named him one of the greatest male stars of all time. And most recently, the pinnacle of his distinguished career when he was awarded the Presidential Medal of Freedom, the highest possible honor for a civilian, by President Barack Obama.

So many triumphs the three of us shared. Both Sidney and I knew we would never see his kind again. It was the end of an era.

It was my intention that I would close out this book with the Martin Baum-Sidney Poitier chapter. But so many different projects and events took place, since the Shapiro-Lichtman Agency closed their doors in 2007 and the three of us went home and put our "Personal Talent Managers" hat on.

New clients, new ideas for TV series, major motion picture deals to put together both here, London and most recently, a World War II film, to be discussed at a later time. My friendship with Larry King continues and we are trying to work on several different deals.

Last year, at the suggestion of my former client and ambassador to

Mexico, John Gavin and his wife and client, Constance Towers, and two extremely talented writers and friends of the Gavins, M.B. Baker and Thomas Hastings, all got together to update the Jack Valenti novel, "Protect and Defend." We are working to bring the story of the sub-plot onto the front pages of all newspapers around the world, dealing with the drug and gun war here at our borders and deep into Mexico D.F. with our leading character, the United States Ambassador to Mexico, and with one of our most talented and respected Mexican actors and directors Edward James Olmos, not only as one of our producers, but stars and possibly our director to go into production in 2016.

The personal relationship with Joanna and Sidney Poitier has not been as active as we would like it to be because of many different business and social reasons, and most importantly, Sidney's constant drive to keep writing his beautiful books and most recently, his first novel, "Montaro Caine."

What follows is a short chapter filled with today's "A" names and a beautiful evening we spent with the Poitiers and Ms. Oprah Winfrey at Sidney's book party that she hosted for "Montaro Caine."

Chapter Fifty-Eight

An Evening With Oprah and Sidney at the Bel-Air Hotel

As my wife, Carolyn and I drove into the valet parking area, at the famous Hotel Bel-Air in Westwood, on my left were three Rolls, a Bentley with the top down, an Aston Martin, two Ferrari's, a hot, very red Lamborghini, and a half a dozen new BMWs. I wondered, as I was greeted by one of at least 10 young UCLA college students/valets all in light brown denim outfits, where they were going to park our old car? There were also three supervisors and several men dressed in black and dark glasses (at 6:30 p.m. in the evening) with very small ear plugs, speaking into their cuffs of all places.

As we got out of my 2004 SUV Lexus and started to walk over the beautiful swan bridge, there were two very lovely young ladies, wearing long black gowns, with clip boards in their hands. "Will you be joining us for the book party?" one of them asked softly. I nodded as she asked for our names. "Oh, of course Mr. Moss, how nice to see you both. This way please!" As she led the way over the bridge, I looked down below as I always do to see if the two beautiful swans were there to greet the guests from all around the world to this most unique hotel.

As we approached the small ballroom ahead of us, in the midst of a plush garden, I noticed a line at the door growing larger. I also noticed to my left, an open door leading to a room that adjoined the ballroom. I took Carolyn by the arm and said "Let's go in this way!" As we entered the room, we were surrounded by what looked like a couple of hundred of Sidney's books and a makeshift table with three young men from the Book Soup store on Sunset Blvd., and their computers already selling "Montaro Caine" to the arriving guests.

Sidney's book cover was black with an enormous gold coin in the center and you could see what looked like large and small stars and moons with a few lines going from one planet to another, while the coin looked like it was spinning around the solar system. Sidney Poitier's name was on the top of the book cover, over the gold coin and then on the bottom it said, "Montaro Caine—a novel."

As Carolyn and I slipped into the ballroom I spotted Sidney at the door, surrounded by numerous friends, waiting to have their photo taken with him for posterity. I had Carolyn by the arm and we slowly backed into the doorway off to the side so that as soon as another photo was taken, we were next in line.

All of a sudden, Sidney looked over at Carolyn, trying to pull up the name of this lovely lady that he had not seen for some time. "Oh my dear lady, what a delightful surprise!"

As Sidney found her name and reached over to her, he said, "Carolyn, come over here." He wrapped his arms around both of us and said, "You too, my dear fellow!" The flash bulbs started to flash...one after another. In a split second I had flashbacks of "Blackboard Jungle" when we first met, and then of being backstage in Chicago for tryouts of "Raisin in the Sun." Then of the Oscar in his hand for "Lilies of the Field." And of our wedding at the home of the legendary "King of Tortes," famed attorney, Melvin Belli, where Chief Justice of the California Supreme Court, Stanley Mosk, presided over our beautiful ceremony in San Francisco, with Joanna and Sidney standing up for us. All of this took less than four seconds, I believe. I could feel the next couple gently pushing their way into our spot wanting their moment to be photographed with this great legend of the motion picture world to be memorialized for eternity, like the stars that were on the cover of his book.

As we moved away, I spotted Joanna sitting at a small table with Barbara Davis (the widow of the great oil giant, Marvin Davis) and Quincy Jones, a true icon of the music world who I go back with when he was married to Peggy Lipton when she was starring in Aaron Spelling's new TV series, "Mod Squad." Joanna, seeing Carolyn, jumped up and reached over to kiss her. They were so excited to see one another. At the same time I reached over as "Q" stood up so I could embrace him…"been a longtime Budd. You look great!" "So do you, 'Q."

Joanna was dressed so elegantly in her silk flowing gown from India. There were so many different colors in her dress. Reds, soft blues. And even the brightness of yellow and oranges…she had a dozen or so gold chains overlapping large pearls and even small silver and purple stones that were in her hair to augment those that were around her neck.

As one of the waiters walked by, I managed to grab two glasses of champagne for us. As noisy as it was, we chatted and I asked Joanna where the girls were? "I saw them briefly over near Oprah." And there she was, one of the world's most recognized and respected women. The word icon and legend don't do her justice and yet, there she stood, speaking to a few friends, dressed in a subtle, multicolored, blue and white silk dress with puffed sleeves. She could have been just coming from a day's work at the office.

Anika and Little Sydney, as we called her over the years, looked so beautiful. I was with Sidney in New York in '72 when we went to a hospital near Gracie Mansion, home of the mayor of New York, for the delivery of Anika, and now there she was, ever so tall and looking like Joanna did when I first met her with Sidney on the set of "The Lost Man." The girls spotted us and came over for a giant hug. They both said, almost at the same time, "How is Geoff?" We had spent so much time together as the kids were growing up.

We even spent a couple of weeks together on the big island of Hawaii at our favorite hide-a-way, Kona Village. A true Hawaiian village where everyone had their own grass hales right on the beach. It was so private and secluded that one morning at breakfast Sidney said, "We might go home a few days early." "Why?" I asked. "It's a little too quiet for us. People are so nice here but not one person has come over to me and asked for my autograph!" Fond memories of days gone by.

All the usual suspects were there to greet Sidney and Joanna. Janet Jackson was there. Sherry Lansing too, who at one time was the most powerful woman in Hollywood. She was the first woman president of 20th Century Fox Studios and then of Paramount. Today, she is one of the most honored and respected philanthropists in our industry. I go back with Sherry to when she was just a school teacher at El Rodeo Elementary School in Beverly Hills and an aspiring young actress who ended up working with some of the most talented producers in Hollywood. I always would get a warm kiss from her. Then there was Norman Lear with his ever present beach hat; my loving friend, George Schlatter and "the power behind the throne" wife, Jolene; and Jackie Collins, actress turned successful author. There was also Sidney's closest friend from his early days in Hollywood, Walter Mirisch, who is truly one of our industry's most respected and honored producers, and an Oscar winner, including for two of Sidney's biggest grossers, "Heat of the Night" written by Oscar winner, the late Stirling Silliphant, also a close friend and former client going back to General Artists days, and "They Call Me Mr. Tibbs," and on and on. There were the "Young Turks" from CAA, the Morris office and other top agencies and all their young starlets-in-training, waiting to be spotted by one of the many moguls that were there...

And wherever you turned, there was the Master Chef Wolfgang Puck, making sure that everyone had plenty to eat and drink. Carolyn and I found the sushi table and stayed very close to it for a long time. Carolyn, who does not like rice, found the chef and the sashimi platter. All you could eat of the freshest Ahi tuna and yellowtail. I found myself washing it down with cold sake on the rocks until finally there was a clinking of the glasses as Oprah walked up onto the mini-stage off to the right of the overcrowded room.

For the next ten minutes she spoke about this man she fell in love with as she was growing up. This man who became her mentor and guiding light in her life and career. Then, Sidney came up onto the small stage and sat with Oprah for almost an hour. She asked him about his early life and growing up in the Bahamas.

Sidney reflected about when he was first born. He was a seven-month-old premature baby. The doctors almost from the beginning did not give him much hope to live. His father even went out and found an old shoe box to use as his coffin, to bury him when he died. In the weeks that followed, much to everyone's surprise, not only did he survive but he started to improve so much that his mother took Sidney to an old soothsayer that she had heard about in the hills overlooking the bay at Nassau. She needed to hear from the spirits if her son was going to survive.

This old black woman held baby Sidney in the palms of her wrinkled hands for almost an hour without saying a single word. The odors of strange burning leaves filled the air. Suddenly, she started to shake and with a deep penetrating and almost piercing sound she made a moaning sound and cried for almost ten minutes rocking this tiny infant back and forth. Finally she held the baby above her head and said to his mother, "Your son will live. He will become strong and he will become a wise and knowledgeable man. One day be will grow tall and soon he will travel the Earth and will walk and talk with kings and queens from around the world!" The soothsayer walked over to Sidney's mother, and with trembling hands, lowered the baby into her arms and then slowly walked out of the cabin and into the woods.

There was a silence that filled the room. Oprah's hands were shaking as she reached over to touch Sidney's face. He too looked like he had been on a journey. She started to look around the room; there was not a dry eye in the audience. Sidney then told us his life story and journey that finally brought him to Miami where he lived with his uncle before he travelled on to New York City to the magical place called Harlem, and then finally to Hollywood, with all of his loving and caring friends over the last 80 some years. A truly beautiful and touching evening.

As the evening was slowly coming to an end, Carolyn and I were speaking with Janet Jackson and Quincy. Oprah was walking over with a friend to introduce her to Janet and "Q" when "Q" said afterwards, "And this is Budd Moss and his wife, Carolyn. Sidney goes back with Budd to the early days of 'Blackboard Jungle.'" I jumped in and said, "I was even with Sidney when he was in tryouts for 'Raisin in the Sun' in Chicago.

I had just started working as an agent for Marty Baum and Abe Newborn at General Artist when Sidney got his Oscar for 'Lilies of the Fields.' Then there was 'To Sir With Love,' 'Patch of Blue,' and 'The Defiant Ones.' I even got to sit on the set with Tracy, Hepburn and Sidney when they were filming 'Guess Who's Coming To Dinner?' And finally Sidney and Joanna stood up for us when we got married at the home of Melvin Belli." Oprah really seemed interested having never spoken to someone who had gone back that far with Sidney.

Kiddingly I said, "You should read my book "And All I Got was 10 Percent!" This caught her and Quincy off guard as she let out a loud laugh...Oprah looked at me and said, "They say you can usually tell a book by its cover but I don't think this is true in your case! You must send your book to my office tomorrow," as she turned and waved goodbye to all of us. Needless to say, the book was on her desk the following afternoon by special messenger. I was honored just to have been asked to send her my book.

I put a note into the folder to read the draft of Sidney's "Farewell to my Wizard, Marty Baum" when he spoke at the CAA memorial service a few years ago. Knowing that Oprah has one of the most successful publishing companies, I hope I can find my way there not only to publish my volume two of "HOLLYWOOD," but possibly re-do volume one with her blessings.

Oh, and by the way, "Montaro Caine" was one of the most exciting and interesting books I have read in a long time. Sidney takes you on the most unusual voyages you can imagine. Every page has a unique twist and turn, and just when you think you have found out the hidden secrets, you find yourself having to start all over again… a must read!

As the guests started to leave the ballroom and wave their goodbyes to Oprah, Sidney and Joanna, I noticed the lovely ladies that greeted us when we first arrived were at the door passing out gift bags. While Carolyn and Joanna had a moment to promise they would call and have lunch, I slipped by several of the guests and took two bags with thanks, back to the table and noticed that in each was a copy of "Montaro Caine." I told "P" that I was going to come over to the house real soon for him to sign my book. With the greatest of pleasure, Buddy, Carolyn and I had a warm hug from him and also received that world famous Oprah smile, then we headed back over the swan bridge to find our SUV amongst all the classic cars in front of the hotel. Within minutes we were down the hill, turned on to Copa del Oro to Sunset Blvd., crossed over to Hilgard and down to Strathmore and home. What a memorable night to share once again with Sidney, Joanna and Oprah.

Epilogue

As I was finishing my second book, "HOLLYWOOD," I could not help thinking of those great human beings that for one reason or another have crossed my path over this long journey I have been on.

First and most important I want to personally thank Addison Fleming, my assistant from Loyola Marymount University who morning, noon and night was always available to me as I was writing and rewriting chapter after chapter until I got it right. A special thanks to Anita Venezia for suggestions and for looking over our shoulders. Bill and Gayle Gladstone and Kenneth Kales, my publishers. My Washington D.C. connections: from the beautiful and talented Ruby Moy and Helen Cameron, both who worked for my loving friend, Jack Valenti, who did not know the word "No" when I needed something done in our nation's capitol. Beverly Mckittrick, special assistant to former Senator Paul Laxalt, whose advice is still there when I need it. Cindy Steele Vance, former congressmen and senators, all too many to mention.

In New York, at the top of the list, probably the most famous of all Broadway agents, Robby Lantz and his Oscar-winning client Milos Forman, Adam Davidson, and Dennis Aspland, Laurence, who had the courage to stay with me and Jack Valenti and his novel, "Protect and Defend" over the years as we tried to bring his brilliant book to the screen. Broadway's legendary giants, Gerry Shoenfield, Jimmy Neiderland, Sr., and his son Jimmy Junior. Actors and writers over the years who became special friends in the "Big Apple," whenever there was advice that was needed or a drink to be had. Tony winner Carole Shelly, Larry Blyden, Noel Behn, producer Jean Doumanian, The Fat Lady, Elaine who always had a table for me at her saloon, even when there was a two-hour wait, usually next to Woody and Mia. Carol Dudley Katzka, Sandy Newman, the beautiful Gloria Garfunkel, and her super daughter, Stacy. Marianne O'Hara, the Kerenyi's, Julia and Carter Walker the 3rd. Frank Lyon, and Laura. The "Mystery Man" at 45 East End Avenue. We never knew who he really was. The talented actress Judy Lewis and legendary mother Loretta Young, Irma and Bert Bacharach and Burt Jr., Shanna Valeska, Marcia Belmont, Gayle Burn and Adrianne Angel, and still today, New York's most honored celebrities who don't say no to any charity, Michele and Larry Herbert and their talented young director son, Loren. If there is a red carpet event, you can find them there.

My life over the years has been filled with hundreds of the most caring and giving friends that have included: Lady Janet Suzman and Master Joshua, Marcella Roulette, Paul, Suzie and Annie Mantee, Sandy and Cathy Ellis, Hal Thunes, Mark Lichtman and the ever- present Jo. Marty, Judy and Susan Shapiro and Caroline Carmenitti and her mom and dad in Cannes, my mentor, the late, great Martin Baum, Antonio and Fiorella Cagnolo, Carolyn Shea, Yetta and Gene Slott, Lynn and Bill Selcer, Leesa Mayer, Jackie Bisset, Bo Derek, Caroline Carminati, actress and brilliant coach Kathryn Daley, Connie and Jack Gavin, Edward James Olmos, Nic Izzi ,Sue Stich, Dr. Susan Perlman, Dr. Stewart Middler, my Larry and Shawn King bagel club headed up by Sid Young, Cal Fussman who helped me endlessly by dotting many of my "i's" and crossing my "t's" as I stumbled through seventy thousand words of my book, along with Julie McCarron, Keith Addis, Janet and Buzz Berger, the special Bob Woolf family, especially Stacey, Dominick Dunne, Carrie Snodgress, Hope Lange, Richard Roman Hall, Gene Washington, Merlin Olsen, Jim Plunkett, Joe Theismann, Emma Bering, Dominic Pace, Brianna Barcus, Princess Yasmin, Judy Ault, June Allyson, Harold and Grace Robbins. Barry, Bruce, another legendary giant (if only in his mind), Irwin Schaffer, and Larry King's biggest cheerleader, Mr. Laugh-in himself, George Schlatter, Jolene and of course, the power behind the throne, Marta. Bobby Blake, I think I am one of the last people that can still call him that. Karen Cadle, the most talent producer, Kirk and Anne Douglas, Yanou Collart, from Paris, to Monte-Carlo to Cannes, to London, Rome or China, the best PR woman in the world. Yetta and Gene Slott and family, special, special friends through the Tom and Patti Bosley years that moved away to Florida much too early. We miss them all the time. Tina and Gerry Frank, the Wilsey family from Palo Alto. Linda Gray, Larry Hagman, Sherry Lansing, Jerry Juroe, Paramount's most special PR man A.C. Lyles—he will never forget your name once he has met you. Shirlee and Henry Fonda, Mr. and Mrs. Jonathan Silverman, Juliet and Maxwell Caulfield, Dr. James and Susan Grotstein, Airman William and Dot Gwinn, special actress France Nuyen, Maggie Blye, Sally Kellerman and Dyan Cannon, who forgot to thank me for their Oscar nominations, Manny, my great barber, Tony Quinn, whom I will never really be able to thank for our years of friendship and introducing me to actress Ruth Roman in Tijuana, Mara and her mom, the best photographer in the world. Got hundreds of actors that can vouch for her. Terri Madrid, Gary Coleman, my beloved Joyce and Ralph Grunauer and their special family. Richard Roman Hall, whom I miss every day of my life, Stefanie Powers, Delia Salvi, one of the truly great drama coaches going back to my Los Angeles City College days. Dan Tana Ron Rice and his Hawaiian Tropic world class beauties, Peggy Walton Walker, Pat and Dick van Patton and their special sons, Nels and Jimmy and Vince, Sylvia Lee Rainey, who kept me in line at General Artist Corp., Nicole Lenzi and Carrie Landfield who helped get the Burton Moss Agency open. The infamous Sue Mengers, who became Hollywood's most famous woman agent. My special Hilda and Sam Rolfe, who shared our wedding together with Joanna and Sidney Poitier at the home of Melvin Belli and the judge that made sure the marriage was going to stick—Chief Justice, Stanley Mosk (even though Hilda today still thinks the marriage won't last, some 45 years later). Joanne Garfield. Marsh Hunt, who opened the doors for me in San Francisco when I was in the air force, R.J. Wagner from high school days and the Valenti family, Mary Margaret, Courtenay, Alexandra and

John. Even today I want to give Jack a call and tell him I miss him. Last but not least, my three beautiful brothers, Dann, David and Greg, who will one day know why I did what I did, and in many ways I miss them every day.

I know there are still so many loving friends that I probably missed and will remember as soon as this book is published.

Budd Burton Moss

HOLLYWOOD

Bibliography

1 "1996 Palm Beach Film Festival Diaries." *1996 Palm Beach Film Festival Diaries*. N.p., n.d. Web. 13 Jan. 2015.

The National Security Archives 2002 Ambassador Robert Hill quote

Caren Roberts-Frenzel, C. (2001). *Rita Hayworth: A Photographic Retrospective*. New York: Harry N Abrams Inc.

54106582R00263

Made in the USA
Charleston, SC
23 March 2016